Trout Streams of
Southern Appalachia

Trout Streams of
Southern Appalachia

Fly-Casting in Georgia, Kentucky, North Carolina, South Carolina, and Tennessee

Jimmy Jacobs

Backcountry Publications
Woodstock, Vermont

An Invitation to the Reader

With time, access points may change, and road numbers, signs, and landmarks referred to in this book may be altered. If you find that such changes have occurred near streams described in this book, please let the author and publisher know, so that corrections can be made in future editions. Other comments and suggestions are also welcome. Address all correspondence to:

Fishing Editor
Backcountry Publications
P.O. Box 748
Woodstock, VT 05091

Library of Congress Cataloging-in-Publication Data

Jacobs, Jimmy.
    Trout Streams of southern Appalachia : fly-casting in Georgia, Kentucky, North Carolina, South Carolina, and Tennessee / Jimmy Jacobs.
      p.   cm.
    Includes index.
    ISBN 0-88150-303-7
    1. Trout fishing—Appalachian Region, Southern.   2. Fly-fishing—Appalachian Region, Southern.   I. Title.
SH688.U6J34   1994
799.1'755—dc20
                                    94-3412
                                       CIP

© 1994 by James L. Jacobs

Third Printing 1996

Published by Backcountry Publications, a division of The Countryman Press, Woodstock, Vermont 05091
Distributed by W.W. Norton and Company, Inc., 500 Fifth Avenue, New York, NY 10110

Cover design by Donna Wohlfarth
Text design by Rachel Kahn
Cover photograph of Conasauga River by Art Meripol, courtesy *Southern Living*® Magazine. Reprinted with permission.
Interior photographs by the author, unless otherwise credited.
Maps by Paul Woodward © 1994 The Countryman Press
Mayfly drawing by Tammy Hiner

Printed in the United States of America

10 9 8 7 6 5 4 3

To Brent and Zane
for their patience on our research trips

ACKNOWLEDGMENTS

This book would not have been possible without the help of the fisheries managers and biologists of Georgia, Kentucky, North Carolina, South Carolina, Tennessee, the National Park Service, and the United States Fish and Wildlife Service. The wealth of technical information supplied by Don Pfitzer is greatly appreciated. My gratitude to LeRoy Powell and Bill Vanderford for letting me tag along on fishing trips. Thanks to John E. Phillips for his encouragement and tips on the book business.

Special thanks to Jim Casada, Soc Clay, and Don Kirk for their years of writing about the trout streams of the South. Their work was invaluable in pointing the way to creating a method from the madness of my research.

To the unnamed anglers whose brains I picked on the banks of streams and rivers or at Trout Unlimited meetings throughout the region, a heartfelt thank you.

S O U T H E R N
A P P A L A C H I A

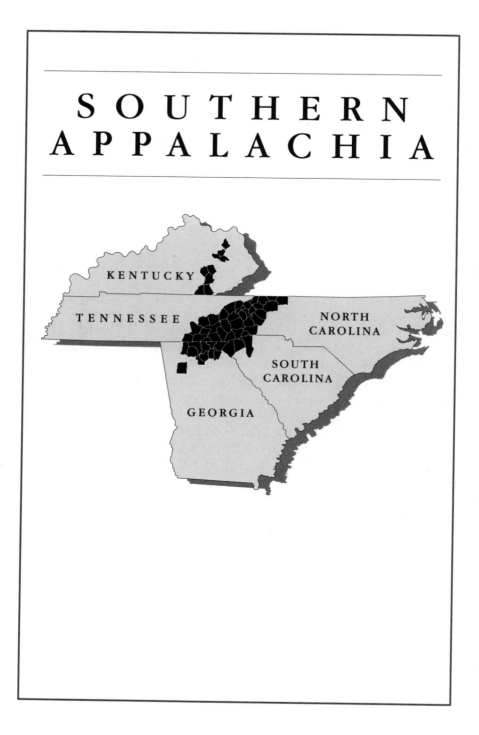

Contents

Preface

Mention fly-fishing for trout in the southern Appalachian Mountains and you are likely to get a befuddled look in return from your listener. Even outdoorsmen who regularly fish the region for these cold-water species are likely to treat you as though you have been standing in a cold stream so long that hypothermia has brought on hallucinations. The tradition of fly-casting for trout in the southeastern states is not a long or deep one. Although there has always been a hard core of fly-fishers in the region, their numbers have been small. Only recently has the fraternity begun to spread rapidly.

Still, even with this newfound interest, bait- and spin-fishermen outnumber fly-fishermen in the South by a wide margin. There are a couple of reasons for this disparity, the main one being the region's tradition of "meat" fishing. The folks who inhabited these mountains in past decades were usually more concerned with putting fish on the table at mealtime than with the sporting aspects of fishing.

Another reason for the slow growth of interest in fly-fishing has been the nature of the streams themselves. The small, freestone brooks of the Southeast, with their heavily foliated banks are, in the vast majority of cases, quite difficult to fish with fly tackle. In fact, many anglers transplanted to the region from the Northeast or western states swear that these creeks are unfishable for the fly caster. These immigrants usually end up doing their fishing on the few large streams available or head for the man-made tailrace fisheries of Dixie, leaving the vast majority of the area's trout waters unmolested.

With the advent of the 1990s, however, researchers have discovered that fly-fishing is now one of the ten fastest-growing outdoor activities among upscale, suburban dwellers. Due to the southeastern states' inclusion in the sunbelt, these are the folks who are flocking into the region. For those reasons, it seems obvious that fly-casting for trout will continue to grow in the southern Appalachians. This is especially true since the increased number of anglers puts pressure on the resource to the point that designating some streams as catch-and-release, artificial-lure-only, or even fly-fishing-only is the current trend. Establishing such restrictions encourages more people to take a stab at fly-fishing.

This book is targeted to aid both the folks already fishing for trout in the southern Appalachians with the long rod and the novice fly caster or newcomer to the region. The book does not endeavor to identify every brook or pothole in the region that contains trout. Neither does it reveal a list of previously unknown fly-fishing destinations in the Southeast.

What it will do is take a look at the trout streams found on public land in the mountainous Appalachian regions of Georgia, Kentucky, North Carolina, South Carolina, and Tennessee that offer fly-fishing possibilities. Of course, there are some anglers who argue that any creek or brook containing trout in this area can be successfully fished with a fly rod and artificial fly. I, for one, am a proponent of that ideology. On the other hand, I also admit that many of these streams provide less than classic fly-rodding conditions. Fly-fishing the bulk of the small headwater streams of the southern Appalachians often more closely resembles some sadomasochistic ritual than an entertaining outdoor pursuit. Clawing through rhododendron thickets or crawling through streamside briar patches in order to poke your rod through the bushes and dap a fly on the surface of pools the size of a washtub does not fit the definition of fly-fishing for most anglers.

To believe that there are some broad, free-flowing streams on public land in the Southeast harboring foot-long wild trout that are as yet unknown to many anglers would be naive. Rather, many of the names mentioned have a familiar ring to them. The purpose of this tome is less revelation than simple description. We will consider which of these creeks, recognized as trout water by their respective states, are ideal for fly-fishing.

In setting the parameters for this overview, only streams that can be fished by the general public have been considered. Even the best blue-ribbon stream, offering predictable insect hatches and voracious trout, is of little interest to the average fisherman if it is also posted and off limits. This applies in the case of streams that have some public access, but also have sections that are posted. The creek needs to have enough freely accessible public water to make it a destination worth investing the commuting time. Simply being able to fish the pools beneath several widely dispersed highway bridges or a short stretch of roadside right-of-way does not qualify a creek or river as a prime fly-casting destination.

It should also be noted that although a number of highland reservoirs have been stocked with trout in the southern Appalachian region, these are not covered. While many offer excellent trout fishing and, in a few cases under certain circumstances, fly-fishing is possible, the vast majority of angling on impounded waters consists of deep-water bait-fishing or trolling. For that reason we are confining our study to the area's free-flowing waters.

Unlike the hosts of some television fishing shows, I do not claim to be an expert on all, or even most of the waters covered in the following pages. Those guys can spend half an hour on a reservoir or river and speak as though they had invested a lifetime in solving the mysteries of those particular waters. Rather, I can only claim to have spent some time on the streams discussed, and 25 years fishing the streams and rivers of the southern highlands.

I have become intimately acquainted with many of the waters. Additionally, over a two-year period of intense research, I have driven more than 25,000 miles over highways, byways, and pig paths in search of public trout waters in the region, as well as logging another couple of hundred miles on hiking trails. Still, much of the fishing information has been collected from the state fisheries managers and other anglers, coupled with my own on-stream observations and experiences.

Hopefully, whether the reader is a novice fly caster or a veteran of many seasons but newly transplanted to the region, the following chapters will provide him or her with some useful information. That knowledge should open a new and exciting world of trout fishing in a region of remarkable beauty—and in the process save the angler a great deal of time usually lost in the search for appropriate fly-casting waters.

Changes Since the First Printing

In American life, about the only constant on which we can count is that things are constantly changing. You would think, however, that a guidebook to trout streams would be the exception: After all, nature changes the location of streams only about every 20,000 to 30,000 years, with an ice age. Even humanity has shied away from trying to move entire creeks. On the one hand this could be attributed to our inability to figure out exactly how to do so. On the other—and more likely—it could be that we just haven't come up with a good enough reason to make such a transfer.

Nevertheless our species has managed to take some actions that require a note or two regarding the accuracy of some details in *Trout Streams of Southern Appalachia*.

In Georgia, the summer of 1995 saw many streams that had previously been managed under standard trout regulations change over to year-round streams. Among these streams are all or portions of Dukes, Holly, Mill, Mountaintown, Noontootla, Panther, Rock, and Stamps Creeks, which are described in this book. The Conasauga River is also on this list, although additional regulations mandate artificial-lures-only from November 1 to the last Saturday of March each year. Night fishing, which is usually legal on year-round trout streams in Georgia, is not permitted on the Conasauga.

During 1994 and 1995 North Carolina designated four new creeks or rivers as delayed-harvest waters. Three of these offer enough public access to be mentioned in this volume: The Tuckasegee, the Watauga, and the North Fork of the Mills Rivers. Also, that portion of the Ararat River regulated under delayed-harvest rules was slightly redefined.

Another change of regulations in the Old North State established a new category of trout stream known as Wild Trout/Natural Bait Water. (Previously, all wild trout streams had been limited to artificial-lures-only.) This new category includes three streams covered in this book: Buck Creek in the Little Tennessee River watershed, Long Creek in the Cheoah River system, and the North Fork of the French Broad River.

Odds are that by the time you read this, one or more of the states covered in this book will have made additional regulation changes. For this reason, it is always an excellent idea to get a copy of the current trout fishing regulations from any of the states in which you intend to fish. These regulations are generally available at any sporting goods outlet that sells fishing licenses, or from the regional offices of the fisheries management agency in the state.

1

Trout Fishing in Southern Appalachia

The first problem involved in describing the fly-fishing waters of southern Appalachia is to define the geographic limits of the area. If you simply take out the world atlas and look at a topographic map of the eastern United States, the Appalachian Mountain range is fairly easy to recognize. It is the backbone of the East, cutting a swath from Maine down to northeastern Alabama. For our purposes, however, it is not quite that simple.

THE REGION AND ITS TROUT

Are we speaking very narrowly when we say southern Appalachia? If so, then our coverage would be just of the areas that qualify as mountains in that particular chain. On the other hand, there are a number of gray areas involved. Some adjacent areas, which are rather high in elevation and share many of the same cultural traits and values, adjoin the mountain range. What of the Cumberland Plateau of eastern Kentucky and Tennessee—or the Foothills region of the western Carolinas?

A traveler venturing into these places sees very little change in the people, yet technically, he has exited the southern Appalachians. On the other hand, the terrain in some of these areas is quite different. The creeks and rivers of the limestone formations of the Cumberland Valley and adjacent high ground of the plateau vary greatly from the tumbling freestone flows of the true Appalachian area. Yet the Carolina Foothills are virtually indistinguishable from the Appalachians, except for the lower elevations of their peaks.

For these reasons, I have fudged on the exact boundaries of southern Appalachia. In doing so I have tried to include all of the high-

The native southern Appalachian brook trout were the original inhabitants of the highlands of Georgia, Kentucky, Tennessee, and the Carolinas.

lands of the target states that are contiguous to the Appalachian chain and also have similar features.

At the same time, I have not attempted to cover all of the tailrace waters or other streams that occur in these areas. While these waters may be in close proximity to the uplands, they are often very different in nature. They would more properly be covered in an inventory of the various states' streams and rivers that support cold-water fisheries for at least portions of the year.

Having put that geography lesson behind us, let's move on to the history of trout fishing in southern Appalachia. Undoubtedly, the Cherokee and their predecessors in the region were familiar with the fish that inhabited the highland streams of the South. In many of the larger creeks and rivers ancient fish weirs built by these people are still visible.

In the course of gathering food from the streams, they would have come in contact with the brightly colored native brook trout that inhabited the waters. These fish, which are actually members of the char family, are the only trout indigenous to the region.

For the first European settlers, who entered these highlands beginning as early as the 1600s, the brook trout represented a source of food, just as it had for the natives. Catching the fish was more a matter of sustenance than sport. A seine was more likely used for the job than a hook and line.

Even into the early 1900s when fishing had taken on some of the trappings of civilization and was looked upon as a source of enjoyment, it was a sport that was expected to put food on the table. Only in the last couple of decades has an ethic of catch-and-release, and the idea that angling is simply fun, begun to make any inroads to the region.

The anglers of southern Appalachia are not the only ingredient of the fishing that has changed in modern times. The trout population has undergone a metamorphosis as well. The native brook trout has given way as the dominant species to the rainbow trout. These hardy expatriates from the western shores of North America were introduced to the southeastern streams as early as the 1880s and have found the waters to their liking. As they have spread their range they have crowded out the less hardy brookies, pushing the native species higher and higher into the more remote headwaters.

Adding to this trend was the simultaneous spread of brown trout into the region. This species, native to Europe, followed close on the heels of the rainbow trout, being stocked as early as 1905 and laying claim to many of the lower-elevation stretches of creeks and rivers. Being even more tolerant of less-than-ideal habitat requirements, brown trout are now masters of most of the marginal-quality waters and share prime waters with the rainbows.

In addition to the pressure from these more competitive species, the native brook trout have also been adversely affected by the lowering of water quality in the creeks of the southeastern states. Higher water temperatures due to the denuding of streamside vegetation by logging or farming began the decline of the brookie population, and the resultant silting and lowering of water purity increased the species' retreat from its traditional home waters.

Today the native brook trout is relegated to the extreme headwaters of the region, usually at 2500 feet of elevation or higher. Its last great stronghold is in the Great Smoky Mountain National Park and even there the decline continues. Since the mid-1970s many of the park's best brook trout waters have been closed to angling to reduce stress on the remnant population. On the southern fringe of suitable trout habitat in the Appalachians, the brook trout of South Carolina and northern Georgia are hanging on by their proverbial fingernails. As a result of these changes, the profile of the average southern Appalachian trout stream has been altered. The bulk of the creeks in the region are small to medium in flow and width (less than 25 feet wide).

The stream usually has a canopy of foliage shading the surface. This tunnel effect aids in keeping summer water temperatures low enough to sustain the cold-water species.

The fish in this average creek are predominately brown trout in the lower elevations, with the species also being present in most of the deep, calm pools of higher elevations. In the midsection of the stream the rainbow trout takes over as the most plentiful fish. It shares the pools with any browns present and is dominant in the faster runs and pocket waters of ripple areas. If brook trout still exist in the stream, they are found in the headwaters where the creek is small (often little more than a tiny brook), cold, and clean. There is usually a natural barrier (or in some cases a man-made one) such as a sizable waterfall that protects these native fish from upstream encroachment by rainbows and browns. Needless to say, there are a great many streams without a natural barrier. The upper ends of these creeks are now dominated by rainbow trout, the brookies having disappeared completely.

SAFETY

Although most novice outdoorsmen think of wildlife when the subject of hazards in the field comes up in conversation, by far the most dangerous critters we are going to meet in the southern Appalachian Mountains will be ourselves. Carelessness, negligence, and foolhardiness rate as the most common causes of injuries to sportsmen, including trout fishermen.

Anytime you are on the stream enjoying a day of fishing, it is wise to pay attention to your surroundings. Although statistics show that we are less likely to be injured while fishing than we are at home, there are accidents out there waiting to happen on the stream as well.

For that reason, especially when entering remote wilderness settings, it pays to be prepared. By always planning in advance we can minimize the opportunities for one of these unfortunate circumstances to sneak up on us.

So what are the things we should be watching for and avoiding? The two that most folks mention first in southern Appalachia are usually bears and poisonous snakes. Both are feared far out of proportion to any danger they pose. Bear attacks on humans that have been documented in the southern highlands are very rare indeed, and ordinarily involve a person coming too close to a sow with a cub, or a sightseer feeding a bear.

Black bears, which are the only species native to the region, are extremely wary about contact with people and will avoid it whenever possible. This, of course, does not include the "moochers" and "garbage dump" bears of the Great Smoky Mountains National Park and other areas. Bears that have been fed and seem friendly to people are the ones that most often end up taking a swipe at the hand that feeds them. In a quarter century of wandering the most remote areas of southern Appalachia I have yet to even see a bear in the wild.

The story is much the same for poisonous snakes. They do exist, but their threat to the angler is greatly overrated. Although timber rattlesnakes and copperheads do inhabit the region, neither can be called common.

Again, in 25 years, I have only seen three poisonous snakes in the mountains, and two of those had already been killed by other folks. The key to this record is that I do not go looking for the critters. If you go to the mountains to dig into rock piles or turn over fallen logs, you can improve your odds of finding a serpent. While you are doing that, however, I will be out on the stream accosting the trout, thank you!

Also, I have heard dozens of anglers describe their encounters with water moccasins on trout streams of the region. Every one of these folks was convinced he had survived a meeting with the infamously belligerent and highly poisonous cottonmouth. Undoubtedly, virtually all of these encounters actually involved a northern water snake. Cottonmouths are truly fearsome creatures to encounter. They will usually stand their ground and be quite aggressive when they feel threatened. Fortunately, the ground they "stand" is located along coastal plain, black-water streams, and bayous. Finding a cottonmouth moccasin in a mountain trout stream is about as likely as sighting Bigfoot in downtown Asheville.

Along this same line, many reports of copperheads by fishermen are sparked by sightings of banded water snakes, which have similar markings and coloration.

About the only precaution necessary to avoid dangerous serpents is to not poke your hands into crevices. In the case of rattlesnakes, the most likely scenario for meeting them is after dark, since they are nocturnal hunters. When wandering around camp at night in warm weather, a flashlight to check your path is a good precaution. Still, in the case of bears or snakes, the odds are that you will be struck by lightning or win the Georgia or Kentucky lottery before suffering a serious wound from a bear or poisonous snake in the southern mountains.

Now that we have covered what is overrated as a threat, let's turn to the things that can, and even likely will, cause you trouble in southern Appalachia. Number one among the dangers of the area (and also the most frequent killer) is the common rock! Cover it with slick algae or just plain water, place it near a waterfall, and some hiker, sightseer, or fisherman will eventually take that one step closer for a better look. No year passes without dozens of injuries from falls and some deaths occurring across the southern highlands as a result of falling from rocky precipices. Most of the more dangerous spots have warning signs, but it seems that many folks see these as open invitations to tempt fate. A couple of visits to spots like Linville Falls in North Carolina or Cumberland Falls in Kentucky to watch our collective foolhardiness and you will agree with the sage possum of the Okefenokee created by the late cartoonist Walt Kelly. As Pogo so adroitly noted, "We have met the enemy and he is us!" Forget the bears and snakes, the rocks are the killers!

Even if you do avoid getting close to dangerous drops, the rocks still have a shot at getting you. Wading rocky trout water is ideal for supplying plenty of scrapes, scratches, bruises, sprains, and the occasional broken bone. Your first line of defense against these hazards is felt-soled wading boots.

Southern trouters are prone to discard waders when the summer heat arrives, opting for wading in more comfortable attire. All too often they wear old tennis shoes. A pair of wading boots may not look stylish with your shorts, but they can help you avoid some unnecessary pain.

In the arena of wildlife, the two most consistently dangerous critters encountered in southern Appalachia by anglers are hornets and yellow jackets. Either of these wasps can make you miserable and under some circumstances their stings can even be lethal. Few southern trout anglers can claim to have never tangled with either of them.

Hornets love to hang their nests over the water and during spring and summer the leaves camouflage their presence. On a couple of occasions I have bumped into these hidden paper hives without ever seeing them beforehand.

If the airborne nests do not get you, you still have to deal with subterranean yellow jacket hives. These wasps often build their nests in the banks of creeks, where anglers will have the opportunity to step on them when getting in or out of the creek, not to mention while stalking a fish from the shore. More times than I care to think about I have taken unscheduled dips into deep, fishy-looking pocket water to escape their swarm.

Of course, try as we may, an unfortunate incident may still lie in our future. The best precautions for meeting these emergencies are to let someone know where you are going (or better yet, take them with you), know the location of the nearest hospital, and take along a basic first-aid kit for the minor injuries. Also, a great tool for survival is a whistle. It can make the difference between languishing in pain or being found in the case of a serious mishap.

One last word of caution is necessary before leaving this subject. If you feel compelled to take along a snake-bite kit and you do manage to beat the odds and get bitten by a poisonous snake, keep your wits about you. Snake bites are rarely fatal and if you are within an hour's travel of medical help, forget the kit and get to a hospital. The danger of cutting a vein or artery, or applying an improper tourniquet, can be more serious than the bite. Use the kit only as a last resort when in true wilderness situations.

EQUIPMENT

There was a time in the South when about the only way to get a native son's dander up was to turn your nose up at grits or to be-smirch the reputation of General Robert E. Lee. Ah, for the good old days! It seems that now all you have to do is mention that you like a 7-foot fly rod for mountain streams and the next thing you know you are on the figurative field of honor at dawn with dueling pistols. Every fisherman seems to have his own ideas of what equipment is needed, permissible, and taboo for fly-casting the tightly foliated southern Appalachian creeks. And speaking from my own experience, I think they are all correct!

When it comes to rods, the two major schools of thought are that a 6- to 7-foot rod is best because it takes less room for casts, or that a 7½- to 8½-footer is more suitable because it allows longer roll casts and extended reach for dapping. Like I said, I agree with both schools of thought. There is no perfect rod for all highland anglers. The ability to handle the wand you prefer is the key.

The same can be said for fly lines as well. Some fishermen argue that the light, tapered lines allow for more delicate presentations of the fly. Others reply that a heavier weight-forward line allows more momentum to be supplied with the necessarily short back casts. Again, this argument is best settled by individual taste. I have even had anglers visiting from other parts of the country contend that the streams are so small and tight there is no need for a fly line at all. They say they would be just as well off tying the leader directly to the end of the rod. Of course, they might then be mistaken for cane-pole fishermen, which could offend the cane polers at the very thought that fly-fishermen were now stealing their secrets.

When the discussion gets down to the leader, the debate does not end. Should it be 10 feet or 6 feet, 4X or 6X? My own rule of thumb is to use the shortest, heaviest leader that the conditions allow. On North Carolina's Lost Cove Creek, the gentle, crystalline pools and wary brown trout demand fine tippets and yards of leader, but on the rough-and-tumble sections of Tennessee's North River you could probably raise a rainbow to a well-presented fly attached to an anchor chain.

Finally, regarding the fly reel, discussions of drags and reel capacity are more entertaining than practical. I know successful southern fishermen who have taken large trout from highland streams, but who have only seen the backing on their reels when they put on new fly lines. Long runs are not a concern when the fish does not have anywhere to make those long runs. Of course, there are some exceptions, like the larger tailwaters or Tennessee's Tellico River. The angler who tackles these rivers may end up using his reel to fight a fish, but most of the rest of us will simply use it to store our fly lines.

In closing, let me stress that in southern Appalachia it is far less a matter of choosing the right gear than it is a case of being able to handle the chosen equipment under tight fishing conditions. If you can land your fly in a 30-inch square from 30 feet, you can cover 80 percent of the fishing situations you will meet.

MAPS

One of the difficulties of putting together a guidebook such as this is the need to provide information on finding the creeks and rivers. It is much more pleasurable to wax poetic about the fishing than to provide directions for getting to it. That is where maps come into the picture.

The maps in this book will give the reader an overview of each river system or watershed described and show the main highways leading to that system. Given the breadth of territory shown on most of these maps, it has not been possible to show all the local roads that provide access to the rivers and, especially, their smaller tributaries. Hence, these maps should be used in conjunction with reliable local maps.

Unfortunately, there is no one map in each of the covered states that provides all the information needed. Some are very good at providing secondary-road names. Others do better at giving the route and county-road numbers. Still, you often do not know which of these will be most useful until you reach the area and see how the road signs at intersections are marked. Additionally, within a single state there is not always a consistent pattern to the signs. Then add to this the factor that most cartographers drawing road maps pay only passing attention to streams.

On the other side of the coin, United States Geological Survey (USGS) maps are great at showing terrain and streams, but the road names and numbers are a lesser priority. The road may look easy to find on these maps, but quite different through the windshield.

When dealing with a large, multistate region like southern Appalachia, the problem is compounded even further. For these reasons, it is necessary to compile a veritable library of maps when looking for trout waters.

Maps produced by state game and fish agencies, private mapping companies, the USGS, the United States Forest Service, and the National Park Service are all part of solving this puzzle. In the interest of simplification, however, each stream covered in the following chapters will be keyed to the USGS 7.5-minute quadrangle maps on which it appears. In states where it is applicable, the page in the DeLorme Mapping Company's *Atlas & Gazetteer* for the state will also be shown. Finally, on streams in South Carolina the page on which the creek appears in the *South Carolina Wildlife Facilities Atlas* will be noted.

In all, there are at least a dozen companies or agencies producing maps that can be useful for locating trout streams on public land in portions of southern Appalachia. These are listed in the appendix in the back of the book, along with descriptions of what type maps they offer.

Having laid a groundwork with this thumbnail sketch of southern Appalachia's trout waters and their inhabitants, as well as safety and equipment concerns, we'll next consider the insect life found in the region and what flies best simulate those bugs.

2

Hatches and Flies

One of the stereotypes of fly-fishermen is that they are obsessed not only with angling but also with the study of the bugs on which trout feed. The impression implies that a college degree in entomology is a prerequisite for becoming a successful fly caster.

The need for this type of information is based on having to "match the hatch" when the trout are being very particular about what they are eating. If you can't identify the critters, how can you hope to present a fly to the fish that imitates the bugs they are feasting upon? This kind of feeding situation is usually found on fertile waters that support large populations of aquatic insects that appear at fairly predictable times. Often, under these situations, trout ignore anything cast to them unless it is the same size, color, and shape as the insect on which they are dining.

The type of fishing situation that we have just described is much more common on spring and limestone waters, or very fertile freestone streams. The bulk of such waters are found in the Northeast or western states, but not in southern Appalachia. The vast majority of southern streams are rather infertile freestone flows.

While these streams support a veritable smorgasbord of insect life, only a relatively small number of individuals of each species are present. Even more important, with a few notable exceptions, the insect hatches that do occur are sporadic and very unpredictable. Add to this the rough-and-tumble nature of most of the small creeks of the region and the result is a population of trout that are accustomed to seeing a wide variety of insects that are being swept by them in a hurry. Of necessity these fish have become very opportunistic in nature, grabbing almost any passing tidbit that resembles any of a number of insect types usually found in their home waters.

Under these conditions a rudimentary knowledge of insect types can be helpful in picking the flies you present to the trout, but those choices are not usually the difference between catching fish and getting skunked. More often, skill at stalking, reading the stream, and casting in tight circumstances are more crucial to the fishing than choice of a fly to match a particular fish's feeding preference. The bottom line is that when the fish are feeding, any fly that looks buggy is usually pounced upon, assuming it is correctly presented.

Having made this point, let's take a look at what is likely to be found in the way of insect life in the creeks and rivers of southern Appalachia. The results of this survey provide the hints necessary to pick a few flies with which to stock your box before testing the waters of the region.

First of all, with regard to the size of flies needed, patterns tied on size 12 or size 14 hooks for dry flies are generally all the variety needed. In nymphs and wet flies, sizes 8 to 14 are adequate to most situations. Some circumstances can occur that require larger or smaller flies, but the bulk of the fishing conditions encountered in southern Appalachia can be mastered with these sizes.

Undoubtedly the most common aquatic insect life in the streams of the southeastern states are members of the *Trichoptera* family. Commonly known as caddis flies, these make up the backbone of the aquatics found in the bulk of the creeks. Examining a few rocks turned over on the stream bed usually reveals the nymphal forms of some of the case-building members of this family, and adult members can often be seen emerging throughout much of the spring, summer, and fall.

Trout on many streams show a preference for dry flies that display the distinctive swept wing of the caddis family, undoubtedly because these resemble the most common adult insect the fish see on those waters. On many days, the trout do not, however, show a strong preference for a particular color of caddis. If they are rising to a slate-gray pattern, they are also likely to come after a green one.

A good basic selection of caddis fly imitations that have proven useful on the streams of southern Appalachia includes the Elk-Hair Caddis, the Chuck Caddis (tied with wings made of woodchuck hair), and the Royal Trude.

Due to their case-building lifestyle during the nymphal stage, caddis fly nymphs are difficult to imitate with a fly. Though trout readily feed on the nymphs (including the cases), these are ordinarily attached to a rock or stick and not found moving or floating free in the stream. Getting your fly to stay still on a rock and look convincing is a difficult proposition under virtually all the water conditions encountered in the region. For that reason, few anglers try to imitate the larval stage of the caddis.

The second important aquatic insect to the fly-fisherman in the Southeast is the mayfly. These members of the *Ephemeroptera* family are nearly as widespread as the caddis flies during the warmer months throughout the southern Appalachians. The mayflies appear in a wide variety of colors and are most easily recognized by their upright wings.

There is very little difference in the habitat in regard to where the caddis or mayfly are found in the southern streams. Very often, they can be found hatching at the same time on the same waters. Unfortunately, in most cases, the mayfly hatches are no more predictable on southern Appalachian streams than are the caddis. Some notable exceptions do occur and are covered in discussing the specific streams on which they take place.

A good basic selection of flies that imitate adult mayflies and cover most situations encountered on southern streams includes the Royal Wulff, the Adams (in both regular and female patterns), and the Light Cahill.

Mayfly nymphs are bottom dwellers, but unlike the caddis family they are free roaming. For that reason, they are a more important food source, at least as far as the fly-angler is concerned, than are the caddis larvas. These nymphs are small, with hook sizes 14 to 16 being standard for imitating them. Good all-purpose fly patterns for this chore are Gold-Ribbed Hare's Ears, Pheasant Tails, and Tellico Nymphs.

Next among the insect types that make up the forage base of trout in southern Appalachia is the family *Plecoptera,* or stone flies. Although found in great abundance and variety in the region's streams, their life cycle relegates them to the position of a less important food source for trout.

Living on the streambed among the rocks, stone fly nymphs crawl out onto the shore or the above-water surfaces of the rocks when they are ready to emerge as adult flies. As a result, the adult flies rate as a relatively rare source of forage for trout. The nymphs, on the other hand, are readily available, especially when moving toward the surface to emerge. Many of these stone fly nymphs can be quite hefty by aquatic insect standards and hooks as large as size 8 are often used for tying flies to imitate them.

Three of the most popular fly patterns throughout the southern Appalachians are (left to right) the Humpy, the Royal Wulff, and the Adams.

Ted's Stone, which is a brown chenille imitation, and the Montana Stone (a black version) are both large, heavily weighted flies that have proven successful at getting down deep to tempt trout on southern streams.

The final category of insects that are important on the trout's menu in the South are the terrestrials. Oddly enough, these nonaquatic, land-dwelling insects make up the closest thing to a dependable "hatch" that can be found on streams throughout the southern Appalachians. During the summer months a steady supply of beetles, ants, crickets, and grasshoppers fall or are blown into the streams. Needless to say, the trout have become accustomed to looking for them.

Surveys of the contents of trout stomachs have revealed that by far the most common insect eaten is the ordinary black ant. They were found in virtually every trout that was checked and often in great numbers. Imitations of these, in either dry or wet patterns, are high on the list of flies to take fishing.

Two final food sources that can be imitated with an artificial fly need to be mentioned: minnows and crayfish (more commonly referred to as crawfish or crawdads in the South). With regard to catching larger trout, these big forage items are quite important to the fly caster. To imitate them, streamer flies are the obvious choice.

Virtually any streamer pattern has a good chance of attracting trout on southern streams, assuming it is presented in the right place and worked through the water enticingly. Quite often the choice hinges on the particular pattern in which the angler has confidence.

From a personal standpoint, the Muddler Minnow has worked well on a number of creeks and rivers. Tied with tan body hair of the white-tailed deer and weighted with a few wraps of lead wire, this fly can achieve a negative buoyancy that seems to attract strikes. In other words the deer hair prevents it from sinking to the bottom, while the lead keeps it from floating to the surface. Even when no action is imparted to the fly, its ability to suspend in the water gives it an edge over other streamers. Additionally, the tan deer hair is very similar to the most common color found in the crawdads of the mountain streams.

Having made these statements about successful fly patterns on southern Appalachian waters, it is now time to make like one of the crawdads we have been discussing and back away from my picks. Virtually every southern fly caster has favorite patterns which, assuming that they are put on the water regularly, produce fish. The ones mentioned have worked well for me for a number of years, plus I have found them in the fly boxes and at the end of leaders belonging to many other successful southern trouters.

Still, to the highly experienced fly caster who has challenged trout in many regions of North America and beyond, this discussion of insects and flies may seem a bit superficial. But, in this part of the country, stream approach, casting accuracy and buoyant, highly visible dry flies lead to much more angling action than waiting for the sporadic, unpredictable periods of feeding activity. The fly caster simply needs to be just as opportunistic as are the fish.

SECTION ONE

GEORGIA

The fact that there are any trout streams at all in Georgia comes as a surprise to many anglers—even some living in the Peach State. Yet, among the states covered by this volume, only North Carolina can claim more miles of cold-water streams than Georgia. With approximately 4100 miles of creeks and rivers classified as trout water by the Georgia Department of Natural Resources' Wildlife Resources Division (WRD), virtually all of the northern third of the state lies within the range of the fishery. Beach Creek, which lies just north of Columbus in the western portion of the state, is easily the most southerly trout water found in the United States.

Granted, much of this water is marginal trout habitat and supports only hatchery-stocked fish during the spring, but Georgia can boast of more than 1500 miles of primary trout water, where the fish are able to reproduce naturally. Even using this figure, the Peach State is still second only to North Carolina in miles of trout water.

Like the waters of her sister states, Georgia's creeks and rivers are home to both wild and stocked brook, brown, and rainbow trout. On the bulk of the streams the rainbow is the dominant fish, but some others are predominantly brown trout fisheries. In a few instances the native brook trout still sits atop the food chain. A program instituted in the late 1960s renovated several streams and reintroduced the brookie to some of its original haunts.

The vast majority of the streams that qualify for our discussion are located in north-central to northeastern Georgia. These are located on the roughly 700,000 acres of land that comprise the Chattahoochee National Forest and many of the creeks are found on Wildlife Management Areas (WMA) that the U.S. Forest Service leases to the state. Under either circumstance, whether managed by the state or federal authorities, these lands are open to the general public for fishing.

On the other hand, virtually all of the creeks located in the northwest or west-central regions are on privately owned, usually posted property. For obvious reasons, we will not be talking about these waters.

Additionally, Georgia has three tailrace fisheries. The waters of the Savannah River below Lake Hartwell on the Georgia–South Carolina border, the Chattahoochee River below Lake Sidney Lanier north of Atlanta, and the Toccoa River from Blue Ridge Lake to the Tennessee border all harbor trout. Of these, however, only the Toccoa falls within our area of concern. The Savannah is virtually a lake fishery since the completion of Lake Richard B. Russell a few miles downstream of Hartwell, and the Chattahoochee tailrace begins on the edge of the Piedmont and knifes its way deep into that region. Many consider this tailrace to be Georgia's premier trout fishery, but few would argue that it is in the southern Appalachian region.

A line drawn on a map along US 411 from the Tennessee border to Chatsworth, then southeastward to Jasper would mark the western boundary of natural trout water in Georgia. From Jasper the line could be extended eastward through Dawsonville, Dahlonega, Cleveland, and Clarksville to mark the southern edge of the natural fishery. While not every creek within these boundaries qualifies as trout water, nothing outside it can be called a part of the natural trout fishery.

A couple of streams that fit our criteria of being on public land and having trout in them do exist outside the boundary we just covered. The first is Johns Creek on the Johns Mountain WMA in northwest Georgia. This limestone stream appears to be ideal trout habitat, but, unfortunately, fails the test on closer inspection. Its waters are only marginally suited for trout and the stockers released there are heavily pursued by bait-fishermen. The combination makes for a rather disappointing fly-casting destination.

The other stream is the Middle Fork of the Broad River. This tributary of the Savannah River lies south of our imaginary boundary on the Lake Russell WMA and is a rather slow-flowing, meandering lowland creek. It is stocked heavily with trout during the season on a put-and-take basis, but water temperatures in the summer and heavy fishing pressure eliminate most fish before they learn that there are other foods besides cheese and kernel corn. Again, this is a stream hardly worth the fly-fisherman's efforts to reach.

Having mentioned these exceptions, we now turn our attention to the waters of the Peach State that offer a great deal of attraction for the long-rod angler.

Before diving into that discussion, however, we do need to mention the state's fishing regulations and access laws. The Peach State has a regular trout season that opens on the last Saturday in March and runs through the last day of October each year. Most of the state's marginal trout waters are not included in this season though, and are open to year-round fishing.

The statewide creel limit on trout is eight fish per day, regardless of species. There are no minimum or maximum lengths on trout that may be kept, but some exceptions do exist on certain managed streams. These will be discussed as we talk about those creeks and rivers. A regular state fishing license and a trout stamp are required to be in the possession of all anglers 16 years of age or older. Unless otherwise noted, fishing in all the Georgia waters discussed is governed by these general trout regulations.

In Georgia a person having title to land bordering a stream also owns the streambed to the middle of the creek. If they own both shores, they own the entire stream bed and can deny access to both wading and float-fishers. Bear in mind that you must have permission to fish on private land in Georgia and the county sheriffs will answer landowners' calls to enforce this law.

The Georgia DNR publishes the "Trout and Freshwater Fishing Regulations" booklet annually. Besides the general regulations, it gives special rules that apply on managed waters, as well as lists of regular and year-round streams by county. A copy of the brochure can be picked up at most sporting goods outlets and tackle shops in the northern portion of the state, or you can order one by writing to the Georgia Department of Natural Resources, Wildlife Resources Division, 2070 US Highway 278 SE, Social Circle, Georgia 30279 or calling (404) 918-6418.

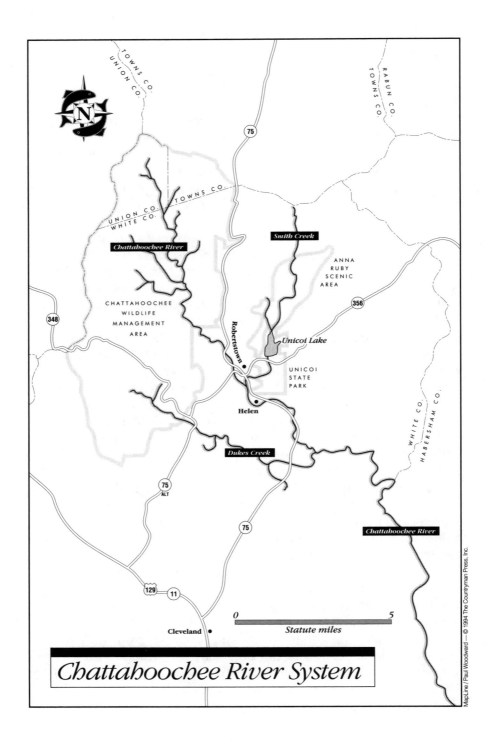

TOWNS CO.
UNION CO.

RABUN CO.
TOWNS CO.

TOWNS CO.
TOWNS CO.

75

UNION CO. TOWNS CO.
WHITE CO.

Chattahoochee River

Smith Creek

ANNA
RUBY
SCENIC
AREA

356

CHATTAHOOCHEE
WILDLIFE
MANAGEMENT
AREA

348

Robertstown

Unicoi Lake

UNICOI
STATE
PARK

Helen

WHITE CO.
HABERSHAM CO.

Dukes Creek

75
ALT

75

Chattahoochee River

129   11

Cleveland

0   5
Statute miles

Chattahoochee River System

MapLine / Paul Woodward — © 1994 The Countryman Press, Inc.

3

Chattahoochee River System

Undoubtedly, the Chattahoochee River is Georgia's best-known trout stream. Most of that renown centers, however, on the tailrace fishery mentioned earlier. The portion of the river further north in the Appalachians is overshadowed, but offers a varied and quite good fishery of its own. Trout are found in the river from its headwaters downstream to just above Lake Sidney Lanier, as well as a number of feeder streams. The waters we are concerned with are the headwaters of the river on the Chattahoochee Wildlife Management Area or in the town of Helen and two feeder streams that are located on public lands—Dukes and Smith creeks.

The river rises in Chattahoochee Gap in northeast Georgia's White County and flows southward. Located at the lower end of the public water is the town of Helen. This tourist mecca makes a good headquarters for exploring the Chattahoochee trout waters. Once a sleepy and dying timber town, in the 1960s the hamlet transformed itself into an Alpine village with a Bavarian theme. It now sports a wide variety of accommodations, eateries, and gift shops. Be warned that during the entire trout season you are also likely to find heavy traffic on GA 75 going through the town. Late in the season when the fall foliage and Oktoberfest celebration extend their grip over the sightseeing public, the traffic jams can rival those of downtown Atlanta as Georgia's worst.

Another option for a central point from which to sample this area's creeks is Unicoi State Park on GA 356 just to the east of Helen. The park has both RV and tent camping facilities as well as a modern lodge and restaurant.

CHATTAHOOCHEE RIVER
USGS Jacks Gap, Cow Rock, Helen

The Chattahoochee River offers three distinct sections in the area that is open to public fishing upstream from Helen. The portion of the stream actually in Helen and the small adjoining municipality of Robertstown is a medium-size stream open under regular trout regulations. It is heavily stocked with catchable rainbow, brown, and the occasional brook trout. There is plenty of room for fly-casting through this entire stretch, but if the weather is good, expect to share the stream with a large number of folks in inner tubes.

There is little if any natural reproduction of trout in this lower area, with water temperatures getting rather warm during the summer months. This is definitely a put-and-take fishery that favors bait-fishermen, who utilize it heavily. Still it can be interesting at times.

While accompanying friends on a shopping trip into the town on a June Saturday, I happened to glance off the bridge (as if I ever walk or drive across a bridge without looking down at the water) that spans the river at the southern edge of town. A couple of dimples on the water were reason enough for me to excuse myself and head back to the car.

I soon had my fly rod assembled and was standing under the bridge. For the next hour I drifted Light Cahills in size 12 down the current between each group of tubers that passed. My efforts were rewarded with five brown trout in the 8- to 9-inch range as well as an ovation from some obviously bored husbands of shoppers who lingered to watch one of the conquests. Granted, the trout were freshly stocked, but it sure beat the alternative of making the rounds of the gift shops.

The second section of the river is located north of the town on the 24,000-acre Chattahoochee WMA that stretches across Towns, Union, and White counties. There is a sizable amount of private land posted between Robertstown and the WMA boundary. On the WMA the river is flowing at a higher elevation and is a legitimate trout stream. There is some natural reproduction, but most of the fish are hatchery stockers. Both wild browns and rainbows can be found mixed with the released trout.

For the most part the river provides room for casting, though it is tight in places. Road access is very good with gravel Forest Service Road (FS) 52 paralleling the river for most of its length. A great deal of primitive camping occurs along the stream and fishing pressure is heavy. On opening day and holiday weekends it can be elbow-to-elbow along the shore. The vast majority of these anglers are bait- or spin-fishing.

Shortly after entering the WMA going north on FS 52 there is a WRD hunting check-in station on the left of the road. Just upstream of this structure the river bears away from the road and runs for a distance through a small, steep-banked gorge. Due to the tough access to this area, it gets light pressure and usually provides better fishing for the wild trout.

Continuing up FS 52 leads to the final section of the Chattahoochee. Just above the junction with a small stream called Henson Creek, there is a waterfall of about 30 feet. From this point upstream the Chattahoochee is one of Georgia's renovated brook trout streams.

In the early 1980s the Chattahoochee became the state's sixth and final stream to be restored as a brookie fishery. All competing trout were removed from this stretch using the poison rotenone, which affects only gilled life-forms. Native brook trout were then transplanted from other streams to repopulate the river. The barrier falls keep rainbows and browns from reentering this portion of the Chattahoochee.

The Forest Service road becomes almost impassable before it reaches Henson Creek and only foot access is possible above that point. Fishing pressure is generally light in the headwaters, where the river is a small stream. Casting is very tight and this would probably not even be mentioned as a fly-casting destination if it were not for the presence of the native fish. These colorful trout average only 5 or 6 inches, but some 8-inch brookies can be found by the angler willing to employ the stalking and dapping tactics needed.

Jasus, Low Gap, and Spoilcane creeks are other small feeder creeks on the WMA that hold trout, but are too small to be of much interest to the fly-fisherman. In the case of Spoilcane, it also meanders on and off public lands, making it difficult to fish.

The lower portion of the Chattahoochee is virtually all accessible off GA 75, which runs through Helen and Robertstown, while the WMA portion of the river can be reached via FS 52 off of GA Alternate 75 at Robertstown.

DUKES CREEK

USGS Cow Rock

Dukes Creek is a major feeder stream of the Chattahoochee River in the headwaters section. The portion of the creek open to public fishing is located in the Chattahoochee WMA, but the creek does not join the river until both have exited the public lands.

Dukes Creek is a small flow that tumbles down an extremely scenic course through a steep gorge. This central portion of the stream is known as the Dukes Creek Falls Scenic Area and is characterized by a number of cascades. The most impressive, however, is formed where small Dodd Creek exits the Raven Cliffs Wilderness Area to drop over 100 feet into the main stream.

Access to the gorge is difficult and the angling pressure is low as a result. Although the creek is relatively small, its extremely rocky bed keeps the canopy of foliage at a distance from the water and provides plenty of casting room. The trout are almost exclusively wild rainbows, up to 9 or 10 inches. Due to the light fishing pressure, there is the chance that a larger trout may turn up occasionally, but expect to catch a lot of 6- to 8-inch fish.

The gorge can be reached via the Dukes Creek Falls Trail. This steeply descending, 1.0-mile trail that features frequent switchbacks has its trailhead and parking lot on GA 348 (Richard Russell Scenic Highway).

SMITH CREEK

USGS Tray Mountain, Helen

Smith Creek is a small tributary of the Chattahoochee that merits mention due to its location, in spite of its size. The creek rises on National Forest land, tumbles over Anna Ruby Falls and flows through Unicoi State Park.

Casting is very tight on the creek but it does hold both stocked fish and a good population of small wild rainbows. Although it is not a major fly-fishing-destination stream, since it runs through a park that is ideally situated for camping while exploring the Chattahoochee drainage, Smith Creek is a convenient place to practice some small-stream casting.

From the head of the lake in the park, there is about one-half mile of water upstream in the state park, which is stocked with catchable-size trout. Above the park there is another mile and a half of creek below the parking area at Anna Ruby Scenic Area. The boundary between the park and the scenic area is clearly marked. This upper portion of the creek is not stocked but, as mentioned earlier, does have some wild fish. No fishing is allowed from the parking lot up to Anna Ruby Falls.

There is a two-dollar-per-day parking permit required in Unicoi State Park, which can be paid on the honor system at locations throughout the park. You do not have to pay the state parking charge if you are going on up into the Anna Ruby Scenic Area, but you still do not get a free ride. The Forest Service charges a two-dollar fee for entering the Anna Ruby Falls area. There is a fee-collection booth, but when it is not manned the honor system applies.

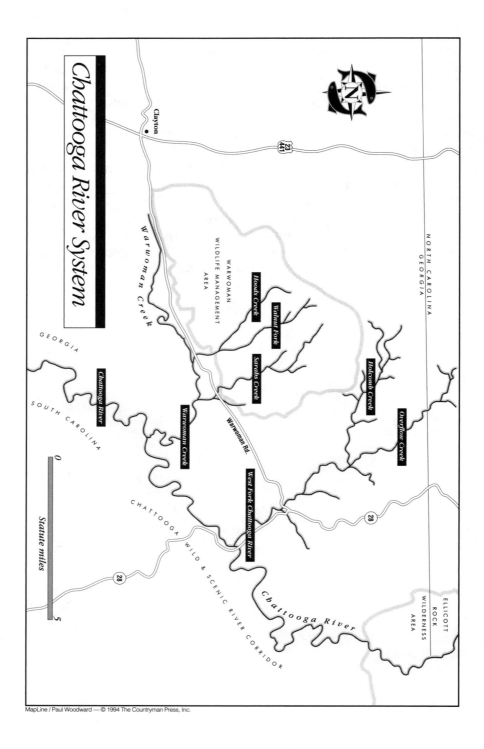

Chattooga River System

Clayton

23
441

Warwoman Creek

WARWOMAN
WILDLIFE MANAGEMENT
AREA

NORTH CAROLINA
GEORGIA

Hoads Creek

Walnut Fork

Sarvhs Creek

Holcomb Creek

Overflow Creek

GEORGIA

SOUTH CAROLINA

Chattooga River

Warwoman Creek

Warwoman Rd.

West Fork Chattooga River

28

CHATTOOGA WILD & SCENIC RIVER CORRIDOR

28

Chattooga River

ELLICOTT
ROCK
WILDERNESS
AREA

0

Statute miles

5

4

Chattooga River System

There are a number of factors that make the Chattooga River system unique among Georgia's trout waters. The system contains two large, natural trout rivers, a wilderness area, a wild and scenic river corridor, and plenty of year-round trout-fishing water. Probably better known for its whitewater canoeing, the Chattooga also attracted a great deal of attention during the mid-1970s when it was the site of the filming of the hit movie *Deliverance*. There are also some very interesting small tributary streams on the Warwoman WMA that add spice to the angling on the Chattooga system.

All of the streams discussed in this river system are located in the Chattahoochee National Forest, except for the Chattooga itself, which forms the border between Georgia's national forest and South Carolina's Sumter National Forest.

CHATTOOGA RIVER
USGS Tamassee, Satolah, Whetstone, Rainy Mountain

The Chattooga River rises in North Carolina's Nantahala National Forest and flows southward to form the border between Georgia and South Carolina, eventually emptying into Tugaloo Lake at the headwaters of the Savannah River. A large, free-flowing river, the Chattooga is acclaimed by both Georgia and South Carolina as one of their premier trout fisheries. In addition to being located on U.S. Forest Service land, the river flows down the Chattooga River Wild and Scenic River Corridor.

From the standpoint of the fly-angler, the portion of the river up-

The author caught and released this 15-inch rainbow in the Ellicott Rock Wilderness Area on the Chattooga River.

stream of Burrells Ford on FS 646 to the North Carolina line is the most interesting. At one time this part of the river was managed as a wild brown trout fishery. Today, no stocking is done in this area and the bulk of the fish are still browns. Some rainbows show up in the lower section of this part of the river, either from stockers migrating upriver or fish dropping down from some of the tributaries.

Brown trout in the 9- to 14-inch range are fairly common, but some recent concerns have been expressed by fisheries biologists that the aquatic insect populations are suffering from low water quality in the river. This in turn has led to a less productive fishery. Still, the Chattooga produces some large browns as well, with bruisers up to 10 pounds having been reported. These large fish are most susceptible to streamers fished in the early morning, late evening, or on overcast days.

The browns on the upper Chattooga have a reputation for being mercurial and at times quite selective. Probably this behavior can be traced to the natural inclination to wariness that brown trout exhibit, plus the fact that they are in big water where the volume of food allows the luxury of being picky about the next meal. At times on summer evenings, midge hatches come off that require dry flies in sizes 18 to 20 to fool these fish. At other times, the bushiest size 12 attractor in your fly box will provoke explosive strikes on the same waters.

The bulk of the land along both banks of the Chattooga above Burrells Ford is located in the Ellicott Rock Wilderness Area and the only access is by foot along the Chattooga River Trail. At the juncture of the Georgia–North Carolina–South Carolina state lines, the border is marked by Ellicott Rock. The rock itself is right at water level on the South Carolina side of the river and is inscribed with a carving dated 1813, placed there by surveyor Andrew Ellicott to mark the boundary. A sign on the trail indicates the location of the rock.

The major factor concerning Ellicott Rock important to fishermen is to be aware that a North Carolina fishing license is required for fishing further upstream. Below the rock, either a Georgia or a South Carolina license is valid on the river under a reciprocal agreement, regardless of the shore on which you are standing. If you fish any of the feeder streams, however, you need a license from the state you are entering.

Even as far north as Ellicott Rock, the Chattooga is a large stream, characterized by tumbling chutes and small falls breaking up long, deep, clear, and often slick-surfaced pools. Casting room is no problem, with plenty of space to really lay out some line. Yet, as with most southern streams, careful stalking to the best position to present a fly is a much better idea than stretching out 60 or 70 feet of line.

The portion of the Chattooga River below Burrells Ford takes on a totally different character from the upper region. Although the entire river down to Lake Tugaloo is listed by Georgia as trout water, the part lying below Russell Bridge at GA 28 is very marginal. This still leaves roughly 10 miles of river that contains trout fishing. The best of this fishing is found in the first couple of miles downstream from Burrells Ford to the Big Bend Falls area.

Beginning at Burrells Ford the river downstream is stocked regularly with catchable rainbow trout, as well as periodic plantings of fingerling brown trout. Since the Chattooga Wild and Scenic River Corridor still surrounds the river, access is very limited downstream of the bridge at Burrells Ford. In fact, stocking of trout is accomplished in this stretch by carrying tanks of fish in by helicopter and dropping them from the air.

The only problem that the stocking creates for the fly-angler is when fishing immediately after a planting of the fingerling browns. It is almost impossible to drop a fly on the water at that time without it being attacked by a 4- or 5-inch brown. Even if larger fish are present, they rarely have time to get to your offering.

This area of the Chattooga offers big, deep pools broken by shallow riffles that are easily waded. From the standpoint of casting and stream approach, it is ideal for fly-fishing. But, you should expect to hike a mile away from either Burrells Ford or GA 28 to find the best fishing.

As mentioned earlier, access to the upper portion of the Chattooga is available on FS 646 off GA 28 on the Georgia shore. Once across the stream and into South Carolina, the same road carries a designation of FS 708 and runs off SC 107 in Oconee County.

All foot-trail access via the Chattooga River Trail between the GA 28 bridge and Ellicott Rock is found on the South Carolina side of the river. For several miles above Russell Bridge the Bartram Trail shares this footpath. Further upriver, after the Bartram veers off, the Foothills Trail joins to share the path with the Chattooga River Trail for a distance. The highway crossing Russell Bridge at the lower end of the legitimate trout water is marked SC 28 on the Carolina shore and GA 28 on the Peach State's side of the river.

The creel limit for trout on the Chattooga River is eight per day, regardless of which shore you are on. There is no minimum length for these fish. The entire length of the river between Georgia and South Carolina is open to year-round fishing.

A primitive campground is located at Burrells Ford, but requires about 0.25 mile of walking from the parking lot at FS 706 on the South Carolina side of the river. Some backpack campsites are also available in the Ellicott Rock Wilderness, particularly at the junction with the East Fork of the river.

WEST FORK CHATTOOGA RIVER
USGS Rabun Bald, Satolah

The West Fork is the main tributary of the Chattooga on the Georgia side of the river. It is formed by the juncture of Holcomb, Overflow, and Big creeks at Three Forks in Rabun County, and its entire length is within the Chattooga Wild and Scenic River Corridor.

The West Fork is a big stream from its beginnings and, by the time it joins the main river, rivals the Chattooga in size. The West Fork contains trout throughout its course.

Catchable-size trout are stocked in the river from the FS 86 bridge downstream. This gravel road, which is also marked on road signs and maps as Overflow Creek Road, and the paved GA 28 combine to parallel the stream closely all the way to the Chattooga, making access easy. The mile or two of water above the FS 86 crossing requires some walking to reach. The head of the West Fork at Three Forks can be reached via the Three Forks Trail off FS 86 several miles beyond the bridge. This upper portion of the river is home to a good population of wild rainbows and some browns as well.

With plenty of wide-open water, casting room is not a concern on the West Fork. However, like most of the big water in southern Appalachia, the West Fork is not as productive as are the smaller streams when blind-casting attractor dry-fly patterns. Nymphs, wets, and streamers are usually a better choice unless some type of surface feeding activity is visible. Like the main river, the West Fork is open to year-round trout fishing.

HOLCOMB CREEK
USGS Rabun Bald, Satolah

Most easily accessible of the three streams that join to form the West Fork of the Chattooga, Holcomb Creek is also the most westerly of the creeks. Rising near Beegum Gap, its extreme headwaters meander through a rather level cove. The creek is very small, heavily foliated, and impossible to fly-cast comfortably. It is a place, however, where it is possible to dap for native southern Appalachian brook trout.

Further down, the creek tumbles over Holcomb Creek Falls, is joined by several feeder flows, and opens enough to allow some casting room. Still only a small stream, wild rainbow trout predominate. Access to this portion of the stream is rather poor. The lower part of the creek is paralleled by FS 86 and fishing up from that point is the easiest approach. There are some heavily used primitive campsites available along the creek parallel to FS 86.

The lower end of the creek along FS 86 is a medium-size flow that has had a number of in-stream structures installed over the years to improve the habitat for trout. This part of the creek gets some stockings of catchable rainbows and is pretty heavily fished by bait-anglers. The final mile or so of water below, where the Forest Service road leaves the stream and veers into the Wild and Scenic River Corridor, is more secluded and requires a hike along the Three Forks Trail. These lower sections afford plenty of room for fly-casting.

To locate the Three Forks Trail travel 4.0 miles north on FS 86 from its junction with Warwoman Road. The trail crosses the road at this point and it is a little over a mile by foot down to Three Forks.

OVERFLOW CREEK
USGS Satolah

Overflow Creek is the other of the streams that form the West Fork of the Chattooga and is listed in the Georgia trout regulations. It is a medium-width stream that forms the most direct headwaters of the river. Rising in North Carolina, it flows south across the state boundary to Three Forks.

If you fish far enough upstream you are likely to encounter some native brookies in Overflow, which contains nothing but wild fish. Be careful in fishing upstream of the FS 86B crossing of the creek. The North Carolina border is only a short distance upstream and you have to have a North Carolina license if you cross over.

To get to Overflow Creek, follow FS 86 for 1.0 mile past the Three Forks Trail. At this point there is a road junction with FS 86B. There are, however, no signs of any kind to identify the road at this intersection. A right turn here puts you on FS 86B which crosses Holcomb Creek at 0.2 mile.

By continuing another 3.5 miles on FS 86B you cross Overflow Creek where it flows through an extremely large metal culvert.

WARWOMAN CREEK
USGS Satolah

Warwoman Creek and its tributaries make up the other major trout fishery feeding the Chattooga, besides the West Fork streams. Rising in the Warwoman Dell area near the town of Clayton, Warwoman Creek flows for a number of miles as a small stream through a valley dominated by private farmlands. None of this upper area that is paralleled by Warwoman Road is open to the public. Finally, however, the stream bends away from the paved road and enters U.S. Forest Service land for its last mile down to the Chattooga River at Earls Ford.

Through this public land the creek is of medium size and flows sluggishly through deep pools broken by short rapids. The quality of the trout habitat is only fair, but the stream is heavily stocked with hatchery-reared fish. It is also heavily fished, as evidenced by the worn condition of the banks and the number of campsites along it. Access is easy along a half mile of the public area from Earls Ford Road. This dirt track runs off Warwoman Road and at 0.75 of a mile crosses the creek to enter the National Forest before proceeding on down to the Chattooga. The last half mile or so of the creek leaves the road and gets less fishing pressure.

On occasions Warwoman Creek produces a surprise such as the 8-pound, 23-inch rainbow pulled from its waters in April 1992. Though taken on bait, this holdover fish still demonstrates the potential for a trophy from this creek.

Warwoman is large and open enough to accommodate the fly caster, assuming it is visited when the bait-anglers are not crowding the shores.

SARAHS CREEK
USGS Rabun Bald

Sarahs Creek is the largest of Warwoman's feeder streams and, in fact, offers more fishable water. Rising on the slopes of Georgia's second-highest mountain, Rabun Bald, Sarahs Creek runs most of its course through the 15,800-acre Warwoman WMA before exiting the managed area and emptying into Warwoman Creek. All of the WMA is located north of Warwoman Road in Rabun County.

Sarahs Creek rates as a medium-size stream and is the only one on this particular WMA that receives any hatchery fish. Stockings of 8- to 12-inch rainbows take place throughout the regular trout season. Some small wild trout are also found in the stream. Pools on this flow are often several yards long, up to 30 feet across and a couple of feet deep. Some structures have been installed in the creek to improve the habitat for the fish.

One surprising thing about the creek is its rather gentle grade, even though it is located in one of the more mountainous areas of Georgia. Through most of the public-access lands, Sarahs Creek meanders along a relatively flat valley, only occasionally dropping over very mild riffles. There is also, however, a more rugged and tumbling section of water downstream toward the edge of the WMA. It features at least one scenic waterfall.

Unfortunately, the appealing fishing conditions and easy access to Sarahs Creek mean it is also a very heavily visited and fished stream. It is quite popular with horseback riders who use the primitive campsites along the creek as a headquarters for weekend mountain rides.

As a result of this heavy visitation, the U.S. Forest Service has identified the Sarahs Creek valley as being one of several national forest recreation areas in Georgia that are considered at risk from overuse. There is the possibility that some regulations governing use of the area could be instituted in the near future.

Sarahs Creek can be reached via FS 156 off Warwoman Road to the east of Clayton. At the intersection a small sign marked 156 is present (along with a road sign showing an incorrect spelling of the road's name as Sarah's Creek Road; additionally, small signs on Warwoman Road on both sides of the intersection are marked Sarah Creek).

At roughly 2.0 miles the creek appears on the left and continues to parallel the road. In the middle of the primitive camping area a paved ford carries the road across the creek.

WALNUT FORK
USGS *Rabun Bald*

Walnut Fork is a small creek to the west of Sarahs Creek. It rates as only a marginal fly-fishing site due to the tight casting conditions. However, since it is managed under an artificial-lure-only fishing regulation, the number of wild rainbows and browns found in the creek makes it worth mentioning. In fact, brown trout of 8 to 9 inches are not uncommon in the small pools of Walnut Fork.

To locate Walnut Fork, turn off Warwoman Road onto Henry Page Road at 7.5 miles east of Clayton. This is a good dirt road for 0.5 mile to the end of the private lands adjacent to the WMA. From here, a very rough track runs 0.25 mile down to the WMA boundary and the creek. In wet weather this track is difficult for all but four-wheel-drive vehicles. Where this road fords the creek, it becomes a trail suited for foot travel only along the eastern bank.

The other option for reaching Walnut Fork is to go to its headwaters by traveling over the ridge from Sarahs Creek valley via FS 155. This dirt track intersects FS 156 just north of the camping area on Sarahs Creek. FS 155 is marked with a small sign at the intersection. Follow this road for 1.3 miles to a sign on the roadside marked Walnut Fork—Artificial Lures Only. At this point the creek is not visible, but you can hear it on the left of the road. Another 0.6 mile further up, the road crosses the creek at a primitive camping area.

HOODS CREEK
USGS *Rabun Bald*

Hoods Creek is a tributary of Walnut Fork, entering that stream from the west. Its entire length is located on the Warwoman WMA. In size, Hoods Creek rates as small, but it does contain wild brown and rainbow trout. The rainbows, which average 6 to 9 inches, predominate.

Along its entire course, angling on Hoods Creek is limited to the use of artificial lures only. As with other Georgia streams, the imposition of this regulation limits the interest of a great many fishermen and the angling pressure is light. Like its sister stream, Walnut Fork, the special regulations are the principal reason it is included in our discussion, since it is so small and heavily foliated as to make fly-casting quite uncomfortable.

Hoods Creek can be reached by following the directions for Walnut Fork. Follow the trail above the ford for a couple of hundred yards to the junction of the two streams. Both creeks are well marked with signs at their confluence.

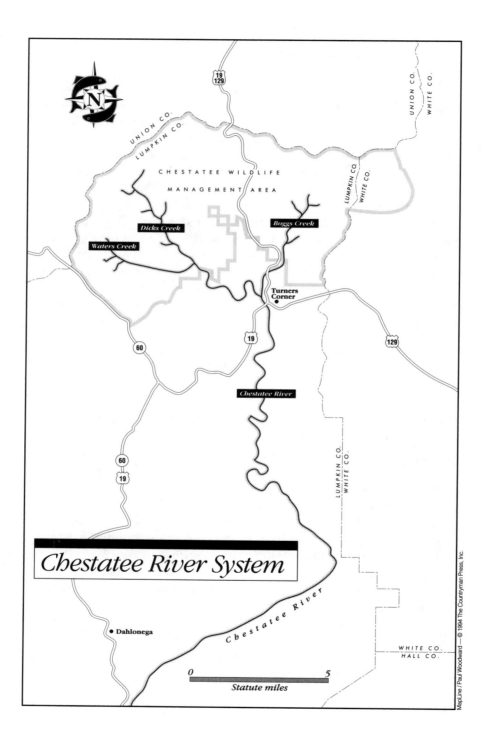

Chestatee River System

Statute miles

5

Chestatee River System

The Chestatee River system is the first that is discussed on which the main river is not an important factor. Flowing just to the west of the Chattahoochee's headwaters, the Chestatee River is a major tributary of the Chattahoochee. Although the Chestatee does contain trout for several miles in its upper reaches, none of the river is on public land. The little access afforded at bridge crossings does not make it a viable fly-casting destination.

Several of the Chestatee's headwater streams, however, are located on the Chestatee WMA in Lumpkin County, almost directly north of the old gold rush town of Dahlonega. This extremely mountainous WMA contains 25,000 acres of land that surround three streams qualifying as fly-fishing destinations.

From west to east these creeks are Waters, Dicks, and Boggs. Though limited in number, they do offer some extremely varied angling opportunities.

Good sites for headquartering your venture onto the Chestatee's headwaters are Dahlonega, which offers a number of motels and campgrounds, or Vogel State Park on US 19/129 just north of the WMA. The state park offers rental cabins, as well as tent and RV campsites. Some primitive campsites are also available at the U.S. Forest Service's Waters Creek Campground on Waters Creek Road near the edge of the WMA.

DICKS CREEK
USGS Neels Gap

Dicks Creek is a medium-width creek that is the principal headwater stream of the Chestatee River. It is also one of the most popular angling destinations in north Georgia. Most of the public-access trout water found on Dicks Creek is located on the Chestatee WMA, but a small stretch in the Waters Creek Campground downstream of the managed area is also open to fishing.

One reason for the heavy fishing pressure is the abundance of hatchery-reared trout released in the creek. The large number of bait-anglers pursuing these put-and-take trout can be discouraging to the fly caster. On weekends or holidays it is difficult to fish more than a few yards without having to detour around other anglers. The number of fishermen does thin out as you get higher up the mountain where the creek is smaller. But, of course, the lesser volume of water and smaller width permit the canopy to close in, making casting difficult.

Some wild fish, both browns and rainbows, are present throughout the stream. These are more often found in the riffle areas between the deeper pools that are the haunts of the stocked trout. Dicks Creek also gives up an inordinate number of large holdover trout each year. Browns and rainbows of over 20 inches are landed during virtually every trout season.

Part of the reason for the presence of these large fish is the size and depth of the pools on the lower end of the creek near the edge of the WMA. Particularly below Dicks Creek Falls the stream is very accommodating to bigger fish.

Another contributing factor to the appearance of the lunker trout is the fact that Waters Creek (which is a trophy trout stream that will be discussed shortly) empties into Dicks Creek. Some of these fish probably migrate down from that feeder stream.

Trying to stalk these big fish in the lower part of the creek is made more difficult by the number of waders, swimmers, and tubers who take to the water during good weather. The trick for fishing Dicks Creek properly is to hit the water early or late in the day, and early and late in the season when the temperatures keep folks out of the water.

This is a popular camping destination also, with a large number of primitive sites available far up the creek. Access to Dicks Creek is via Waters Creek Road (FS 34) off US 19 north of Dahlonega. The road changes to dirt above the junction of Dicks and Waters creeks, but continues to parallel the creek for several miles.

WATERS CREEK

USGS Neels Gap

Waters Creek is one of the most celebrated fly-fishing sites in Georgia, and with good reason. Although only a small stream, it teems with rainbow, brown, and brook trout that reach gargantuan proportions. A little careful stalking can put one at the edge of pools where trout of 18 to 24 inches are clearly visible.

The reason for this population of big fish lies in the strict trophy-stream regulations that have been in effect on the creek for 20 years. The Georgia Wildlife Resources Division, the United States Fish and Wildlife Service, and Georgia Trout Unlimited have cooperated over that period in developing one of the truly unique fisheries of the Southeast.

Besides the usual in-stream structure work to improve the trout habitat, much more has been done to enhance the likelihood of fish surviving to trophy proportions.

Access is limited to Waters Creek, with all anglers being required to surrender their fishing licenses upon checking in to fish. The license is then returned when the fisherman checks out to leave Waters Creek. Angling is allowed only on Wednesdays, Saturdays, and Sundays during the regular trout season. Fishermen cannot begin fishing until 30 minutes before sunrise and must be off the stream by 6:30 P.M. EST (or 7:30 P.M. EDT). They must also have a Wildlife Management Area Stamp in their possession, in addition to the regular state license and trout stamp. The WMA stamps, usually only required for hunting on WMA lands, cost $19 for residents and $73 for nonresidents, but must be purchased before you arrive at the stream. The WMA stamps are not sold at the Waters Creek checking station. They can be obtained at any tackle shop or sporting goods outlet that sells fishing licenses.

Once all of these requirements are met, the angler still must make sure his equipment is legal as well. Fishing is restricted to artificial lures with single barbless hooks that may not exceed size 6. Landing nets carried on the creek must not exceed 2 feet in length.

Finally, the creel limit on trout for Waters Creek is one fish per day. Brook trout must exceed 18 inches, while brown and rainbow trout must be over 22 inches to be legal. Additionally, an angler is limited to only three fish per season.

Given all of this red tape, it naturally follows that not many people go to the trouble to fish Waters Creek. Still, in an average season between 1500 and 2500 anglers will check in at Waters Creek on just over 20 angling dates. These figures represent angler/days since a fisherman visiting the creek on three different Saturdays is counted three times.

Using these figures, Waters Creek's 2½ miles of fishable water gets moderate to heavy pressure on weekends, and slightly lower use on Wednesdays. Of course, the pressure is high because of the possible reward. During the 1987 angling season Waters Creek gave up 76 keeper trout. That figures out to just over 30 trophy fish per mile! Among the keepers taken from the creek during the 1986 season was the Georgia state record brook trout. Russell Braden landed the trout that weighed 5 pounds 10 ounces.

Unfortunately, a much publicized poaching incident occurred in the late 1980s, with as many as 100 trophy fish having been gigged or netted from the creek. As a result, trophy fish declined in the following years, but fish in the 15- to 20-inch range became more numerous. Since then, only three or four legal fish have been removed from the creek each year, although up to a dozen more are reportedly landed and released. The creek is beginning to approach the recovery point from that unfortunate event.

As if man had not provided enough trouble for Waters Creek, nature got into the act in the fall of 1992 when the stream valley was hit by a tornado. Many trees were downed across the creek, making fishing difficult. Then the blizzard of March 1993 finished the job by knocking down an estimated 250,000 board feet of timber in the lower stretches of the creek. While the trout were unaffected, angling has become extremely tough.

No stocking of rainbow trout is done in Waters Creek since natural reproduction is sufficient to sustain the population. In the case of browns and brookies, some fish are planted. These are in the 10- to 14-inch sizes to allow them time to grow and become streamwise before they can fall victim to anglers.

Over the years, rainbows of up to 12 pounds, browns of 9 pounds, and brook trout of 5 pounds have been landed from Waters Creek. Another reason for the size of these fish is the supplemental feeding program that is practiced on the creek. Automatic fish feeders are suspended over the water at several locations and food pellets are dropped into the stream twice each week.

This feeding program has spawned one of the more unusual flies of the southern Appalachians. The "cork" fly is simply a hook adorned with a piece of cork, designed to imitate a floating food pellet. The fly raises the dander of many purist fly casters, but its effectiveness over the years cannot be disputed.

A more traditional approach is to drift small nymphs or wet flies through the pools on the creek. Using dry flies ordinarily produces plenty of action from fish up to 12 inches, but is seldom very effective on the big boys.

Anglers have developed specialized techniques for fooling the trophy trout of Waters Creek. The usual method is to stake out a pool where a fish is visible and spend literally hours working that single trout. After several presentations, the angler settles back to let the pool and fish calm down before trying another fly or presentation. Standard to this type of fishing is complete camouflage clothing so the angler can hide among the streamside foliage.

As mentioned earlier, Waters Creek is a small flow, not offering much casting room in most places. There are some stretches open enough for easy casting, though. An angler who concentrates on the riffle areas and pocket water is less likely to hook a huge fish, but catches more trout.

Access to Waters Creek is limited and controlled. The creek is paralleled by FS 144, which intersects Waters Creek Road at the junction of Waters and Dicks creeks. The approach to Waters Creek on FS 144 passes the local rangers residence and then the checking station at which all cars are required to stop.

BOGGS CREEK
USGS Neels Gap

The final creek in the Chestatee River watershed to be discussed is Boggs Creek. It is a small stream that rises on the slopes of Hogpen Mountain near the Appalachian Trail. The creek is also the most easterly of the trout waters on the Chestatee WMA. The point at which Boggs and Dicks creeks join is generally regarded as the beginning of the Chestatee River.

The creek is open enough to allow limited casting room, especially on the lower section near the edge of the WMA. Both rainbow and brown trout are stocked in the stream and it receives heavy use by local anglers. Occasionally a respectable brown trout of over 20 inches is wrestled from one of the large pools on Boggs Creek, but most fish are only 8 to 10 inches. A few scattered stream-reared wild trout are also present and become more prevalent further upstream.

Boggs Creek can be reached via FS 443, just off the east side of US 19/129 north of the crossroads at Turners Corner. There are a few heavily used primitive campsites between the forest road and the creek immediately above the edge of the WMA.

6

Conasauga River System

The Conasauga River system is the most westerly of the drainages that contain trout waters on public land in Georgia. It also contains some of the most pristine and rugged lands in the Peach State. At the core of this trout fishery is the 34,000-acre Cohutta Wilderness Area, the largest federally mandated, roadless tract in the eastern United States. The wilderness area is located within the larger Cohutta WMA that stretches across Fannin, Gilmer, and Murray counties and is managed by the state of Georgia. This preserve covers over 95,000 acres, making it the largest WMA in the state. The bulk of these managed lands is owned by the U.S. Forest Service as part of the Chattahoochee National Forest.

All of the trout streams in the river system that are on public land are located on the Cohutta WMA. From stream valleys at 1500 to 1800 feet above sea level, the surrounding Cohutta Mountains rise steeply to heights of over 4000 feet. This primitive land is populated by white-tailed deer, wild hogs, black bears, and a host of smaller animals. As would be expected, the wild and inaccessible nature of the area makes for some exciting trout-fishing opportunities.

To make the angling even more appealing, the fact that much of the water is difficult to reach means the creeks get only light fishing pressure. This is the domain of the angler who doesn't mind walking a few miles to find wild, stream-bred rainbows and browns that are rarely accosted by fishermen.

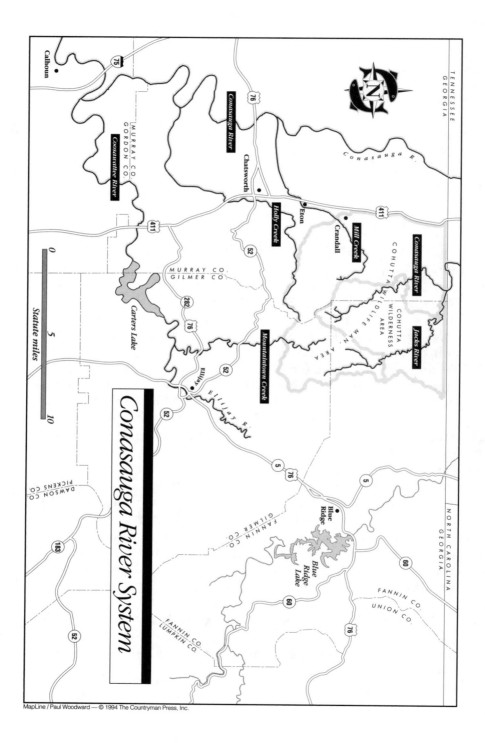

Conasauga River System

Statute miles
0
5
10

Calhoun

Conasauga River

Coosawattee River

MURRAY CO.
GORDON CO.

Chatsworth

Holly Creek

Eton

Crandall

Mill Creek

Conasauga R.

Conasauga River

Jacks River

COHUTTA WILDLIFE MANAGEMENT AREA

COHUTTA WILDERNESS AREA

MURRAY CO.
GILMER CO.

Carters Lake

Mountaintown Creek

Ellijay

Ellijay R.

DAWSON CO.
PICKENS CO.

GILMER CO.
FANNIN CO.

Blue Ridge

Blue Ridge Lake

FANNIN CO.
LUMPKIN CO.

FANNIN CO.
UNION CO.

TENNESSEE
GEORGIA

NORTH CAROLINA
GEORGIA

75
76
411
52
282
76
52
52
52
5
76
5
183
52
60
60
76

MapLine / Paul Woodward — © 1994 The Countryman Press, Inc.

CONASAUGA RIVER
USGS Dyers Gap, Hemp Top, Tennga

The Conasauga River is the most pristine major trout stream located in Georgia. In fact, several years back *Trout* magazine, the national publication of Trout Unlimited, named the Conasauga one of the top 100 trout streams in the United States. Rising in the southern portion of the Cohutta Wilderness Area, the stream attains the volume to be considered a large stream as it flows north to the Alaculsy Valley.

From its headwaters to the exit from the wilderness area, the Conasauga flows through a valley untouched by human activity for several decades. No buildings, agricultural fields, or even road crossings are located on this upper section of the river. As a result, even during periods of heavy rains when the river rises, the Conasauga very seldom is stained. On one weekend during a rainy April, I found the river out of its bank, flowing through the streamside trees. Yet, I still managed to catch several trout with dry flies from water that was only slightly discolored.

In all, there are roughly 15 miles of the Conasauga in the Cohutta Wilderness Area. These waters teem with wild rainbow trout and also produce some wild browns. Rainbows up to 20 inches turn up occasionally, and browns to 9 pounds have been recorded over the years.

Although the fish are plentiful, it does not follow that the fishing is easy. Another result of the natural setting of the river is that the water quality is excellent—and it is extremely clear. Especially during low-water periods in the summer and fall the flow appears transparent. It is possible to walk up on pools and find as many as a dozen fish visible. Of course, the trout can see you about as well as you can see them. One unguarded step along the creek bank sends them scurrying for cover.

To fish the Conasauga effectively requires a great deal of stealth and stalking. Fortunately, portions of the stream bed have plenty of large boulders that provide cover for the cautious angler. Except in the headwaters there is also adequate casting room available.

Although the Conasauga Valley is often crowded with hikers and backpackers during the spring through fall on weekends, very few of these will be anglers. Many of these campers have a spinning rod with them, but they seldom fish much and rarely with great success. Needless to say, the Conasauga is not a place for the novice angler. The fishing is challenging, but can be very rewarding to the fly caster.

There are two stretches of water downstream of the wilderness area that are on Forest Service land and, thus, open to public fishing. By the time the river reaches this area it is beginning to become marginal trout water. There is also some private land on the river separating these tracts in the Alaculsy Valley. The only road access to the Conasauga is found in the valley via the road that is variously marked on maps as FS 16, County Road 103, or Old GA 2.

Further upstream in the wilderness area the only access to the Conasauga is via foot trails. The Conasauga River Trail parallels the stream through most of the wilderness. Its trailhead is located on FS 64 in Betty Gap. Along the length of the river, three other trails descend from the west off FS 17 to intersect the river trail. From south to north they are the Chestnut Lead (2.0 miles), Tearbritches Trail (4.0 miles and extremely steep), and Hickory Creek Trail (3.0 miles). Primitive camping is allowed all along the river.

JACKS RIVER
USGS Dyers Gap, Hemp Top

The Jacks River is the major tributary of the Conasauga in the headwaters region, and, in fact, it is a slightly larger stream than the Conasauga. The two rivers flow parallel, with the Jacks on the east.

The Jacks is formed by its West and South forks that join near Dyer Mountain on U.S. Forest Service land within the Cohutta WMA, but upstream of the Wilderness Area. Both of these forks have populations of wild brown and rainbow trout, but are small and bushy creeks. Although possible, fly-casting is very tight on these headwaters.

After crossing a patch of privately held land below the junction of the two forks, the Jacks enters the Cohutta Wilderness Area as a medium-width stream. For the next 15 miles it descends a valley covered with poplar and hemlock trees, and the river gains much in size. Throughout the wilderness area the river presents wide-open water for the fly rodder.

The Jacks River rivals its sister stream, the Conasauga, in number of fish, and probably produces a larger average fish. Rainbows of 12 to 14 inches turn up regularly and browns up to 9 pounds have been caught as well. Of equal importance to the angler is the fact that trout of 9 to 11 inches are common. As in the case of the Conasauga, all the fish are wild, since no stocking has taken place on these waters since the 1960s.

To reach the best fishing areas on the Conasauga River requires several miles of hiking on mountain trails, but the fishing is worth the effort.

A common pattern for fishing the Jacks throughout the season is to hit the deep slow pools in the early morning before the mist rises off the water. Probe these with a big size 8 or 10 weighted stone fly nymph. The rainbows usually attack the nymph viciously and an occasional brown will also show up. Once the sun burns off the mist, switch to dry flies like the Royal Wulff or Adams and hit the riffle areas between the pools. Using this pattern, up to 20 or 30 fish can be landed and released on a good day.

Access along the river is via the Jacks River Trail, which follows the bed of a turn-of-the-century railway used to haul timber out of the valley. In places the railroad cross ties are still visible sticking out of the trail, and bits of twisted cable and other ancient debris are also present. Near the midpoint of the trail the river drops over the extremely scenic, 60-foot Jacks River Falls.

This is one area that generally is crowded due to the number of campers present. Most are swimming or wading in the river rather than fishing. As with the Conasauga, a relatively small number of the people making the trek to the stream come for the fishing. The campsites around the falls are another area that the Forest Service identifies as threatened by overuse. A better choice is to camp either up- or downriver from this area and pay the falls a visit while fishing.

The Jacks River Trail begins at Dally Gap on FS 22, reaches the river at the mouth of Bear Branch, then continues downstream to the

PHOTO BY BOB TOWNSEND

The Jacks River offers plenty of room for casting in a very
remote wilderness setting.

junction with the Conasauga River. The trail crosses the Jacks 44 times during this descent, with many crossings up to waist deep. The Hemp Top/Penitentiary Branch Trail, which also originates in Dally Gap, is a 6-mile trail that approaches the river from the east about a mile above the Jacks River Falls. Finally, the relatively level 3-mile Beech Bottom Trail runs from FS 62 in Tennessee, crosses the state boundary, and joins the river trail just upstream of the falls. This last trail is by far the easiest approach to the falls.

The only access by road to the Jacks is at its junction with the Conasauga on FS 16 or in the headwaters at a couple of points just off FS 64 on either the South or West forks.

HOLLY CREEK
USGS Dyers Gap

Holly Creek is a medium to small stream located just on the southern edge of the Cohutta WMA. It has the distinction of being the only stream in the Cohuttas that receives regular stockings of hatchery trout.

Roughly two miles of the creek are on public land and the flow is paralleled by FS 18. In the lower section of the creek the road runs immediately beside the stream and some large deep pools attract plenty of bait casters and swimmers. This is the portion that is heavily stocked with catchable rainbows, browns, and occasional brook trout.

Upstream from this area, the creek leaves the road and courses through a ravine. Through here wild rainbows predominate. A small feeder stream, Emery Creek, will enter from the north about 0.25 mile above the road. Emery offers some tight fishing for abundant wild trout in the 6- to 8-inch range.

Although the road is still close to the stream through the ravine, it is high up the ridge. Further upstream, the creek and road come back together, but the headwaters of Holly Creek are on the south side of the road, outside the WMA and on private property.

After exiting the WMA at the lower boundary, Holly Creek quickly becomes marginal water as it runs through private lands to empty into the Conasauga, which has looped through Tennessee and is now flowing to the south.

MILL CREEK
USGS Crandall, Tennga

Mill Creek is a small stream that flows off the western side of the Cohutta WMA to join the Conasauga on its southward course. This creek merits only a passing mention, not only because of its small size, but because it is mostly marginal water.

Although it appears to be a tumbling mountain brook as it parallels FS 630 coming off Grassy Mountain, it doesn't live up to its promise. The water is relatively warm and redeye bass are more common than trout. In fact, the bulk of the trout encountered are hatchery rainbows that have moved up from stockings below the WMA.

In a nutshell, Mill Creek is only of minor interest to fly casters.

MOUNTAINTOWN CREEK
USGS Dyers Gap

Unless one is a fan of maps, it comes as a surprise to see Mountaintown Creek listed as a stream in the Conasauga System. Although it is located in the southeastern quadrant of the Cohutta WMA, its southward flow appears to take it away from the Conasauga. After leaving the WMA, the creek eventually empties into the Coosawattee River,

The author casting for early-season trout on Mountaintown Creek.

which joins the Conasauga to form the Oostanaula River.

Mountaintown Creek is the only stream in the river system managed under special regulations. A short portion of the water near the edge of the WMA is open under general trout rules, but upstream of Hills Lake (designated Soil Conservation Structure No. 2 in the state trout regulations) fishing is restricted to artificial lures.

As usual, this regulation limits the fishing pressure, plus the relative inaccessibility of the stream lessens it still further. Both wild rainbow and brown trout are present and fish of up to 12 inches are fairly common in the creek. The portion of the water immediately above the lake has had some in-stream structures installed by TU chapters, improving the amount of holding water available. Mountaintown is only a small stream on the WMA, but offers surprisingly open casting conditions for its size.

A rough road, only suitable for four-wheel-drive vehicles when the weather is wet, runs from FS 90 up to Hills Lake. A small sign at the junction with FS 90 is marked with the lake's name. There is also a primitive campground on the creek below the lake at Bear Creek. This can be reached via FS 241. Mountaintown Creek Trail follows the creek upstream above Hills Lake, providing access to the headwaters.

7

Etowah River System

The Etowah River system covers a wide-ranging drainage that contains a number of trout streams on public land located on three different state WMAs. The main river has its headwaters in north-central Georgia just west of the town of Dahlonega. The main stem of the river and several feeder streams rise on the Blue Ridge WMA of Dawson, Fannin, and Lumpkin counties. Containing roughly 42,000 acres of U.S. Forest Service land, the Blue Ridge WMA is the oldest such preserve in Georgia, having been established in 1937.

The management area is bisected from west to east by the Appalachian Trail and all of the streams south of the ridge that parallels the trail flow south as tributaries of the Etowah. Those creeks on the north slope drain into the Toccoa River.

Once the Etowah leaves the Blue Ridge WMA it enters Dawson County and traverses the Dawson Forest WMA. By the time the river reaches this point it is no longer trout water, but its major feeder creek on this WMA is the Amicalola River, which does contain trout and is on public land. The portion of the Amicalola that has trout flows through land owned by the state of Georgia.

Further to the west, the Etowah is impounded in Lake Allatoona. The headwaters of Stamps Creek, which empties into the lake, are on the Pine Log WMA in Bartow and Cherokee counties, where they are stocked with trout.

Although a number of other feeder streams of the Etowah do contain trout, none of these are located on public land. Eventually the Etowah joins the Oostanaula River at Rome to form the Coosa River, flowing to Mobile Bay.

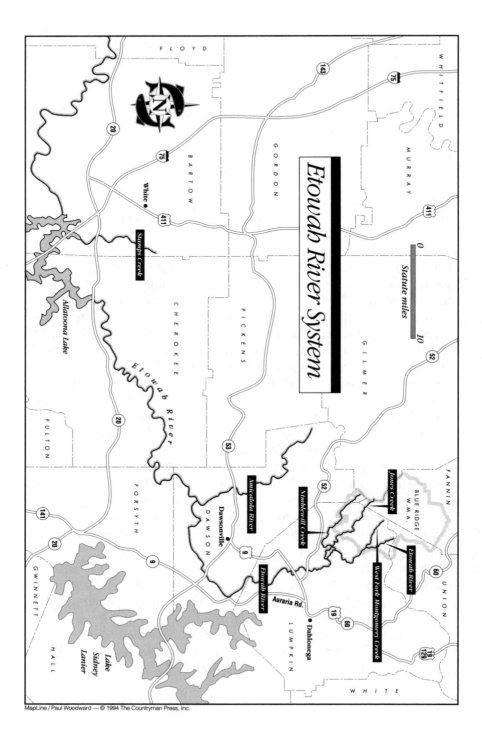

Etowah River System

Statute miles

0   10

MapLine / Paul Woodward — © 1994 The Countryman Press, Inc.

The many campgrounds and motels around Dahlonega make good spots from which to check out the best of the trout streams in the Etowah River drainage.

ETOWAH RIVER
USGS Suches, Campbell Mountain, Dawsonville

There are two sections of the Etowah River that merit discussion as likely fly-casting destinations. The first is the extreme headwaters section on the Blue Ridge WMA. Only about a mile of the river at the southern edge of the WMA, and upstream of FS 28-1, is large enough to be of interest.

The Etowah is a small stream on the Blue Ridge WMA, but has a few large pools and open stretches spread along its length. Immediately above the FS 28-1 crossing, a spur road follows the river for a few hundred yards through a number of primitive campsites. The campers traditionally have not treated this area very well and it is often trashy.

The pools through this section are heavily stocked with catchable-size rainbows through the season and it receives fairly heavy fishing pressure. Stocked fish continue to show up in the creek for about a half mile above the camping area, along with some wild trout. Most of these wild fish are small rainbows, but brown trout also make an appearance.

At this point the river tumbles down a set of small cataracts, above which wild trout predominate. A bit further up a larger cascade called Black Falls appears with a sizable plunge pool at its bottom. This marks the upper limit of the water of interest to fly-anglers. Further still, the creek runs through the U.S. Army's Frank Merrill ranger training camp. Through here the creek is small, narrow, and heavily canopied, besides being off-limits when the camp is in use.

One point of confusion that occurs on the Etowah concerns it name. On the maps the portion we are talking about above FS 28-1 is labeled as the Etowah, but some local people identify it as Montgomery Creek. Some longtime residents still hold to the even older name of Hightower River. To add a final note of confusion, the main fork of the stream above the junction with the West Fork of Montgomery Creek is also referred to as Black or Black's creek.

The second section of the Etowah that presents some fly-fishing options is located south of the Blue Ridge WMA and to the southwest of Dahlonega. From the GA 9E highway bridge downstream for

8.0 miles to the Castleberry Bridge Road crossing to the west of the crossroads of Auraria, the Etowah supports stocked put-and-take trout and a few carry-over or even wild fish.

Through here the stream is big water better suited to float fishing than wading. Since both shores are bordered by private land, anglers are limited to staying on the river. This, however, is a stream that has traditionally been navigated by canoeists and rafters without major conflicts with the landowners along the banks. The only access is at the put-in and take-out bridges.

Although a few trout turn up below Castleberry Bridge, it marks the downstream limit for productive casting. The bulk of the fish encountered on the lower Etowah River are stocked rainbows, but these waters offer excellent opportunities to tie into a big holdover brown trout as well.

WEST FORK MONTGOMERY CREEK
USGS Noontootla, Suches

Located on the Blue Ridge WMA, the West Fork of Montgomery Creek is a major headwaters tributary of the Etowah. It is also a very deceptive stream that is often overlooked by most anglers. There are a number of reasons for this lack of notoriety.

At the point where it empties into the Etowah about a mile above FS 28-1 the creek appears to be quite small. Part of this deceptive look is caused from having run for quite a distance along a level valley that allows some of its flow to soak into the soil rather than remaining on the surface. The other more important reason is that the creek splits around a small island as it enters the river, giving it the appearance of two very small feeders emptying close together.

If the creek is followed for a short distance upstream, it begins to gain elevation with a series of waterfalls, some of which are 30 to 40 feet high. These also provide plunge pools at their feet that contain plenty of room for good trout. Browns of up to 18 inches have been taken from this creek, and rainbows of over 10 inches are fairly common. There are no stocked trout in this stream.

Angling can be tight on most of the stream, since it rates as only a small flow, but breaks in the canopy allow some casting throughout its length. In the areas of the waterfalls the pools are large enough to allow a bit more leeway for casting.

Access to the West Fork of Montgomery is limited to foot travel upstream from FS 28-1 along the Etowah, or downstream from the crossing of FS 141 in the headwaters of the creek. If you approach the stream from this latter option, you'll need to walk downstream until the creek becomes open enough to fish.

Fishing pressure on the West Fork is usually quite light due to the difficulty of reaching it and the absence of any stocked fish to attract the casual angler.

JONES CREEK
USGS Campbell Mountain, Nimblewill

Jones Creek is another small tributary of the Etowah River that is found on the Blue Ridge WMA. Its small size and tight fishing make it only a marginal fly-casting destination, but the quality of the angling on the stream requires that it be discussed.

Fishing on Jones is restricted to artificial lures and the creek contains only wild stream-bred brown trout. Among the smaller mountain waters of Georgia it is by far the best for these wily immigrants from the Old World. Even though browns in excess of 12 inches turn up in the creek, the average fish only runs from 6 to 8 inches. They are, however, quite vividly colored, with golden hues, brilliant red spots, and orange tips on their fins.

Although the special regulations and the difficulty of catching the wild browns discourages many anglers from troubling these waters, Jones still receives moderate pressure from a number of regular fans. On opening days and holiday weekends this creek can be a bit crowded.

The creek's waters are usually quite clear and the pools not large or deep (with some exceptions) so the always cautious brown trout are even more difficult to fool on this creek. It is sometimes necessary to cast to the pool above the one you are on, in order to avoid spooking the fish. This, naturally, is not always possible due to the canopy of foliage and small size of the creek. Fortunately, Trout Unlimited volunteers have spent many hours in recent years improving this fishery by installing in-stream structures.

All in all, Jones Creek is a tough fly-casting stream that is best left to the experienced angler seeking the ultimate challenge.

Access to Jones Creek is off FS 28-1, which crosses the stream at the southern edge of the WMA. By traveling past this crossing to the

Stocked rainbows, like the one Brent Jacobs is displaying, are the mainstay of the trout fishery on the Amicalola River.

east and turning north on FS 77 (Winding Stair Road) and then to the left on FS 77A, a primitive camping area near the midpoint of the stream can be reached. Several of the larger, deeper pools on the creek are located near this campground.

NIMBLEWILL CREEK
USGS Nimblewill

Nimblewill is the final of the Etowah's feeder streams on the Blue Ridge WMA to be covered. It is a small stream that runs along the southwest edge of the WMA. The main attraction of this creek is its easy access and the large number of rainbow trout that are stocked here.

Although some wild fish are present, this is a put-and-take fishery that is heavily utilized by both local and visiting anglers. By the time one gets far enough upstream to find mostly wild trout, the flow is too small for comfortable fly-casting. The fly caster also has to deal with crowds of bait-fishermen on weekends, so weekday fishing is a much better option. Another possibility is to visit the stream after the Labor Day holiday, when stocking has ceased and most fishermen have put away their rods for the year.

Stocked trout run from 8 to 11 inches on Nimblewill and the wild rainbows that are present rarely exceed 8 inches. Some browns also turn up in creels from time to time.

Much of the creek is open enough for limited fly-casting, if one can find room among the bait-fishermen to lay out a line. Nimblewill is also a relatively level and gentle stream by mountain standards, thus providing easy wading or walking along its bank.

There are a number of primitive camping sites along the stream and these are also heavily used during periods of good weather during the spring and summer. Solitude is a rare commodity on Nimblewill.

FS 28-2 parallels the creek for its entire fishable length on the WMA. While convenient, this easy access contributes to the crowds that congregate on this stream.

AMICALOLA RIVER
USGS Juno

The Amicalola is identified as a river on some maps and a creek on others. Regardless, in the section where it contains trout, it qualifies as big water, deserving of the river designation.

Rising on the slopes of Amicalola Mountain, the river flows its entire 15-mile length in Dawson County before emptying into the Etowah. The river's name is derived from the Cherokee Indian word for "bubbling or white water" and as the name implies, much of the river is rough, tumbling water that is quite scenic.

The part of the river that contains trout in fishable numbers is located on a portion of the Dawson Forest WMA that is owned by the Georgia Wildlife Resources Division and composed of a slender corridor along the stream. The river is only marginal trout water and contains few if any wild fish.

Better known as a canoeing and rafting stream, most of the access is available at the put-in and take-out points utilized by the boaters.

In fact, float fishing is by far the easiest method of covering the water. The lower limit of trout water is at the GA 53 highway bridge. Below this point trout are rare and the river becomes a serious whitewater canoe stream that is dangerous to venture on unprepared.

Both hatchery-reared brown and rainbow trout are stocked in the Amicalola and some carryover from year to year occurs. As a result, an occasional large trout turns up. Although the river is big enough to provide plenty of casting room, much of it has no easy bank access or is too deep for easy wading.

Other than the access points at Six-Mile put-in and GA 53, the only other point of entry and exit on the trout water is at Devils Elbow, about 4.0 miles above GA 53. At this point, Devils Elbow Road crosses the stream. The Six-Mile put-in is located just off Amicalola Church Road on the west side of the river and has a number of primitive campsites on the river bank.

STAMPS CREEK
USGS *White East*

Ask Georgia anglers to list the trout streams feeding the Etowah River and it is unlikely that one in a hundred will have Stamps Creek on their list. This small stream lies far to the west of the Etowah's other tributaries that harbor trout. Located on the Pine Log WMA in Bartow County, this small stream empties into the Etowah's waters where they are impounded in Lake Allatoona.

Descending through a gently sloped valley, its crystal-clear waters are marginal habitat for trout, but they do receive stockings of hatchery fish several times each season. The lower portion of the stream near its exit point from the WMA is also wide and open enough to permit some casting room. From these standpoints it fits all of our criteria of being open to the public, big enough for fly-casting, and containing trout.

Yet, it is at best a very marginal destination. There are no wild fish in the creek, unless you count sunfish, or Coosa and spotted bass. When the hatchery truck pays a visit, word spreads quickly and local bait-anglers are soon crowded along the creek to clean out the stockers.

If, in spite of this dismal description, you still want to sample this creek, it is located just to the east of US 411 at the town of White, via Stamps Creek Road.

8

Tallulah River System

Although the Tallulah River has cut a deep and impressive valley through the northeast corner of Georgia, not much of the stream that remains is of interest to the trout angler. Beginning soon after the turn of the century a series of dams and reservoirs were constructed to harness the potential power of the river.

Besides the loss of a free-flowing river, some of the most powerful waterfalls in the southeast disappeared under these lakes or were reduced to mere shadows of their former selves due to loss of water volume. In particular, the waters that once rushed through the now almost dry Tallulah Gorge near the southern end of the river were said to have roared with such a volume that they were heard up to several miles away.

Today short sections of the river still flow in the original course, but only the headwater section fulfills the criteria for this book. Additionally, the Tallulah's major headwater tributary, the Coleman River, merits coverage, as do Moccasin and Wildcat creeks. The latter two empty into the Tallulah where it is impounded in Lake Burton to the west of the town of Clayton. The final stream in the drainage that meets the criteria for discussion is Panther Creek, which actually empties into the river after the Tallulah and Chattooga have merged to form the Tugaloo River.

While all of the streams in the watershed lie on U.S. Forest Service land in the Chattahoochee National Forest, the Coleman River is also located on the Coleman River WMA. Moccasin and Wildcat creeks cut their courses through the Lake Burton WMA.

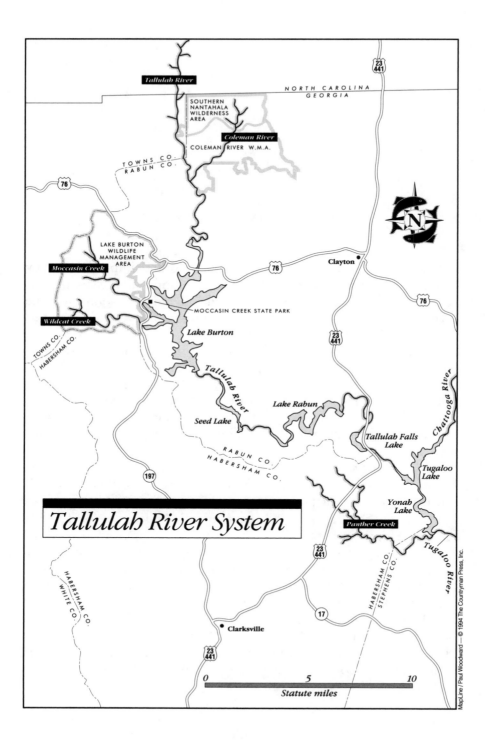

Tallulah River

NORTH CAROLINA
GEORGIA

SOUTHERN
NANTAHALA
WILDERNESS
AREA

Coleman River

COLEMAN RIVER W.M.A.

TOWNS CO.
RABUN CO.

76

LAKE BURTON
WILDLIFE
MANAGEMENT
AREA

Moccasin Creek

76   Clayton

76

MOCCASIN CREEK STATE PARK

Wildcat Creek

TOWNS CO.
HABERSHAM CO.

Lake Burton

23
441

Tallulah River

Lake Rabun

Chattooga River

Seed Lake

Tallulah Falls
Lake

RABUN CO.
HABERSHAM CO.

Tugaloo
Lake

197

Yonah
Lake

Tallulah River System

Panther Creek

Tugaloo River

23
441

HABERSHAM CO.
STEPHENS CO.

HABERSHAM CO.
WHITE CO.

17

Clarksville

23
441

0   5   10

Statute miles

MapLine / Paul Woodward — © 1994 The Countryman Press, Inc.

TALLULAH RIVER
USGS *Hightower Bald*

The Tallulah River flows in a long arc from the North Carolina border at the tiny Georgia hamlet of Tate City to the South Carolina border at the river's junction with the Chattooga River. Along this roughly 60-mile route the river passes through impoundments at Lake Burton, Seed Lake, Lake Rabun, and Tallulah Falls Lake before ending in Tugaloo Lake.

All of the remaining free-flowing portion of the Tallulah is found in its headwaters section above Lake Burton. Unfortunately, even in this area, only about five miles of the river bordering on the Coleman River WMA is located on public land.

Rising on the southern slopes of Standing Indian Mountain in North Carolina, the river is not open to public fishing until it crosses the state line and gets south of Tate City. Through this area the Tallulah is a large- to medium-size stream and particularly in the downstream area has some large, deep pools.

Although the river has naturally reproducing populations of both brown and rainbow trout, its popularity as a fishing destination results in frequent stockings of hatchery trout to supplement the resource. Part of this popularity of the river can be traced to the presence of the Forest Service's Tallulah River, Tate Branch, and Sandy Bottom campgrounds on the stream. Access to all of these is via FS 70, which parallels the river through the public land.

The lower section of the river up to the confluence of the Coleman River contains most of the deep pools. The stocked fish in these deep waters are rarely inclined to rise to dry flies, so wets or nymphs generally attract more action. As you move upstream into the area where the Tallulah becomes a smaller creek, wild trout, especially rainbows, are more numerous.

Another bit of good news on the Tallulah is that the river is open to trout fishing throughout its length on a year-round basis. This becomes of major importance if you want a little solitude on the river. During the spring and summer months the Tallulah is crowded, particularly on weekends. During the cooler months, however, the river is virtually abandoned by anglers.

Most of the stocked fish are rainbow trout in the 8- to 10-inch range, while the wild fish average 6 to 8 inches. Some large browns undoubtedly inhabit the larger pools, where their carnivorous habits protect them from the cheese and corn offerings of the numerous bait-fishermen.

The Tallulah River is reached via FS 70 from Persimmon Road, which in turn branches off US 76 between the towns of Hiawassee and Clayton.

COLEMAN RIVER
USGS Dillard, Hightower Bald

The Coleman River is the largest of the feeder streams emptying into the headwaters section of the Tallulah River. This does not, however, mean that it is a large flow. In fact, the Coleman rates as only a small stream, but it is, nevertheless, one that is worth considering for some interesting fly-casting.

The Coleman rises on the flank of Dicks Knob just south of the North Carolina border. These headwaters are in the portion of the Southern Nantahala Wilderness Area that is located in Georgia, just to the east of the Tallulah River. Along its entire length, the Coleman also flows through the state-managed Coleman River WMA. Finally, in the last 1½ miles of its course, the surrounding lands are in the Coleman River Scenic Area. Between the edge of the wilderness area and the upper reaches of the scenic area, the creek flows through a couple of patches of privately owned property.

From the standpoint of practical fly-casting, the only portion of the river of interest is that from its mouth on the Tallulah, upstream through the scenic area to the FS 54 bridge. As noted, it is a small stream, but it flows through a rocky course that allows some room for casting in this lower section. The pools are small and crystal clear, so expect to have to stalk them cautiously if spooking the trout is to be avoided.

No planting of hatchery trout takes place on the Coleman River, but it is possible that a few stockers may find their way up into the lower stretches of the stream from the Tallulah River. The dominant species in the Coleman River is the rainbow trout, but some wild browns are also present. In the headwaters of the stream, in the wilderness area, native brook trout still thrive, but they seldom wander down into the lower areas of the river. Most fish encountered are under 10 inches, but an occasional brown of larger proportions does appear.

The portion of the Coleman River from its mouth up to FS 54 is

*Man-made waterfalls, like this one on the Coleman River, have been
constructed to prevent rainbow and brown trout from moving
upstream into the area inhabited by native brookies.*

open to fishing using only artificial lures. Due to this restriction, fishing pressure is quite light on the stream, in spite of the large number of anglers and campers on the Tallulah at the junction of the two rivers. Other reasons for this light angling pressure are the close proximity of the Tallulah's easier-to-catch stockers, plus the difficult fishing conditions created by the clear water and small size of the Coleman.

Access to the lower portion of the Coleman is via FS 70 along the Tallulah. The rivers join just upstream of the Tallulah River Campground. From that point the Coleman River Scenic Trail follows the creek for over a mile upstream.

MOCCASIN CREEK
USGS Macedonia, Lake Burton

The first of the impoundments that the Tallulah River passes through is Lake Burton, and Moccasin Creek drains into this reservoir from the Lake Burton WMA on the western side of the lake. This small stream has, for a number of reasons, been overlooked by most fly casters in recent years.

Moccasin Creek in the state park of the same name provides angling that is accessible even to anglers in wheelchairs.

Foremost among the reasons is the misunderstanding surrounding the regulations that apply on the creek. After exiting the Lake Burton WMA the creek is dammed to supply water to a state fish hatchery and then for its final couple of hundred yards down to the lake it flows through Moccasin Creek State Park. Within the park, fishing is restricted to persons over 65 or under 12 years of age, or holders of honorary licenses. The creek is heavily stocked throughout the trout season in this regulated section, and equally heavily fished.

The fishing restrictions mentioned are posted on signs upstream to the northern side of GA 197 at the edge of the park, as well as being noted in the "Georgia Fishing Regulations" brochure. The last sign on the stream is between the dam for the hatchery intake and the dirt road that leads upstream to the WMA. The presence of this sign discourages casual anglers, who are not familiar with the regulations, from proceeding upstream.

The result of this situation is that the upper reaches of Moccasin Creek on the WMA, which are open to everyone during the regular state season, go almost unfished. What few anglers follow the road up past the WMA deer-hunting station to its dead end find a small, shallow stream that seems hardly worth the effort to fish. A hike of a few hundred yards or so up the valley along the trail that follows an old logging train roadbed changes the complexion of the stream, however, as the creek tumbles over waterfalls and descends into deep plunge pools.

The creek valley is scenic enough to be enjoyed even if no fish are present, but Moccasin Creek has the added bonus of plenty of wild rainbow and brown trout. The bulk of these are 6 to 8 inches long, but larger fish are definitely present. Fish of 12 inches are not particularly uncommon, and ones up to 18 inches have been taken. Particularly in the lower portion of the creek the fish are hard to get to because the stream is in the bottom of a ravine that requires a steep climb down from the trail. A particularly large falls and pool are about 200 yards upstream from the first point at which the trail crosses the creek.

Although tight in places, the creek can be fished effectively with a fly rod and in some places it is quite open. The wading is not the easiest encountered in the Georgia mountains, because of large boulders, steep banks, and deep pools.

Upper Moccasin Creek can be reached by going north on the dirt road that is directly across GA 197 from the entrance to the Lake Burton State Fish Hatchery.

WILDCAT CREEK
USGS Tray Mountain, Lake Burton

Wildcat Creek is another small stream that flows off the Lake Burton WMA to empty into that reservoir. It is located 1.0 mile south of Moccasin Creek on the west side of Lake Burton and is slightly larger than its sister stream.

Rising in the Tray Mountain Wilderness Area, Wildcat Creek closely resembles the upper portion of Moccasin Creek in that it is a constant series of cataracts and pools. For this reason it offers better angling water throughout its length. It is also possible to fly-cast Wildcat up to the point where it exits from the wilderness area. From there on it is small, brushy, and canopied.

The major difference between Wildcat and Moccasin creeks, however, lies in the way they are managed. While the upper part of Moccasin is left as a wild trout fishery, Wildcat is a put-and-take fishery that is heavily utilized. The number of anglers, particularly bait-fishermen, that this stream attracts rivals the turnout on the Tallulah itself. Wildcat is one of the most popular creeks for fishing in the Georgia mountains.

Being only a mile distant from the hatchery, Wildcat also gets some healthy doses of hatchery fish. In the portion of the creek near the boundary of the WMA, the large pools found at roadside are ideal for this put-and-take fishing; thus they stay crowded. Late afternoon or weekday fishing are the only options for finding solitude on Wildcat Creek during the spring and summer.

In spite of the heavy stocking of these waters, some wild fish are still found in Wildcat Creek. Needless to say, the further upstream one fishes the more of these stream-bred trout are encountered. For the most part the wild fish are rainbows of under 8 inches. The stockers, on the other hand, run up to 14 inches.

Access to Wildcat Creek is off GA 197 on FS 26-1, which follows the stream up to the edge of the wilderness area. Several bridge crossings provide easy opportunities to get to the creek along its course.

PANTHER CREEK
USGS Tallulah Falls, Tugaloo Lake

Panther Creek is another of those streams that meet our criteria for inclusion, but just barely. It is marginal trout water that flows from US 23/441 down to FS 182 in Habersham and Stephens counties. Then, after crossing some private holdings, it dumps into Lake Tugaloo below the junction of the Chattooga and Tallulah rivers.

Throughout its course below US 23/441 the creek receives stockings of rainbow trout during spring and summer, but little if any reproduction occurs in the stream. Fishing is allowed year-round in Panther Creek.

The stream is a small to medium flow, which has a tendency to become stained quickly in rainy weather. The number of cascades and waterfalls on the creek create enough pools to make fly-casting possible. The bottom line is that Panther Creek is not a bona fide fly-fishing destination, but only of passing interest.

Panther Creek Trail parallels the stream all along its length through the public portions of the creek and is accessible at either end from the roads mentioned above.

9

Toccoa River System

The Toccoa River drains in a northwest direction, covering a large portion of west-central Georgia. Eventually this river crosses the state border into Tennessee where its name changes and it becomes the Ocoee River. The final destination of these waters is the Tennessee-Mississippi river system.

Rising near the small valley town of Suches to the northwest of Dahlonega, the Toccoa is unique among Georgia's large trout streams in that it supports the cold-water species along its entire course in the state. This fishery is made possible on the lower portions of the river because of the cold tailrace waters released from Lake Blue Ridge, which is about two-thirds of the way down the river's course in Georgia.

Several of the creeks feeding into the Toccoa above Lake Blue Ridge also merit mention as trout streams, with these flows being spread over three different WMAs. Cooper Creek and its tributary, Mulky Creek, are located on the Coopers Creek WMA, while Noontootla and Rock creeks are on the northern portion of the Blue Ridge WMA. Finally, Stanley Creek flows down off the Rich Mountain WMA to join the Toccoa.

Although the Toccoa River and its tributaries are not particularly well known among fly casters, some very convincing arguments can be put forth supporting the contention that the river system contains both Georgia's best river and best small stream for trout angling. Such a statement will, of course, stir some heated debates, but as we shall see in discussing the individual streams, there are some outstanding ones in this drainage.

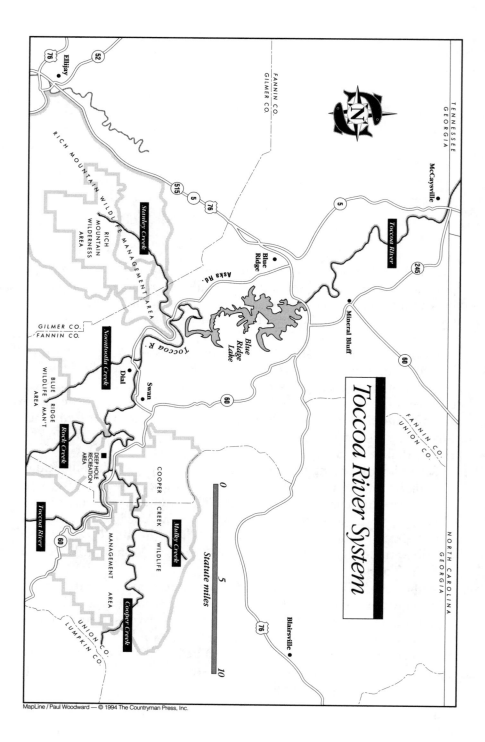

Toccoa River System

Statute miles

0

5

10

MapLine / Paul Woodward — © 1994 The Countryman Press, Inc.

TOCCOA RIVER

USGS Suches, Noontootla, Wilscot,
Blue Ridge, Mineral Bluff

In discussing the Toccoa River itself, we are actually talking about two very different flows. The portion from the river's head down to Lake Blue Ridge near the town of the same name is a free-flowing stream that merits being called a river along most of its course. By the time it begins to parallel GA 60 just north of Suches it is a large stream.

Unfortunately, a great deal of the upper portion of the Toccoa is on private land and inaccessible to most anglers. There are several bridges that afford access, plus sections of Forest Service land at the Deep Hole Campground near the crossroads of Margaret, just downstream of the village of Swan, and on several plots along Aska Road near the headwaters of Lake Blue Ridge. Although these supply only spotty access, as a group they do represent a substantial amount of water, all of which is open enough for easy fly-casting.

There is some natural reproduction of trout in the Toccoa River, particularly in the upper reaches of the stream. Due, however, to the heavy fishing pressure, the river receives substantial stocking of hatchery rainbows and some browns. Because of the size of the Toccoa, many of the stockers hold over, so fish up to 20 inches are taken each season.

By the time the river gets down near Lake Blue Ridge, the water is marginal for trout, and this, as mentioned, is the area where most of the public access is available. For this reason the upper Toccoa can be rated as only a moderately interesting fly-casting destination. Most of the trout taken from the river are by bait-fishermen trying their luck at bridges or around Deep Hole.

The second distinctive portion of the Toccoa is found below Lake Blue Ridge in the tailrace down to the twin cities of McCaysville, Georgia, and Copper Hill, Tennessee, at the state line. Though not as heralded as the tailrace of the Chattahoochee River, the Toccoa has the potential to be on a par with that celebrated Georgia river. If the Toccoa received as much fishing pressure as the Chattahoochee, the fisheries might well be rated as almost equal. Probably the nod still goes to the Chattahoochee because of its record of producing large trout as well as quantities of fish.

That is not to say that the Toccoa tailrace never produces large

PHOTO BY BILL VANDERFORD

*A good, wadeable shoal and easy access to the Toccoa River are available
in the vicinity of Shallowford Bridge off Aska Road.*

trout, of course. At one time the Georgia state record for brook trout
was held by an almost 5-pound brookie that was pulled from this
tailrace. Also, anytime you combine big water with the presence of
brown trout you know there are some large fish available. Since all
three species of rainbow, brown, and brookies are stocked, the river
offers some fascinating possibilities.

For roughly 15 miles from Blue Ridge Dam downstream to the
state border at McCaysville the river is heavily stocked, but, due to
restricted shore access, is relatively lightly fished. Open to fishing the
year-round, the river gets almost no pressure from September to April
each year. The bulk of the anglers trying their luck at any time are
likely to be bait casters fishing from the walls at the foot of the dam.

With a few exceptions, the river is so deep that float fishing is the
easiest method of covering the water. In fact, a couple of guides offer
float services on this stream. There are a few shoal areas that are

wadeable on low water, most notably at the town of Mineral Bluff and just upstream of McCaysville. Much of the river can be reached via the old railroad right-of-way on the western shore, but it is strictly walk-in access.

The key to catching trout on the Toccoa is to be on the water while it is falling, after the flow at the dam has been shut off. The fish feed actively during the falling water, but once it bottoms out, they become tough to find and fool. Most of the fishing is of the wet fly or nymphing variety, but occasional, and sometimes rather large, insect hatches occur, bringing the action to the surface. This action is quite sporadic and unpredictable, but casting attractor patterns like a Royal Wulff or an Adams, especially in shoal areas, usually attracts some fish as well.

Best access to the upper Toccoa River is available off GA 60 northwest of Suches, in the vicinity of Deep Hole Campground, or along Aska Road to the east of the town of Blue Ridge. For the tailrace, there is a TVA park at the foot of Blue Ridge Dam. Other access points are off GA 245 at Mineral Bluff and above McCaysville.

COOPER CREEK
USGS Neels Gap, Coosa Bald, Mulky Gap

Cooper Creek is the largest of the feeder streams on public land that enter the Toccoa River. Like all of the tributaries that are covered, it joins the river upstream of Lake Blue Ridge. Not only the biggest, it is also the furthest upstream of any of the feeders, as it empties in from the northeast side of the river.

A very good case can be made for Cooper Creek to be recognized as the most heavily fished stream in Georgia for its size. Due to the presence of Mulky and Cooper Creek Forest Service campgrounds on its banks, this stream is heavily visited throughout the spring and summer. This is one stream on which you can expect elbow-to-elbow fishing conditions on opening day of the season and on many summer weekends.

Through this portion the creek, which lies on the Coopers Creek WMA, is of medium size, but falls on the borderline of rating as big water. Although the creek is open enough for easy casting, your problem often is finding room among the other anglers to make your casts.

PHOTO BY BILL VANDERFORD

Fishing regulations on Noontootla Creek make it virtually a catch-and-release fishery in the Blue Ridge WMA in north-central Georgia.

Hatchery trout are stocked heavily throughout the creek, but some wild fish are also present. These are particularly concentrated in the limited-access portion of the creek through the Cooper Creek Scenic Area, just upstream of the campgrounds. In the scenic area only foot access is possible, resulting in lower fishing pressure. The bulk of the fish encountered are stocked or wild rainbows, plus some browns of both varieties.

Although the first four miles of the stream from its mouth on the Toccoa up to the edge of the WMA are on private land and closed to the public, the rest of the creek, up to its headwater at Lake Winfield Scott, is in the WMA on Forest Service lands. FS 4 parallels a short stretch of the creek below and up to the campgrounds and the parking area at the edge of the scenic area. The upper portion of the creek is accessible from FS 33, which runs along the water for several miles above the scenic area.

MULKY CREEK
USGS *Mulky Gap*

Mulky Creek is a small stream that flows into Cooper Creek from the north between the Mulky and Cooper Creek campgrounds. The gravel bed of FS 4 follows the creek for most of its course, affording convenient access to the stream.

Although the casting is tight, it is possible to fly-fish much of its lower areas. Pools are mostly small and shallow, with only a few providing really interesting water. There are no hatchery fish released into Mulky Creek and its wild fish population is not overly abundant.

Given this description, the question might come up of why we bother to mention this creek. Mulky Creek is at its best late in the season, particularly in October. When the brown trout in Cooper Creek get the spawning urge, they often find their way into this stream. Finding a brown over 12 inches in Mulky Creek at this time is not all that rare.

ROCK CREEK
USGS *Noontootla*

In moving down the Toccoa River the next fishable feeder stream on public land is Rock Creek. This stream enters from the south off the Blue Ridge WMA, emptying into the river downstream of Deep Hole Campground. Rock Creek is one of the streams that gives Cooper Creek some competition for the title of most heavily fished. With its close proximity to Deep Hole and the presence of the Forest Service's Frank Gross Campground on the creek, many anglers are attracted to the area.

Also adding to the appeal of the stream is the Chattahoochee National Fish Hatchery's location on one of its feeder streams and having Rock Creek Lake impounded at the stream's midpoint. The hatchery ensures that Rock Creek gets some healthy doses of stockers, while the lake, which contains trout, offers fishermen a little variety in the fishing opportunities. Adding to the congestion on the stream is the presence of a plentiful supply of primitive campsites on the lower portion of the creek.

A medium-size flow downstream of Rock Creek Lake, the creek is open enough for casting on all of its downstream course. Above the lake the stream is small, contains both stocked and wild rainbows, and gets slightly less fishing pressure. Below the lake, stocked rainbows and browns constitute the bulk of the fish encountered.

Rock Creek does hold the distinction of having yielded the Georgia state record brown trout back in 1967. That 18-pound, 2-ounce monster was, however, a bit of an anomaly, since it was a brood fish that had escaped from the fish hatchery.

Unless you just crave some company while fishing, Rock Creek is probably not your ideal casting destination. It is particularly popular with bait-fishermen who are posted on most of its deeper pools throughout the fishing season.

Access is excellent to the entire stream via FS 69 off GA 60, just to the south of the village of Margaret.

NOONTOOTLA CREEK
USGS Noontootla

As mentioned in the introduction to this river system, the Toccoa is arguably the best big-water trout fishery in Georgia. By the same token, Noontootla Creek just might be the best all-around small stream in the state.

Rising in Frying Pan Gap deep in the Blue Ridge WMA, Noontootla is managed as a catch-and-release stream. Only artificial lures are legal for fishing the stream, and a very restrictive creel limit of one fish per day that must be at least 16 inches in length is in effect.

Rainbow trout dominate the fishery on Noontootla Creek, but brown trout are also present. Some of the small feeder streams emptying into Noontootla also contain native brook trout. Most of the rainbows run from 6 to 12 inches, but browns make up the majority of the legal keepers each year. Brown trout up to 20 inches appear and are most vulnerable late in the season when they move upstream in answer to the spawning urge. These large fish occasionally even show up in the small tributary creeks.

Noontootla is a medium-width stream on the public lands of the WMA. Although tight in places, casting room is adequate to allow fly-fishing upstream to Three Forks. This is the point at which the Appalachian Trail crosses the creek, as well as where Long Creek empties into Noontootla from the west and Stover Creek joins from the east. Further up the creek valley, Noontootla is small, quite bushy, and difficult to fly-fish.

Due to the restrictive regulations, Noontootla gets relatively light fishing pressure, in spite of easy access from FS 58, which parallels the entire creek through the WMA. Even on summer weekends, angling pressure rates as only moderate. Recent renovation programs along the creek have closed many primitive campsites at streamside. While further discouraging crowding on the creek, this move also helps ensure that Noontootla will retain its high water quality and the scenic beauty of the stream valley.

Although wild trout are plentiful in Noontootla, they can also be finicky and tough to fool. Careful stalking of the pools and a minimum of wading are usually necessary to hook these trout successfully. And, of course, due to the regulations, the possibility always exists that the next fish may be a rainbow in the 13- to 15-inch range or a brown of over 16 inches.

The easiest approach to FS 58 and Noontootla Creek is on Big Creek Road from the west, off GA 52 to the east of Ellijay.

STANLEY CREEK
USGS *Tickanetley*

The final stream in the Toccoa basin that merits discussion is Stanley Creek on the Rich Mountain WMA between the towns of Ellijay and Blue Ridge. Both the Rich Mountain WMA and Stanley Creek look much better on paper than they prove to be in reality. Although the Rich Mountain preserve claims five streams in the Georgia Fishing Regulations, only Stanley Creek has enough of its length on publicly owned land to make it of interest.

Stanley Creek, however, also suffers from much the same problem. This stream is managed under special artificial-lure-only regulations, receives no stocked trout, and is a high-quality fishery. Unfortunately, the sign on the creek identifying it as a special-management stream is located in the front yard of a streamside homeowner! Most of the land through which Stanley Creek's lower stretches run is privately owned and posted. Only the upper couple of miles of the stream are on public land. By the time you get far enough upstream to find public access, the creek is a small, bushy flow that is difficult to fly-cast. As a result,

Stanley Creek gets very light visitation from anglers on its public-land section.

In spite of these problems, Stanley offers some high-quality fishing for wild rainbows. Fish up to 12 inches turn up fairly regularly and small trout are abundant. Some brown trout are caught, but they are not common.

Stanley Creek originates in the Rich Mountain Wilderness Area in the heart of the WMA, and the headwaters portion of the stream provides some interesting fishing, but it is mostly dapping water.

Access to Stanley Creek is via Stanley Creek Road off GA 515 at the village of Cherry Log. Follow Stanley Creek Road through Stanley Gap and descend to the edge of the WMA lands where the Benton McKay Trail crosses. Stanley Creek is to the right of the road on the far side of a wildlife clearing.

SECTION TWO

KENTUCKY

Since Kentucky is the most northerly of the states covered in this description of the trout streams of southern Appalachia, it seems reasonable that it would also have the most natural cold-water fishery. Eastern Kentucky has a long and close association in most people's minds with rugged hills and mountaineers. The cultural heritage of the region is very closely tied to the rest of the southern highlands, and the Cumberland Plateau provides scenery and flora that are often indistinguishable from the rest of Appalachia.

In spite of these similarities and expectations, the only trout naturally occurring in the Blue Grass State were probably found in the thin ribbon of the Blue Ridge Mountains located in the extreme eastern rim of the state. Although some experimental reintroduction of native southern Appalachian brook trout has taken place in small creeks on this eastern rim, these streams do not constitute a valid fly-fishing resource. In fact, the fisheries managers of the state are even rather reluctant to identify the creeks. There are no streams in this area managed by the Kentucky Department of Fish and Wildlife Resources (KDFWR) that are large enough to constitute fly-fishing destinations.

This leaves the Cumberland Plateau as the bastion of trout angling in the eastern part of the state. All of the fisheries that exist to the west of this range cannot be considered a part of Appalachia.

The plateau possesses some subtle differences from the Blue Ridge

Mountains to its east. These differences heavily affect Kentucky's potential as a trout-fishing Mecca. The topography and geology of eastern Kentucky are not ideal for members of the salmonid family of fish.

To begin with, the plateau, which forms a band from Ashland in Boyd County on the Ohio River southwesterly to Whitley City in McCreary County on the Tennessee border, lacks the elevations usually associated with southern trout waters. The highest areas on the plateau are barely 1300 feet, with most being only 1000 to 1200 feet high. The plateau is also composed of mostly sedimentary rock formations. Limestone is quite prevalent, with some shale and sandstone. This differs greatly from the hard igneous and metamorphic stone base of the Blue Ridge to the east.

Due to the lack of elevation, most of the creeks and rivers start out as marginal trout waters. The water's ability to cut through the sedimentary rocks, rather than tumbling over them, has lowered the stream elevations even more and eliminated much of the aeration associated with shoal areas. The resulting waters tend to flow through level courses cut deep into the valley floors. At these low levels, only in few places does the inflow of springs from the limestone provide enough cold water to produce year-round trout habitat.

On the other hand, the presence of limestone has led to the formation of a number of caves in the region. These have provided an environment where some of the state's best trout streams appear and disappear while flowing out of and into these grottos. Such streams provide some of the most unusual and challenging fishing situations found in southern Appalachia.

A final characteristic of the trout fishery in eastern Kentucky is the presence of a number of tailrace fisheries below hydroelectric projects. The lakes involved are not very deep, and the water released into the tailraces is not truly cold. For the most part, the streams below the dams are small and only stocked with trout in the springtime.

After eliminating the streams on the state's list of trout waters that are on private land (in Kentucky, permission of landowners is required to cross or fish on their property), are too small for fly-casting, or that bear little resemblance to a southern Appalachian mountain creek, only five river systems in Kentucky merit coverage. These are the Cumberland, Kentucky, Licking, Red, and Rockcastle river systems.

Having noted the drawbacks faced by Kentucky's highland fishery, let's close this introduction on a positive note. There are streams among the 45 the state lists as trout water in the eastern counties that do offer valid fly-casting destinations, and some can be rated as good prospects. All of these streams are located within the 670,000 acres of the Daniel Boone National Forest, which takes in most of the Cumberland Plateau.

From a management standpoint, the KDFWR has done a very good job of protecting and maintaining the trout streams that Kentucky does have. While the creeks that provide marginal habitat are employed as heavily stocked, put-and-take fisheries, the streams that provide better conditions are utilized to their fullest. Where possible, stockings of fingerling trout are used on year-round, cold-water streams. In most cases this provides fishing opportunities that are very similar to wild-trout angling.

The trout available in Kentucky are mostly catchable-size rainbows stocked by the KDFWR, but the U.S. Fish and Wildlife Service also stocks both catchable and subadult rainbows in National Forest streams. Kentucky authorities plant 4- to 8-inch brown trout in selected streams on a once-a-year basis to provide the put-grow-and-take fishery as well.

There are no minimum size limits for rainbow or brown trout on any of the streams in Kentucky, with the exception of the tailwaters below Dix Dam at Lake Herrington. That stream, which has a 15-inch minimum size limit and three-fish creel limit, is not in the Appalachian region. Brook trout have a minimum size limit of 10 inches and some streams containing them are posted with signs mandating artificial lures and flies. The creel limit for rainbows and browns is eight fish daily in any combination, while the limit on brook trout is two fish.

There is no closed season for trout fishing in Kentucky. To fish for trout in the commonwealth, a regular fishing license and a trout stamp are required. To request a copy of the pamphlet, "Kentucky Trout Waters," containing the state trout regulations, write to the Kentucky Department of Fish and Wildlife Resources, #1 Game Farm Road, Frankfort, Kentucky 40601 or call (502) 564-3400.

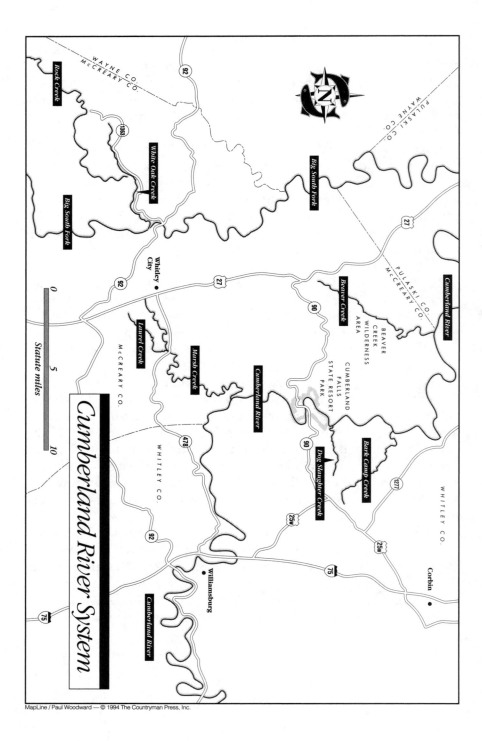

Cumberland River System

Rock Creek

White Oak Creek

Big South Fork

Big South Fork

Cumberland River

Beaver Creek

Laurel Creek

Marsh Creek

Cumberland River

Bark Camp Creek

Dog Slaughter Creek

Cumberland River

Whitley City

Williamsburg

Corbin

WAYNE CO.
McCREARY CO.

PULASKI CO.
WAYNE CO.

PULASKI CO.
McCREARY CO.

McCREARY CO.

WHITLEY CO.

WHITLEY CO.

BEAVER CREEK WILDERNESS AREA

CUMBERLAND FALLS STATE RESORT PARK

0 5 10
Statute miles

10

Cumberland River System

Mentioning the Cumberland River and trout in the same sentence makes most anglers in the Blue Grass State immediately think of the tailwaters below Lake Cumberland in Russell and Cumberland counties. The reaction is understandable since that portion of the river is widely considered Kentucky's premier fishery for trophy trout. It is also some of the most heavily stocked trout water in the state, receiving almost 100,000 fish each year.

If, however, one is talking about mountain trout fisheries in Kentucky, that portion of the Cumberland is located too far west and is not part of southern Appalachia. The upstream portion of the river above Lake Cumberland is the major waterway of southeastern Kentucky and along with its large tributary, the Big South Fork, is fed by the bulk of the better trout streams of the area. Neither the Cumberland nor the Big South Fork, however, are trout streams themselves.

Bark Camp, Beaver, Dog Slaughter, Laurel, and Rock creeks make up the fly-fishing waters feeding into the Cumberland system. Although there are a number of other streams that flow into the river system and contain trout, they either are mostly on private land, are quite small, or do not resemble mountain trout water.

BEAVER CREEK
USGS Hail

Beaver Creek is a small stream that empties into the Cumberland River at the point where the river becomes the border between McCreary and Pulaski counties. Located on the southeast side of the

91

river, Beaver Creek's entire watershed is in McCreary County and the Daniel Boone National Forest.

There are a couple of facts about Beaver Creek that set it apart from most of the trout streams in Kentucky. First of all the stream is located in the Beaver Creek Wilderness Area, which was established by the Eastern Wilderness Act back in 1975. It was the first such federal reserve set up in the Blue Grass State. Secondly, although the stream has been stocked with trout for more than 20 years, there are also some indications that natural reproduction may be taking place in the creek's headwaters.

Part of the reason that Beaver Creek was ideal for inclusion in the wilderness system was that the 5000 acres of land making up the creek valley have been owned by the state since the 1930s. That ownership protected the stream's water quality from falling victim to the pollution associated with mining that has affected many eastern Kentucky waters.

Today only foot or horseback travel is permitted in the wilderness area. Naturally, the wilderness regulations make the fishing pressure quite low. Add to this the stocking of only about 2000 subadult rainbow trout every other year and the fishing on Beaver Creek holds appeal for only the purist, wilderness angler. The meat-on-the-table anglers can find easier pickings on other waters.

Another oddity in the management of Beaver Creek is that only rainbow trout can be stocked there. Since they were the only trout species present when the wilderness area was established, introduction of other species is prohibited. Although rainbows of up to 14 inches have been reported, during the months of low water in the summer, trout are outnumbered by panfish and bass, especially in the lower half of the creek. During the hotter months the water temperatures on the creek hover around the marginal level for trout. In spite of the fact that the lower and middle sections of the creek are open enough to allow some casting room, it is tight fishing. These areas of the stream valley do not have much of a grade so the creek does not have a great deal of shoal water.

A concrete and wood bridge still stands across the stream near the midpoint of its course. The two miles of water below it down to the Cumberland can best be described as marginal. Upstream the creek is small and heavily foliated for the 2.5 miles to where the Middle Fork of Beaver Creek is joined by Freeman Fork and Hurricane Creek to form the main stream. While Beaver Creek offers one of the more interesting wilderness fishing experiences in Kentucky, it cannot be called a blue-ribbon fly-fishing destination in southern Appalachia.

Access to Beaver Creek is via FS 50 to the east off US 27 south of Somerset. Watch for FS 51 entering FS 50 from the east. Follow FS 51 to its end and then take the foot path that is between 0.75 and 1.0 mile long, down to the old bridge. The trail can be fairly overgrown from lack of use in the summer when flies, ticks, and warm temperatures make the walk uncomfortable. Another trail splits off FS 51 (it is marked FS 51C) that leads to the Three Forks area where the main stem of the creek is formed.

BARK CAMP CREEK
USGS Sawyer

Bark Camp Creek is a small, heavily foliated stream that flows through Whitley County to join the Cumberland River. Although it constitutes a difficult fly-casting destination, and because of its small size, a marginal fly-fishery, it still merits mention, since virtually all of it is on Forest Service land.

Through much of its course it is a rocky tumbling flow that offers some good shoal water. In places it drops over some picturesque falls with plunge pools that occasionally yield impressive trout.

Only one Forest Service road (FS 193) crosses the stream and in the vicinity of the bridge some in-stream structure work has been done to improve the trout habitat. This portion of the creek is completely canopied and perpetually shaded, which, no doubt, keeps summer water temperatures cooler. Both rainbow and brown trout can be found around the structures.

Above the road crossing, the creek parallels the road, but is not visible from the gravel track. It is also a very small flow in this upper stretch, and not a practical fly-casting area. Below the bridge the creek is paralleled by a foot trail, FT 413, all the way to the Cumberland River. This trail intersects the Sheltowee Trace National Recreation Trail (FT 100) at the Forest Service's Bark Camp Campground by the river. The trace trail, which winds for 250 miles through eastern Kentucky, gets its name from the Indian name given Daniel Boone by Chief Blackfish of the Shawnee Tribe and means "Big Turtle." Blazes for this trail appear as white turtles painted on trees and rocks along the path.

The U.S. Fish and Wildlife Service stocks Bark Camp with catch-able-size rainbow trout monthly from March through June. Due to the relatively light angling pressure applied and better-than-average habitat conditions, some trout are available all through the warmer months. Kentucky adds a planting of 400 brown trout to the stream, usually in the fall each year.

Trout of 12 to 13 inches turn up regularly, but the average fish in Bark Camp is a stocker of 9 to 10 inches and probably a rainbow. In the deep holes of the lower part of the creek, fish of up to 16 inches have been reported.

To reach Bark Camp Creek, take US 25 to the southwest out of Corbin. Turn to the right on County Road 1277. After passing Young Chapel Church on the left, begin watching for FS 193 on the left as well. Follow this gravel road until it crosses Bark Camp Creek. The end of CR 1277 is at its junction with the Sheltowee Trace at the Cumberland River. It is possible to hike upstream from here to the mouth of Bark Camp.

DOG SLAUGHTER CREEK
USGS *Wiborg*

Lying just over the ridge to the south of Bark Camp Creek, Dog Slaugh-ter is a smaller version of its neighbor stream. Like Bark Camp, it is located mainly on Forest Service land in Whitley County.

The creek is fishable downstream of the point that FS 195 crosses the flow, but for three-quarters of a mile below the crossing the creek is small, level, sluggish, and tightly canopied. After drop-ping over a 20-foot waterfall, the final one-quarter mile down to the Cumberland River is steeply graded with several cataracts, pot-holes, and large boulders. This lower portion runs through a short gorge with steep bluffs on both shores, is fairly open, and offers the best fishing.

Dog Slaughter is stocked with rainbow trout each month from March through June. It presently gets no brown trout plantings. Trout of 10 to 13 inches are taken regularly from the creek.

Access to Dog Slaughter Creek is via FS 195, running north off KY 90 a few miles east of Cumberland Falls State Park. A small sign marked 195 is at the intersection of the highway and this gravel road.

The creek goes under the road through a pipe and the water is not visible from the roadway.

On the south side of the creek there is a parking area that also serves as the trailhead for a path that parallels the creek all the way to the Cumberland. Blazed with white diamonds, the path crosses a bridge over the South Fork of Dog Slaughter just a few yards from the trailhead. There is a trail intersection here and turning right leads to the main branch of Dog Slaughter Creek via FT 714. The trail is moderately strenuous down to the river, where it intersects the Sheltowee Trace. The junction of the creek and river can also be approached by hiking north from Cumberland Falls State Park on the Sheltowee Trace.

LAUREL CREEK
USGS *Whitley City*

Not to be confused with streams of the same name that are in Elliot, Johnson, and Lawrence counties, this version of Laurel Creek is located in McCreary County. While those other Laurel creeks are stocked with trout, they are also on private land. This McCreary County stream is located almost entirely on Forest Service property, as it winds its way down to Marsh Creek, which in turn joins the Cumberland River south of Cumberland Falls State Park.

Laurel Creek is a small stream, but does offers some (very tight) fly-casting conditions. The streambed is fairly rocky and provides some holding water and ripples. Water temperatures in the lower portion seem rather marginal in the summer.

Laurel Creek is stocked only once each year with subadult rainbow trout by the U.S. Fish and Wildlife Service. As a result, fishing pressure is quite low.

Access to the creek is via KY 478 to the east of US 27. An old logging road parallels the creek downstream of the bridge, while the Laurel Creek Trail runs upstream along the flow. The trail starts at a parking area and is blazed with white diamonds. A footbridge carries the path over Bridge Fork then upstream along Laurel Creek.

It is also possible to get to the headwaters of the creek at the dam on the McCreary County Reservoir. It is a very small stream this far up and can be reached via Reservoir Road off US 27 south of Whitley City.

ROCK CREEK
USGS Barthell SW, Bell Farm, Barthell

Flowing south to north, Rock Creek is a tributary of the South Fork of the Cumberland lying in McCreary County. It is probably the best-known and most popular trout creek in the commonwealth. It is also a stream that has been designated a Kentucky Wild River and offers roughly 15 miles of public water that provide a variety of fishing options.

Located entirely within the Daniel Boone National Forest, the creek is large and open enough to allow fly-casting all the way from White Oak Junction upstream to the Tennessee border. One peculiarity of the stream is that it does not actually make it all the way to the junction with White Oak Creek. Just a few yards short of this destination Rock Creek plunges into a limestone cave, leaving the stream bed dry downstream to the junction.

From the cave mouth upstream the creek is paralleled by FS 566 all the way to Bell Farm (a Forest Service campground designed for campers with horses) and consists of a string of deep sluggish pools with an occasional bit of shoal water. Through this area the creek is of medium size and holds a mixture of rainbow and brown trout, along with a healthy dose of smallmouth bass. The distance by road is 8.0 miles along this part of the stream, and there are a few parcels of private land located through here.

Above the Bell Farm camping area, the creek runs along FS 564 for a distance though a large patch of private, posted land. Next the creek follows FS 137 and more closely resembles a mountain stream, tumbling through rocky shoals between deep, but current-flushed pools. There are 7.0 miles of stream along FS 137 to the end of the road. A footpath then follows the creek on up to the Tennessee border. This upper portion of the stream has two Forest Service campgrounds, Hemlock Grove and Great Meadow, located on it. The Sheltowee Trace joins the creek at Hemlock Grove and runs through Great Meadow as it follows the creek on to the headwaters in Tennessee's Pickett State Park and Forest.

The U.S. Fish and Wildlife Service annually stocks 9- to 11-inch rainbow trout in Rock Creek each month from February through October. More than 25,000 fish are usually planted in the stream during the year. Kentucky officials also add another 1500 to 2000 brown trout to the stockings in October. Finally, the federal stockers release about 2000 subadult rainbows in the upper reaches of the creek above Great Meadows each fall. As a result of these plantings, fish are plentiful year-round, and trout of 3 to 5 pounds have been reported in the lower portion of the creek.

For the fly caster, the headwaters, where the fingerling rainbows grow into streamwise adults, hold the most promise. The stream is small above Great Meadows but gets much less fishing pressure than further downstream. It is ideally suited for either dry or wet flies, with adequate room for casting. All in all, the upper portion of Rock Creek has the most natural fly-fishing setting and conditions to be found in Kentucky.

To reach Rock Creek take KY 92 to the west of Whitley City. Immediately after crossing the South Fork of the Cumberland, turn left onto KY 1363. At White Oak Junction take another left on FS 566, which follows Rock Creek up to Bell Farm. At the Bell Farm intersection go left on FS 564 for about a mile to the junction with FS 137. Yet another left turn onto FS 137 leads to Hemlock Grove, Great Meadow, and the headwaters of Rock Creek.

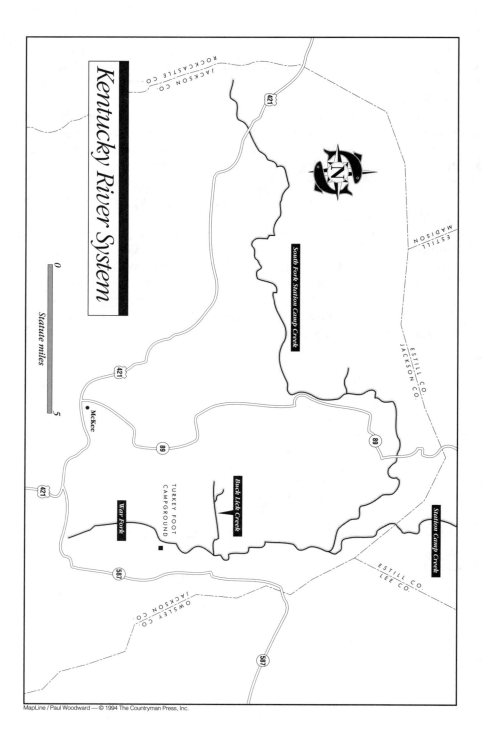

Kentucky River System

South Fork Station Camp Creek

War Fork

Buck Lick Creek

Station Camp Creek

TURKEY FOOT CAMPGROUND

McKee

Statute miles

0   5

JACKSON CO.
ROCKCASTLE CO.

ESTILL
MADISON

ESTILL CO.
JACKSON CO.

ESTILL CO.
LEE CO.

JACKSON CO.
OWSLEY CO.

421

421

89

89

587

587

11

Kentucky River System

The Kentucky River system drains the east-central area of the commonwealth, taking in Estill and Jackson counties on the Cumberland Plateau. Although the river itself does not support a cold-water fishery, there are a couple of tributaries that do contain trout. The river flows to the northwest, eventually emptying into the Ohio River midway between Louisville and Cincinnati.

All of the trout water in the Kentucky River system on the Cumberland Plateau is found in the drainage of Station Camp Creek. This stream, however, is located almost exclusively on private land and does not offer a true public fishery. This leaves War Fork as the only legitimate public trout water in this system.

WAR FORK
USGS McKee, Leighton

War Fork is a small- to medium-size stream that flows from south to north through the eastern edge of Jackson County. Entering the Daniel Boone National Forest along KY 587 east of McKee, the creek appears to offer a substantial length of water down to the U.S. Forest Service campground at Turkey Foot and from there to where the creek empties into Station Camp Creek near the Jackson and Estill county line. As is often the case, however, the maps do not tell the whole story.

In fact, War Fork offers one of the most unusual of the trout fisheries found anywhere in southern Appalachia. From March through June the federal stocking trucks make stops all along the creek, plant-

War Fork provides a most unusual trout-angling opportunity that combines season-long fishing with a wilderness setting. Here the creek emerges from a limestone cave near the junction with Buck Lick Creek.

ing catchable-size rainbow trout. This is particularly true of the area around Turkey Foot. By late June, however, the creek above Turkey Foot and a long stretch below the campground goes completely dry. At this time of year, the creek begins in a large pool just at the head of the picnic area in the campground. The water comes out of the rocky west bank of the creek and flows through a series of pools and gentle shoals for one-quarter of a mile downstream. Just at the foot of the campground, the creek pools up and goes underground again. This portion of the creek receives moderate to heavy fishing pressure in the spring, but the crowds thin considerably in the summer.

What makes War Fork unusual is that it reappears from a cave on the left bank of the creek about two miles downstream near its junction with Buck Lick Creek. Although Buck Lick is listed as a trout stream and is stocked once a year with subadult rainbows, only its small headwater section contains water year-round. Lower down it goes underground, and undoubtedly adds its flow to the water appearing in War Fork at the cave entrance.

Below the cave, War Fork has a steady flow even in summer and the water temperatures are cool enough to support trout on into August and September. There seems a good possibility that some fish carry over from year to year in this lower area. The bed of the creek is solid and rocky, providing deep pools connected by water rushing over shoals. These tumbling, aerated waters are often where the trout hold as the weather warms in the summer.

Although the stream's course is open enough for fly-casting, it appears to get only light fishing pressure on this lower portion. This is probably due to its hidden location, plus the need for a little walking and local savvy to find the water.

Another oddity encountered on War Fork is the appearance of isolated pools along its bed from Turkey Foot down to the Buck Lick junction. These sometimes hold fish in the late spring after most of the creek has dried up. A hike down the dry bed during the latter half of June (depending on how wet the year has been) can lead to the discovery of pools formed by deep spots in the normal creek channel that still hold water and have a trout or two surviving in them. These fish are prime candidates for a streamside fish dinner, since they only last a short time before falling victim to marauding raccoons anyway.

Access to War Fork is available at Turkey Foot Campground by taking FS 4 to the west from KY 587. This gravel Forest Service road crosses War Fork at the campground. The Sheltowee Trace trail parallels the creek downstream from this point to the creek's exit from public lands near its mouth on Station Camp Creek.

To get to the lower portion of War Fork, turn north onto FS 345 at the intersection beside Turkey Foot and go 2.1 miles. At this point a very rough spur runs off the right of the road and ends in a primitive campsite a few yards down the hill. Unless a four-wheel-drive vehicle is available, don't try to drive down this spur. A trail marked with white diamonds goes through the campsite. Follow it to the left going north for 200 yards downhill to the mouth of the cave from which the creek flows. By continuing on FS 345 past this spur, the headwaters of Buck Lick can be reached. The road will then parallel this tiny flow for several hundred yards.

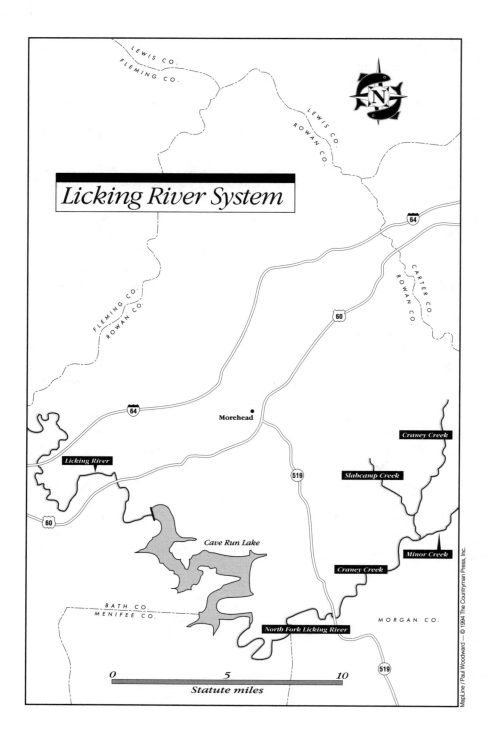

Licking River System

LEWIS CO.
FLEMING CO.

LEWIS CO.
ROWAN CO.

64

CARTER CO.
ROWAN CO.

FLEMING CO.
ROWAN CO.

60

64

Morehead

Craney Creek

Licking River

Slabcamp Creek

519

60

Cave Run Lake

Minor Creek

Craney Creek

BATH CO.
MENIFEE CO.

MORGAN CO.

North Fork Licking River

519

| 0 | 5 | 10 |

Statute miles

MapLine / Paul Woodward — © 1994 The Countryman Press, Inc.

12

Licking River System

The Licking River system is the most northerly in the Daniel Boone National Forest that contains any trout waters. The river and its major reservoir, Cave Run Lake, drain a large portion of Bath, Morgan, Powell, and Rowan counties.

Although the Licking River tailwaters below Cave Run are stocked with trout, they do not constitute a southern Appalachian mountain fishery. Additionally, Brushy Creek and the North Fork of Triplett Creek are tributaries of the Licking that are not covered. In the case of the former, it is quite small and bushy, while the latter flows primarily on private lands.

The remaining trout water in this system that is open to the public is in the valley of Craney Creek, consisting of that stream and its two feeders, Minor and Slabcamp creeks.

CRANEY CREEK
USGS Haldeman, Wrigley

Craney Creek is a medium to small flow that feeds into the North Fork of the Licking River arm of Cave Run Lake just at the high-water mark. This designation of the North Fork can cause some confusion, however. It is based on the map of the Daniel Boone National Forest (North Half) distributed by the U.S. Forest Service. On the other hand, the Rand McNally atlas and road maps show a North Fork of the Licking River cutting across Mason, Robertson, and Pendleton counties much further north and joining the main branch of the river just south of Cincinnati.

Regardless, once you figure out the maps and find Craney Creek it forms the county line between Morgan and Rowan counties. It is also a slow-moving, bottomland stream in the area just before it empties into the lake. Craney Creek does, however, have an unusual amount of broad, shallow riffle water for such a low-elevation location. For more than two miles upstream it continues to alternate between these sandy shoals and deeper pools. All of this portion of the creek is open enough to allow fly-casting.

Craney receives monthly stockings of catchable rainbow trout from March through May each spring, as well as an additional planting of rainbows in October. These stockings are made by U.S. Fish and Wildlife Service personnel.

Access to Craney Creek is off KY 519 south of Morehead, via FS 947. This Forest Service road is paved along the North Fork all the way to the headwaters of the lake, then changes to gravel for a short distance before being blocked by a gate beside the creek. Be aware that the approach along the shore of the North Fork is virtually at Cave Run Lake's water level, so in times of heavy rains, the paved portion of FS 947 is prone to flood.

Above the gate, FS 947 provides foot access all the way up to the junction with Slabcamp Creek. Above that point, Craney is no longer on Forest Service property and flows through private lands.

MINOR CREEK
USGS Wrigley

Minor Creek is a quite small tributary of Craney Creek that flows for about a mile along the Morgan and Rowan county line. It offers little room for fly-casting, and, like Craney Creek, its headwaters are located above the public lands on private property.

Minor is stocked once each fall with fingerling brown trout. Most recently the stockings have consisted of 300 fish annually. Due to this small number of fish, and the equally small size of the creek, fishing pressure is light on Minor Creek. Trout of up to 12 inches are found in the pools on the creek, and browns of 16 inches have been reported.

Access to Minor Creek is gained by walking up FS 947 along Craney Creek. Minor Creek is the first tributary entering the main stream from the east above the gate on FS 947.

SLABCAMP CREEK
USGS Haldeman

Like its sister tributary to Craney Creek, Slabcamp is a small stream, and is located entirely in Rowan County. Fishing is very tight with a fly rod. Slabcamp receives a yearly stocking of 250 brown trout fingerlings in the fall, with fishing pressure and catches reported as being similar to those of Minor Creek.

Access to Slabcamp is also via foot travel along FS 947. It joins Craney Creek from the west, above the junction of Craney and Minor creeks. Although Slabcamp flows through several substantial stretches of Forest Service land, it also crosses some private holdings as well.

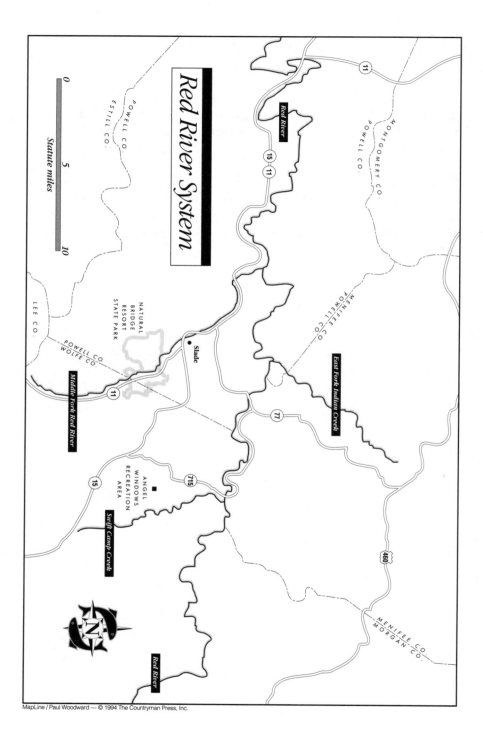

Red River System

Red River

15 11

11

Statute miles
0
5
10

ESTILL CO.

POWELL CO.

POWELL CO.

MONTGOMERY CO.

MENIFEE CO.
POWELL CO.

POWELL CO.
WOLFE CO.

LEE CO.

NATURAL
BRIDGE
RESORT
STATE PARK

Slade

Middle Fork Red River

11

East Fork Indian Creek

77

15

715

ANGEL
WINDOWS
RECREATION
AREA

Swift Camp Creek

460

MENIFEE CO.
MORGAN CO.

N

Red River

MapLine / Paul Woodward — © 1994 The Countryman Press, Inc.

13

Red River System

The Red River system, which flows east to west across Menifee, Powell, and Wolfe counties just south of Cave Run Lake, is second only to the Cumberland River system among Kentucky watersheds providing public mountain trout water. While Indian Creek in Menifee County and Chimney Top Creek in Wolfe County are both in the system and receive token fall stockings of brown trout, they are also small, inaccessible, and of minimal interest to fly casters.

Two of the three fly-fishing destinations on this river system, the East Fork of Indian Creek and Swift Camp Creek, are located in the Red River Gorge Geological Area. Composed of 26,000 acres of National Forest land, the gorge is a landscape dotted with unusual vegetation and more than 50 natural stone arches. Because of the unique nature of the area, anglers, along with all other visitors, should take extra care to avoid damaging either plants or rock formations.

The other trout stream in the system is the Middle Fork of the Red River, which is just south of the gorge.

EAST FORK INDIAN CREEK
USGS Scranton, Frenchburg, Slade

The most northerly of the streams in the Red River system, the East Fork of Indian Creek flows south through Menifee County to join Indian Creek before their combined waters empty into the Red River. The East Fork is a small stream that has a very gentle drop to it, especially in its lower stretches. This lower part is characterized by a series of deep pools, or "blue holes" as the locals call them.

Further upstream the creek has a bit more drop and, consequently, more current. The streambed also has rock and gravel stretches that provide more of the look of trout water. The runs and riffles, however, tend to be broad and shallow, providing little holding water for the fish. This water is quite clear during dry periods, making it still harder for trout to hide in the pools.

The East Fork offers very tight fishing conditions to the fly-fisherman for 3.8 miles up to the second concrete ford across the stream. Above that point the stream is too small for fly-casting.

The East Fork of Indian Creek receives stockings of rainbows from March through May each year, plus a release of 700 brown trout in the fall by the KDFWR. Especially in the upper reaches of the stream, these stockers tend to congregate in the large—but not necessarily deep—pools, where they are easily visible. Needless to say, they attract a lot of attention from anglers.

Another result of this concentration of fish and fishermen is trash. Primitive camping is allowed along the East Fork, with obvious heavy use of the sites at the second ford. The visitors have not been kind to the area. It is badly worn and much trash can be found discarded in the campsites and along the stream.

A final drawback for the fly caster is the presence of heavy concentrations of creek shiners, daces, and darters in the upper portion of the creek. These tiny fish are more than willing to take a fly before a trout has a chance to strike it.

To reach the East Fork of Indian Creek take FS 23 to the northwest off KY 77 where the highway crosses the Red River. At the mouth of Indian Creek on the river, FS 9A turns to the north. Follow this gravel road to its intersection with FS 9B and turn right. FS 9B parallels the East Fork from this point, fording the stream twice and following it to the upper reaches of fishable water.

SWIFT CAMP CREEK
USGS Pomeroyton

Not only is Swift Camp Creek the best of the trout waters in the Red River system, it is one of those locations that is surrounded by such a body of lore that it becomes a "must visit" destination. Tumbling for eight miles through a rugged and scenic valley in northern Wolfe County, the history of the creek has been a magnet to adventurers for centuries.

The upper reaches of Swift Camp Creek have a rocky bed and enough drop to provide some good pocket water. When fishing here, you might want to keep an eye open for the legendary lost silver mine along its banks.

Ever since Jonathan Swift reported discovering a mother lode of silver along a stream described as closely resembling Swift Camp, treasure hunters have ventured along its banks. Unfortunately, shortly after the find in the early 1740s, Swift was imprisoned in England and went blind during his incarceration. Upon returning to Kentucky around 1765 he attempted to describe to companions the exact location of his bonanza find, but the silver was never relocated. Their camp on the banks of the stream produced the only lasting legacy in providing the name for Swift Camp Creek.

Today the real treasure of Swift Camp Creek is its trout fishery. This small stream receives about 4000 catchable-size rainbow trout each year in stockings that take place from March through June. As an added bonus, it is reported that experimentally stocked brook trout still inhabit pools in the upper reaches of the creek.

Swift Camp actually provides two very different fisheries along its course. In the lower section near its mouth on the Red River the stream is deep and slow moving. It is characteristic of a lowland, sluggish flow. But, since this area has the only road access, it gets the bulk of the planted trout. Fishing pressure is heavy in the spring on this portion of the stream that extends to about a half mile above the last road access.

Further up the creek, above a small inholding of private land, the stream again is on Forest Service property. It also has a steeper grade and more shoal water. Though small and offering only very tight casting conditions, this is also the area of the creek where encounters with brook trout of up to 12 inches have been reported.

Access to the lower section of Swift Camp Creek is via KY 715 at the bridge over the Red River. To the south of this point the road runs within sight of Swift Camp before meandering away from the creek. Access to the upper portion of the creek is available over Forest Trail 219, which originates on KY 715 at the Angel Windows parking area.

The trail begins on the opposite (east) side of the road from the parking lot and is not marked with a sign. A few feet down the pathway an intersection is encountered. Turn right and head uphill at this junction. A sign soon appears identifying the path as FT 219. It is a 1.2-mile hike to the creek, with the last half of the trail dropping steeply downhill. FT 219 then turns upstream to follow the creek all the way to the Rock Bridge Picnic Area on Rock Bridge Road (FS 24) near the creek's headwaters. The picnic area is 0.5 mile from the creek.

MIDDLE FORK RED RIVER
USGS *Slade*

Running in a northwest direction across Powell County, the Middle Fork of the Red River contains 14 miles of water that is stocked with rainbow trout. Although virtually all of the stream runs along KY 11 or KY 15, providing easy access to the water, a great deal of the river is on private land. The only portion that can truly be considered public domain is the three miles of the stream flowing through Natural Bridge State Resort Park just south of the village of Slade.

A small, slow-moving stream with occasional shoals, the river courses through a couple of small lakes in the park. Since it is only marginal trout water to begin with, this impounding further limits the river as trout water. A total of about 4000 rainbow trout are stocked in the river each spring from March through May. With the stream running through campgrounds and picnic areas in the park, fishing pressure is quite heavy. The river is also within sight of KY 11 all the way through the Natural Bridge area, adding to its appeal to anglers.

The accessibility of the Middle Fork and its location in the resort park are its major assets. Small, often bushy and sluggish, it is not prime fly-fishing water.

To locate the Middle Fork of the Red River, take KY 11 south from the town of Slade. The river is visible on the south side of the road all the way to the boundary of Natural Bridge State Resort Park. The stream continues along the roadway though the park as well.

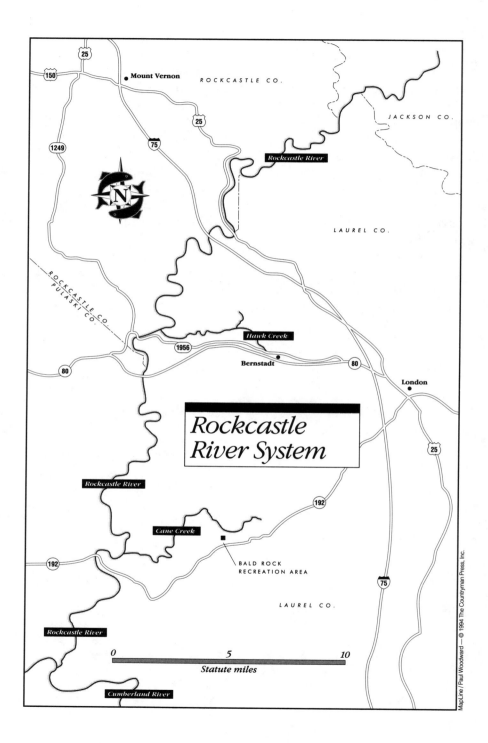

14

Rockcastle River System

The Rockcastle River forms the boundary between Rockcastle and Laurel counties, then as it flows further south it serves the same function between Laurel and Pulaski counties. Eventually, at the common boundary of Pulaski, Laurel, and McCreary counties it runs into the Cumberland River.

The main flow of Rockcastle is not a cold-water fishery and only two of its tributary streams support trout. These are Cane and Hawk creeks, both of which lie to the north of Laurel River Lake in Laurel County.

One word of caution regarding names is in order at this point. Some confusion arises concerning Rockcastle Creek. Although sharing a common name with the river, the two flows are not in the same drainage and are quite far apart. Rockcastle Creek is a trout stream that is located in Martin County in the northeast corner of the state near the Ohio and West Virginia state boundaries. It is a tributary of the Little Sandy River in Boyd County and located almost exclusively on private lands.

CANE CREEK
USGS Loudon SW, Ano

Located in Laurel County, Cane Creek is a medium- to small-size stream that empties into the Rockcastle River. In total there are 10 miles of water on this stream with virtually all of it located in the London District of the Daniel Boone National Forest. It also runs through the Cane Creek Wildlife Management Area. The location of

Hawk Creek is a small stream stocked with fingerling trout. It is also difficult to find or reach, making for light fishing pressure.

the stream on these public lands with no road access makes it a back-pack destination for anglers who like to get off the beaten path.

Of major importance to the fisherman, Cane Creek maintains a good flow of water even in the summer, with water temperatures staying at least at marginal levels for trout. While long, slow pools and runs are common, there are some rocky shoal areas providing both grade and aeration for trout. This ripple water is the most likely hiding place for the trout, especially in the summer months. Although quite tight in its upper reaches, Cane Creek offers room for fairly easy casting in its middle to lower stretches.

The trout found in Cane Creek consist of catchable-size rainbows stocked by the U.S. Fish and Wildlife Service monthly from March through June each spring. One more stocking takes place each October. In addition to these federal stockings, Kentucky fisheries managers release 600 brown trout into the creek each fall.

Access to the mouth of Cane Creek is available via a foot trail from Bee Rock Boat Ramp and Campground on the Rockcastle River. These are located off KY 192 at the border of Pulaski and Laurel counties.

An entry point to the midsection of the stream is via a hiking trail from the end of FS 109. This road runs off KY 192 in a northeasterly direction, a little more than a mile to the southeast of the Rockcastle River. At the end of the road a very poorly marked trail descends about 1.0 mile to the creek to intersect another trail that follows the stream's course.

The entry point for the upper portion of the creek is at the U.S. Forest Service's Bald Rock Campground (the sign at the site identifies it as Baldrock). FS 625 runs into the campground and a foot trail leads from that site to the creek, then parallels the flow along its course down to the Rockcastle River.

HAWK CREEK
USGS Bernstadt, Billows

Hawk Creek is a small stream that runs across U.S. Forest Service land in Laurel County. Dropping through a steeply banked course in its lowest section near its mouth on the Rockcastle River, the first quarter mile of water upstream is surprisingly open for such a small flow. There are some shoal areas mixed with deeper, slower sections.

The stream is stocked with subadult rainbow trout only once a year by the U.S. Fish and Wildlife Service. As a result of this delayed harvest stocking and the remote location with difficult access, fishing pressure is light on this creek.

To reach Hawk Creek, take KY 1249 west from the village of Bernstadt. At 0.25 mile south of the Rockcastle River bridge, turn onto the unmarked dirt road running to the east. This is a very rough track that is suitable for four-wheel-drive vehicles only. The road runs along the Rockcastle for 1.3 miles to the mouth of Hawk Creek. It then turns up the creek for 0.25 mile to a concrete bridge. Above this point access is by foot travel on a streamside trail.

SECTION THREE

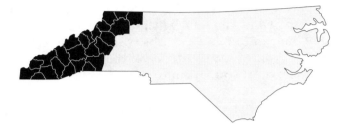

NORTH CAROLINA

If pressed to pick one word to summarize the trout fishery of the
Tarheel State, I would unequivocally opt for "abundance." North
Carolina has more natural trout streams than any of the other states
being discussed and these waters offer more types of fishing opportunities. It also has more agencies managing those streams, using a wide
variety of management techniques.

There are 4200 miles of trout water, all of which are located in the
26 westernmost counties of the state. All of these lie in either the
Appalachian Mountains or the bordering foothills region. More than
half the streams and rivers providing trout habitat are designated as
public fishing waters by the North Carolina Wildlife Resources Commission (NCWRC). Various portions of the streams are, however,
under the jurisdiction of North Carolina State Parks, the U.S. Fish
and Wildlife Service, the National Park Service, or the Eastern Band
of Cherokee Indians.

Brook, brown, and rainbow trout are all present in North Carolina streams and rivers. As in all southern states, the brookie is the
only native fish, but it is rare even in this bastion of cold waters.
Competition from introduced species and degradation of habitat have
been the culprits in the speckled trout's retreat. As early as the 1880s,
rainbow trout were introduced and eventually stocked in virtually
every watershed in the Old North State. In 1905 the rainbows were
joined by plantings of brown trout, which are continuing to expand

their range in North Carolina even today.

Of additional interest to fly casters in North Carolina are two other introduced fish of the salmonid family that anglers occasionally encounter. Kokanee salmon, a landlocked subspecies of the Pacific coast's sockeye salmon, were introduced to Nantahala Lake in the 1960s. As a result there is a spawning run up the Nantahala River each fall. It is a rather sporadic run, and a relative curiosity to fly casters. These fish may be seen in the river in October and November, but the salmon do not feed on their runs, so they must be angered or pestered into striking a lure or fly.

Another relic of earlier stocking experiments is the apparent presence of a strain of steelhead trout in Santeetlah Lake. Although there is no definite evidence of a run of these fish, some big and quite strong rainbows are reported in the lower reaches of Santeetlah Creek during the fall months.

The bulk of the trout waters of the Tarheel State are under the management of the NCWRC. The main thrust of North Carolina trout management is to preserve streams that are capable of supporting wild populations of trout in their present state. Secondarily, efforts are made to provide a variety of fishing opportunities to the state's anglers.

The fishing regulations that apply in North Carolina are quite varied. In water managed by the NCWRC the most basic categories are hatchery-supported waters and wild trout waters. Hatchery-supported streams receive stockings of trout, while no plantings take place in wild trout waters. On hatchery-supported waters all types of tackle and baits are allowed, the season is open from early April through the end of February each year, there is no minimum size on trout, and the creel limit is seven fish per day. These waters are marked with small diamond-shaped, green-and-white signs identifying them as hatchery supported. In the description of streams in the following chapters, the number of fish stocked will often be mentioned. These figures are based on the most recent year's stockings. In all streams, unless noted otherwise, the fish stocked are 40 percent rainbows, 40 percent brookies, and 20 percent brown trout. As a rule of thumb, in North Carolina, stocked trout will average 8 inches long, with 3 percent being 10 inches or longer. One percent of the stockers will exceed 13 inches.

On the other hand, wild-trout waters in North Carolina have a number of varied degrees of regulation. The standard wild-trout regulations allow year-round fishing, limit fishing to the use of artificial lures with single hooks, and impose a four-fish creel limit. The minimum size for a keeper on wild waters is 7 inches for all species. All wild trout streams open under these regulations that are located on private property, or on public lands located west of Yancey, McDowell, and Rutherford counties are marked by blue-and-gold signs indicating their designation.

Some of the designated wild streams are set aside as catch-and-release, artificial-lure-only streams. These creeks are open to year-round fishing, with artificial, single-hook lures. No trout of any size or species may be harvested from these streams. Purple-and-gold signs are prominently posted along these waterways.

Another wild trout designation is catch-and-release, artificial-flies-only streams. These creeks are open year-round, no fish may be harvested and only flies having a single hook can be used. These creeks and rivers are marked with red-and-gold signs.

One final designation used by the NCWRC combines a hybrid set of regulations. These rivers are delayed-harvest trout waters. In these stocked streams, year-round fishing is allowed, but from the first of March until the first weekend of June, special regulations apply. Only artificial lures with single hooks may be used and no fish may be harvested.

After the first weekend in June, these waters revert to the standard hatchery-supported regulations, with no size limits, a seven-fish creel limit, and no bait restrictions. Besides the green-and-white, hatchery-supported signs, notices explaining the rules are also posted at streamside.

Over 300 miles of trout streams in North Carolina are located within the confines of the Great Smoky Mountains National Park in Haywood and Swain counties. These are managed by the National Park Service (NPS) under special park regulations. No trout are stocked in the park and streams are open to fishing year-round. Only single-hook artificial lures are permitted. All brook trout must be released, and a creel limit of five rainbows and brown trout in any combination is in effect. Both of those species must be 7 inches or longer to be kept legally. Anglers having the appropriate trout fishing licenses from North Carolina or Tennessee may fish on any stream within the park boundaries.

The NPS also has jurisdiction over 75 miles of trout water lying on the lands along the Blue Ridge Parkway in North Carolina. About 25 miles of these waters are managed through a special agreement with the NCWRC as general hatchery-supported waters. The rest are managed by the NPS as wild-trout waters, with some set aside as fly-fishing-only destinations. Creel limits and minimum sizes conform to those that apply on similarly managed streams regulated by the NCWRC. Anglers having appropriate North Carolina or Virginia trout fishing licenses may fish in all parkway waters.

Two North Carolina state parks in the western section of the state contain a total of 26 miles of creeks holding trout: South Mountain State Park in Burke County and Stone Mountain State Park in Wilkes County. They contain both hatchery-supported and wild-trout waters, plus some special-regulation streams. Again, the appropriate North Carolina trout licenses are necessary for angling in the parks.

The final management authority for trout in North Carolina is the Cherokee Fish Management Enterprise on the Qualla Cherokee Indian Reservation in Jackson and Swain counties. Thirty miles of rivers and creeks on the 57,000-acre reservation are open for public fishing. These waters are designated as "Enterprise Waters" and operated as a tribal business. The streams are open to fishing from the last Saturday in March through the last day of February each year. The creel limit is 10 fish per day, with no bait or size-limit restrictions. The waters on the reservation are extremely heavily stocked. No state fishing license is required to fish on the reservation, but a daily, short-term, or season tribal permit (available at most stores on the reservation) must be purchased.

A cursory glance at the list of public trout waters in the North Carolina fishing regulations can be daunting. The number of streams and rivers (or portions of streams and rivers) listed reaches the staggering total of 250. This does not count the waters in the Great Smoky Mountains National Park, many of the streams along the Blue Ridge Parkway, those on the Qualla Reservation, or some that are on state-managed game lands or state parks. To try to visit and describe all of them would call for several volumes, not just a section of a single book.

Fortunately for the scribe and unfortunately for the angler, this vast number of public streams loses a bit of its luster under closer inspection. Sixty-eight percent (exactly 170 of the 250) either are too small and bushy for practical fly-casting, or actually offer very minimal public access. A large number of these creeks are listed as having several miles of trout water, but it turns out that only a few hundred yards in the headwaters are on public land, or there will be a few widely scattered road crossings or points of right-of-way access. The rest of the stream's course is through pastures or backyards, behind fences, and posted against trespassing. In North Carolina, as with the other southern states, one must have the landowners' permission to fish on private property, so the bulk of these waters are off limits.

Another problem with cataloging the public trout waters of the Old North State is the nebulous character of the beast. From year to year some of the hatchery-supported creeks will disappear from the list to be replaced by others. Some even fall off the list only to reappear in later years. Add to this the occasional shifting of creeks from one wild-stream category to another and it becomes hard to corral the critter. Fortunately, the better public streams do not suffer from this malady. Their fishing regulations remain relatively stable, thus these streams will be the focus of the discussion.

The following chapters cover the various river systems of North Carolina that support trout, sticking to the rivers and creeks that provide enough clearly defined public water to make them true fly-fishing destinations. Two of the river systems listed by the NCWRC as having trout water, the Dan and New rivers, are not covered because there is no appreciable public access to the streams of either of their watersheds.

There are, however, a few streams described that are on North Carolina's state-managed game lands, but do not appear on the list of public streams. This is because streams that are not stocked and are located on game lands are not listed. It is also worth noting that virtually all of the U.S. Forest Service land in the Nantahala and Pisgah national forests are managed by the NCWRC as public game lands.

To be on the safe side, it is advisable to pick up a copy of the current "North Carolina Inland Fishing, Hunting and Trapping Regulations Digest" before picking a destination. That way you can verify that the targeted stream has not changed designations. This booklet can be obtained at most outlets that sell hunting and fishing licenses, or can be requested by mail from the North Carolina Wildlife Resources Commission, 512 North Salisbury Street, Raleigh, North Carolina 27604-1188.

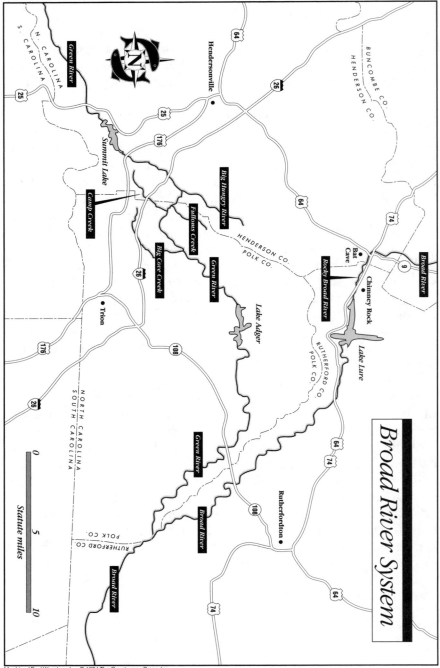

Broad River System

Green River

N. CAROLINA
S. CAROLINA

Hendersonville

Camp Creek

Summit Lake

Big Hungry River

Fullams Creek

Green River

Big Cove Creek

Trion

Lake Adger

HENDERSON CO.
POLK CO.

Rocky Broad River

Bat Cave

Chimney Rock

Broad River

Lake Lure

RUTHERFORD CO.
POLK CO.

BUNCOMBE CO.
HENDERSON CO.

NORTH CAROLINA
SOUTH CAROLINA

Green River

Broad River

RUTHERFORD CO.
POLK CO.

Broad River

Rutherfordton

0

5

10

Statute miles

15

Broad River System

The Broad River rises in the edge of Buncombe County to the south of the town of Black Mountain. It first runs south, then turns south-eastward to drain a large portion of Cleveland, Henderson, Polk, and Rutherford counties before flowing into South Carolina to become part of the Congaree-Cooper river system.

Along its route the river passes through Lake Lure in the edge of Rutherford County. The head of the lake is the downstream boundary for trout water on the river's main branch. This is also the part of the state where the foothills begin to give way to lower elevations of central North Carolina, making most of the water in this river system only marginal trout habitat. In fact, there are no wild-trout fishing opportunities available on the Broad River system. The bulk of the trout water in the Broad system is located in the drainage of the Green River in southern Henderson and Polk counties.

The Green River itself has stretches of trout water, as well as a number of stocked feeder streams. Of these, Laurel Branch, the Little Hungry River, plus Little Cove, Ostin, and Rixhaven creeks are all either too small for fly-fishing or on private land. This leaves the Big Hungry River in Henderson County, plus Big Cove, Camp, and Fulloms creeks as the remaining trout water feeding the Green.

The entire North Pacolet River, plus its tributaries Fork and Big Fall creeks, located near Trion, does not offer adequate public access to be covered.

ROCKY BROAD RIVER
USGS Bat Cave • DeLorme 54

The Rocky Broad River is probably not the best representative of North Carolina's trout streams, so it is a bit misleading to have it as the first in the state to be described. In spite of its name, the Rocky Broad is actually just a portion of the Broad River. From the junction with Hickory Creek near the intersections of NC 9, US 64, and US 74 in Henderson County downstream to Lake Lure in Rutherford County, the river is known as the Rocky Broad. Both above this section and below Lake Lure the river goes by the moniker of Broad River.

The name Rocky Broad is quite fitting for this section, since the river is medium to large in size and tumbles along a boulder-strewn bed. The Rocky Broad lies just on the eastern edge of trout habitat in this portion of the state and is only marginal trout water. All of the fish in the river are stocked, adult trout. A total of 13,000 trout are released into the stream between March and August each year. A contributing factor in this heavy stocking along the two miles of river is the location of the tourist towns of Bat Cave and Chimney Rock at streamside.

Thanks to the resort developments, motels, and abundant gift shops, the area can be quite crowded in the spring and summer. This can also lead to some very slow traffic along the highway through the towns. Another nuisance for the serious angler is the large number of tubers who take to the water during the warm months. Suffice it to say that fishing on the Rocky Broad is not the site's major attraction, but is a bonus provided to the tourists already headed there.

The entire Rocky Broad from one-half mile upstream of Bat Cave down to Goose Pond Hole below Chimney Rock is open to fishing under general hatchery-supported regulations. All of the access is from the right-of-way along the main highway, but there are a number of private, posted tracts along the course. Despite these off-limits areas, there is still enough water to make it a fly-casting destination. Just make sure to keep an eye open for the green-and-white signs marking the river as public trout water.

The Rocky Broad lies at the border of Henderson County on the west and Rutherford County to the east, between the towns of Hendersonville and Rutherfordton. The roadway that parallels the river carries the designations of NC 9, US 64, and US 74, as all three routes share the pavement.

GREEN RIVER

USGS Zirconia, Hendersonville, Cliffield Mountain
DeLorme 53, 54

The Green River is a major feeder stream of the Broad River. Running in an easterly direction, the Green drains the extreme southern edge of Henderson County along the South Carolina border and just north of the Saluda Mountains. Passing to the south of Hendersonville, the river then cuts a swath across central Polk County before emptying into the Broad River on the Polk-Rutherford county line. Near the midpoint of its passage through Polk County the river flows through Lake Adger. The headwaters of this impoundment mark the downstream limit of trout water on the Green.

There are actually two distinct trout fishing areas on the Green River. The first of these is located in Henderson County, consisting of three miles of water from the mouth of Rock Creek down to the mouth of Bob Creek. This stream is listed under the name Bob in the fishing regulations, but on some maps of the area it appears as Bobs. Although paralleled by Green River Road and stocked with 2000 adult trout, virtually all of this part of the river is on private land. Only a few road crossings offer any access.

After the river passes through Summit Lake to the southeast of Hendersonville, it reappears to enter the Green River Game Lands that are owned by Duke Power Company and managed by the NCWRC. On this second section, down to the end of trout water at Bright Creek near the head of Lake Adger, the bulk of the water is open to the public. The Green River receives heavier stockings of catchable-size trout in this lower section.

Below Summit Lake, down to Fishstop Falls, the river is of medium size and offers adequate room for fly-casting. It is, however, quite difficult to reach as it runs down a gorge with very limited access. Although both US 176 and I-26 cross the river in this section, neither offers an easy way to the water. The interstate highway, of course, provides no place to park, while US 176 is far up the gorge wall, has limited parking, and requires a steep descent to the river.

The first practical access to the Green River is via Green River Cove Road at the Fishstop Access point, a canoe landing used by boaters to enter the river. Through here the Green is a big flow, more suited to float-fishing from a canoe or Belly Boat. There are, however, wadeable shoals at several points along the river down to the end of trout water.

These ripple areas alternate with long, calm, and deep pools.

Especially in the area immediately below Fishstop, there are some posted tracts of private land, but as you progress downriver these become fewer in number. Green River Cove Road follows the river down to the Big Rock Access point, which is the last spot where boaters can exit the stream above Lake Adger.

A couple of small creeks entering the Green upstream of Fishstop, and located on game lands, offer some limited fishing as well. Camp Creek, which enters the river from the south, is very small and tight. Only the lower portion around the creek's mouth is on public land, and it can be reached only by foot travel upstream on the Green from Fishstop. Although SR 1919 crosses the creek just upstream of the game-land boundary, the land along the road at the creek is posted and offers no access to the public area.

Camp Creek receives a limited number of catchable-size stocked fish each year, but trying to catch them with a fly rod will be difficult.

Further up the Green and entering from the north side is Fulloms Creek. Like Camp, this small stream receives some stocking, but is difficult to fly-fish. Its headwaters are crossed by SR 1802, but private land bars downstream access to the fishable portion of the creek. Walking upstream from Fishstop is the only viable alternative to get to Fulloms Creek.

To reach the lower portion of the Green River, exit I-26 (Exit 26) onto Holbert Cove Road in the western edge of Polk County. Go north to Green River Cove Road and take a left. After descending steeply the road will pass Fishstop Access and follow the river for several miles.

BIG HUNGRY RIVER
USGS Bat Cave, Cliffield Mountain • DeLorme 54

A main tributary of the Green River, the Big Hungry is located in the eastern edge of Henderson County. It flows through a valley on the eastern side of Cliffield, Laurel, and Rich mountains, which sit on the Henderson-Polk county boundary. The accessible portions of the Big Hungry's flow are on two separate portions of Green River Game Lands.

In all, 2000 trout are stocked in the Big Hungry each year from March to June. These fish are all adults and are spread over both sections of the river.

The upper portion of the Big Hungry is located on lands owned by Champion International Corporation. The river is small here and fishing is quite tight. The stream is paralleled by Deep Gap Road for 1.5 miles on the game lands, and although the road is unpaved and quite rough, it can be traveled by passenger cars. At the end of the road a trail continues up the creek, but the stream is too small for fly-casting at this point. The road ends in a primitive camping area, but a permit is required from Champion International before pitching your tent.

The lower portion of the Big Hungry that is on game land can be reached by traveling east on SR 1802 (Adams Road) from its junction with Ridge Road just east of I-26. Where the road crosses the river the stream is of medium size, filled with large boulders and rather rugged in nature. It offers plenty of room for fly-casting. Looking upstream from the bridge, an old mill dam is visible, presenting a very scenic view.

Trails parallel the river both up- and downstream from the road, offering the only access to this lower portion of the flow.

BIG COVE CREEK
USGS Cliffield Mountain • DeLorme 54

The final feeder stream of the Green River that merits coverage is Big Cove Creek. This small- to medium-size stream flows northward through the western edge of Polk County, a little northwest of the town of Trion.

To the south of the point at which the creek crosses under I-26 the stream is on private land. From the interstate downstream to the Green River, Big Cove is on Green River Game Lands and open to public access. Along its lower course, it also tumbles over Bradley Falls.

Big Cove receives several light stockings of adult trout during the spring and summer, but like all the other water in this river system, it is marginal trout habitat. It also offers only minimal room for casting, especially above the falls.

The only road access to Big Cove is off Holbert Cove Road. The road parallels the creek for 0.5 mile, with access to the rest of the stream limited to foot travel either upstream toward I-26 or downstream to Bradley Falls and the creek's mouth on the Green River.

To reach Big Cove Creek exit I-26 onto Holbert Cove Road (Exit 26) and go north. This road will then bend to the east to join the creek in about 2.0 miles.

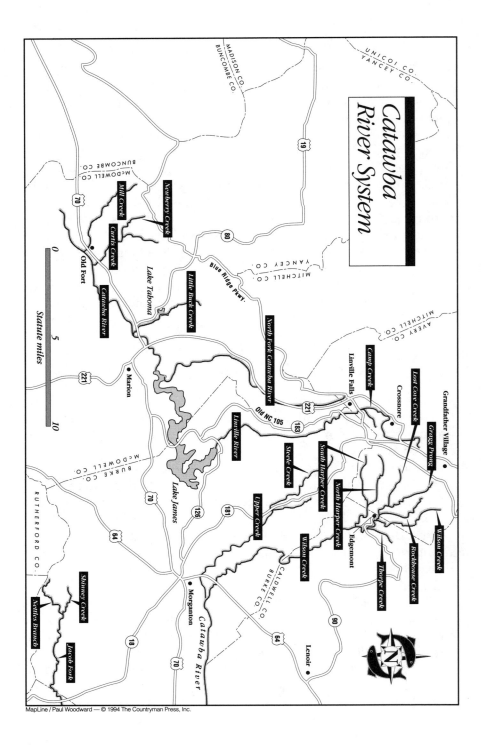

Catawba River System

Statute miles
0
5
10

MADISON CO.
BUNCOMBE CO.

UNICOI CO.
YANCEY CO.

19

80

Blue Ridge Pkwy.

McDOWELL CO.
BUNCOMBE CO.

70

Mill Creek
Newberry Creek
Curtis Creek
Old Fort
Catawba River
Lake Tahoma
Little Buck Creek

BUNCOMBE CO.
YANCEY CO.

MITCHELL CO.
YANCEY CO.

North Fork Catawba River

AVERY CO.
MITCHELL CO.

221

Marion

McDOWELL CO.
BURKE CO.

Linville Falls
Camp Creek
Crossnore
Lost Cove Creek

Grandfather Village
Gragg Prong

Old NC 105
183
221

Linville River

Steele Creek
South Harper Creek
North Harper Creek
Edgemont
Wilson Creek
Rockhouse Creek

Lake James

70
126
181

Upper Creek

Wilson Creek
Thorpe Creek

RUTHERFORD CO.

64

Shinney Creek
Nettles Branch
Jacob Fork

18

70

Morganton

Catawba River

CALDWELL CO.
BURKE CO.

90
64

Lenoir

N

MapLine / Paul Woodward — © 1994 The Countryman Press, Inc.

16

Catawba River System

The Catawba River system offers something for everyone. It has a wide variety of streams, from both the standpoint of size and management techniques. These range from big, legitimate rivers to small brooks; from heavily stocked put-and-take waters to catch-and-release, fly-fishing-only streams. Between these extremes are a number of other variations.

Rising on the McDowell–Buncombe county line in the shadow of Hicks Mountain, the Catawba flows eastward, picking up volume from its major tributaries, the North Fork, the Linville, the Johns, and finally the South Fork. Although the main stem of the Catawba and all four of these feeders have tributaries that contain trout waters, only the Linville and North Fork actually support trout themselves.

As the Catawba flows to the east it is joined by the North Fork and Linville rivers in Lake James in McDowell County, then by the Johns just upstream of Lake Rhodhiss in Burke County. Finally, the South Fork joins the main river in Lake Wylie on the South Carolina border just west of Charlotte in Gaston County. Along this journey, the Catawba picks up waters drained from trout streams in Avery, Burke, Caldwell, and McDowell counties.

There are a number of streams in this system that are listed as public trout water by the NCWRC that do not meet our criteria for size or access. Among the stocked streams, the Henry Fork in Burke County drains into the South Fork, Armstrong Creek feeds the North Fork in McDowell County, while Licklog Creek enters directly into the Catawba in McDowell County. All of these are stocked streams that are small or on private land. Other streams falling into these categories are Mill Timber Creek which feeds the Linville in Avery

County, along with Carroll Creek in Burke County, and Birchfield Creek and Webb Prong in Avery County. These last three are tributaries of the Johns River, with all being stocked except Birchfield, which is a wild-trout stream.

The coverage of the streams that do offer public access in the Catawba system begins at the headwaters of the main stem of the river and moves downstream along its course.

MILL CREEK
USGS Montreat, Old Fort • DeLorme 32

Mill Creek is a small stream flowing down a gentle valley from the northwest into the village of Old Fort. Although some portions of the creek are quite heavily foliated, some other open parts exist. The creek is stocked with trout upstream from the US 70 bridge in Old Fort.

Mill Creek Road parallels the creek upstream from Old Fort, but the first three miles are almost exclusively on private property. Beginning at the Old Fort Picnic Area near the junction of Mill Creek Road and Old US 70 there are a number of right-of-way access points, as well as a long stretch of creek in the Andrews Geyser Park. This county-owned park provides about a half mile of access in its picnic area and around the geyser monument.

Just above the second railway bridge, which marks the upstream limit of trout water, is the Boy Scouts of America Camp Tatham. From Old Fort Picnic Area to Camp Tatham there are about two miles of water on Mill Creek, as well as some private tracts of land.

Although Mill Creek does not constitute a major destination stream, its easy access and the rather heavy stocking of 3000 fish in the span of March through August make it of interest to anglers already in the area.

To find Mill Creek, travel east from Black Mountain to the village of Old Fort and turn left onto Mill Creek Road.

CURTIS CREEK
USGS Old Fort • DeLorme 32

Located in McDowell County and feeding into the Catawba River, Curtis Creek offers a variety of angling opportunities to trout fishermen. When fly casters approach this creek they are also treading on historic ground. A portion of the stream runs through an 8100-acre tract of land that was the first ever purchased by the U.S. Forest Service. On March 1, 1911 the Forest Service took title to the woodlands along Curtis Creek, with the area eventually being incorporated into the 187,000 acres of land in the Grandfather Ranger District of the Pisgah National Forest.

Rising near Big Laurel Gap close to the Blue Ridge Parkway on the McDowell-Yancey county border, Curtis Creek flows as a small stream down to its mouth on the Catawba just east of Old Fort. The creek's valley skirts to the west of Sams Knob, Buckeye Knob, Chestnutwood Mountain and, finally, Piney Mountain on its descent to the river.

Despite its size, Curtis offers adequate room for fly-casting along much of its length. It is stocked with 4000 trout between March and August. These fish are released into the stream from the US 70 bridge upstream to the fish barrier just below Curtis Creek Campground. Above the campground the stream is open under wild trout regulations.

The first half mile upstream of US 70 is on private land, then a mile and a half of public access is available at roadside. This is on the lower section of National Forest land managed by the NCWRC as part of the Pisgah Game Lands. Through here the creek is gently graded, with the easy wading conditions usually found on lowland creeks. Above this public land is another mile of private holdings up to just above the mouth of Newberry Creek, where public land begins again and borders the stream to its headwater.

In this upper portion of public access, Curtis Creek has gained some elevation and is more of a rocky tumbling stream. There is roughly a mile and a half of water from Newberry Creek up to the Curtis Creek Campground, which is operated by the Forest Service. Above the campground in the wild-fish area the creek is small and tight, but can be fished with fly gear for a mile before the stream breaks up into a number of small feeder branches. Most of the trout in the wild area are small rainbows.

Especially on the stocked portion of the creek, don't expect to be alone. This is a popular camping and fishing destination in the Grandfather Ranger District. Access to the creek is easy via SR 1227, which changes designation to FS 482 above Newberry Creek. The road is paved through the lower section of public land and gravel above there. This roadway stays at streamside all the way up to the end of practical fishing water on Curtis Creek.

NEWBERRY CREEK
USGS Old Fort • DeLorme 32

This small tributary of Curtis Creek offers an additional option for anglers. Although it is stocked with trout it does not get the usual mix of fish. Instead, 1000 brook trout are stocked from March to June.

In its lower section near the junction with Curtis Creek, Newberry is on public land and open under hatchery-supported regulations. This part of the stream is only a few hundred yards long, however, with the next quarter mile of the creek on private land. Finally, the creek is again on game lands and open to public use the rest of its length. Up until 1993 the fishing on this upper portion of the creek adhered to wild-trout regulations, but these have now been changed to mandate artificial lures, with catch-and-release rules in effect.

Although small, Newberry is a tumbling stream that offers some limited fly-casting. The creek is followed by FS 482A from its mouth up through the private land to the edge of the wild-trout water. At that point the road is gated and only foot travel is possible upstream.

LITTLE BUCK CREEK
USGS Little Switzerland • DeLorme 32

Little Buck Creek is another of the small tributaries of the Catawba system. Like Newberry Creek, it receives a stocking of 1000 brook trout, with the fish released in March through August.

Rising on the slopes of Woods Mountain in McDowell County, Little Buck empties into Lake Tahoma on Buck Creek, before the waters head downstream to the Catawba. From the lake up to the edge of the Pisgah Game Lands, Little Buck Creek is on private property and mostly posted. Once on the game lands there is about a mile of water along FS 470 that provides some very tight fishing options. The creek is open under hatchery-supported regulations.

The best approach to Little Buck Creek is via US 70 west from Marion, then turn north onto NC 80. This paved road passes to the west of Lake Tahoma. Just north of the lake turn right onto SR 1436. At the head of the lake this road intersects FS 470 (gravel) at Little Buck Creek. Follow FS 470 upstream to the game lands. At one mile past the boundary the road is gated, but by then the stream is too small for casting anyway.

NORTH FORK CATAWBA RIVER
USGS Linville Falls • DeLorme 32

The portion of the North Fork that is trout habitat consists of 11 miles of stream from the headwaters down to North Cove School near the SR 1569 crossing. Of this distance, however, only about two miles of the river is on public land. The rest is on private land, often crossing the backyards of residences.

Rising near the town of Linville Falls and to the southeast of the Blue Ridge Parkway on the edge of McDowell County, throughout its length the North Fork is only a medium to small stream. In all, 4000 trout are stocked in the flow. These fish are planted from March to August. In the area of public access upstream of Linville Caverns, the river is quite small, offering only very tight casting room.

The entire length of the trout water on the North Fork is paralleled by US 221. This is another of the streams that offer some fishing, but not as a primary destination.

LINVILLE RIVER
USGS Linville Falls, Chestnut Mountain, Glen Alpine
DeLorme 33

The Linville River is one of the premier trout streams of the Tarheel State, yet it defies easy description. Rising in Linville Gap to the north of Grandfather Village, the river runs southward into Burke County to mix its waters with those of the Catawba in Lake James. Due to the unique double dams on this lake, the Linville also has a short tailwater section downstream of the lake.

Along this course the Linville has four distinct sections for trout fishing offering a variety of fish and fishing conditions. In the first and most northerly of these waters, the river runs along NC 105 down to the town of Linville, where it borders NC 181 for a short way. From that point the river runs along US 221 through the town of Crossnore and then on to Blue Ridge Parkway lands just north of the village of Linville Falls.

Throughout this upper portion of the river it is small to medium in size, relatively level, and flows gently. Due to the elevation of the surrounding land, it is, however, legitimate trout water. Development, silting, and litter make this a rather unsightly section of the stream, but it apparently has not affected the fishing a great deal. The NCWRC identifies the upper Linville as one of the most fertile streams in the state and heavily populated with trout.

Although there is usually plenty of room for fly-casting on the upper Linville, access can be a problem. There are many private tracts of land mixed with the right-of-way access points. Care is advised to make sure one does not intrude on posted areas along the upper river.

Although both rainbow and brown trout reproduce in the Linville upstream of the Blue Ridge Parkway, the NCWRC also stocks trout to meet the heavy fishing pressure resulting from the easy access along the river. From March to August 7000 mature fish are released, and the entire stretch of river is open for fishing under hatchery-supported rules.

Once on the lands owned by the National Park Service along the Blue Ridge Parkway, the river is much the same as upstream. It is still a gentle flow, it continues to be stocked by the NCWRC under a special arrangement with the park service, and it can be fished under the same set of regulations.

Although rainbows and brook trout that have moved downstream from other stockings will turn up in this part of the river, only adult-size brown trout are stocked through here. The river has also reached proportions that qualify it as big water in this area. These same conditions also prevail on the part of the stream on Pisgah Game Lands downstream of the parkway land and above the Linville Gorge Wilderness Area.

Access through here is more difficult. The river can be approached off crossings on the Blue Ridge Parkway, the parkway spur, and NC 183.

Once the river reaches the Linville Gorge Wilderness Area, its nature changes drastically, as does the terrain surrounding the stream. The Linville Gorge is a mystical place, named for William Linville, who was an early explorer of the region. Linville and his son were killed by Cherokees near the chasm in 1766, leaving the family name forever associated with the river and canyon. Having changed little since William Linville viewed it, the gorge remains one of North Carolina's most remote and unchanged natural areas.

Twelve miles long, dropping 2000 feet in elevation, and surrounded by 11,000 acres of federally mandated roadless areas, the stone cliff walls of the gorge contain a wild and powerful section of the river.

Huge boulders, crashing cataracts, and deep plunge pools character-
ize the Linville—along with brown trout measured in pounds rather
than inches. Although some rainbows are present, this is essentially
the domain of the European immigrant trout. The browns have established themselves in a reproducing population that sits atop the
food chain in the gorge.

Access to the gorge is by foot travel only, with the best approaches
being along Forest Service trails from the western rim of the canyon.
Needless to say these descend sharply, then intersect with the Linville
Gorge Trail (FT 231) that follows the river through the entire canyon. Count on the going being tough in the gorge, even on the marked
trails. These big waters provide plenty of fly-casting room, but for
safety's sake it is an area best challenged in the company of at least
one companion.

Although the river through the gorge is open to fishing under
regular wild-trout regulations, it does receive some stocked fish.
The NCWRC plants 5000 fingerling brown trout in the gorge.
These fish are especially produced for this purpose from half-wild
brood stocks.

To reach the Linville Gorge Wilderness Area, the Kistler Memorial
Highway (Old NC 105) along the western rim is the most practical
entry corridor. Running south off NC 183 near the town of Linville
Falls, this gravel road follows the gorge and the edge of the wilderness area for 14 miles. The road is, however, quite rough at times and
prone to washouts in wet weather.

The first parking area along the road traveling south is at Upper
Falls Overlook. It is worth the delay in fishing to walk the 0.4-mile
trail to Linville Falls, which marks the head of the gorge. This waterfall cuts an "S"-shaped course through solid rock. Another 0.3 mile
of walking on a spur trail to the Chimney Top Overlook will provide
a view of that natural rock chimney, plus the bottom of the falls
where the water spews from the end of the "S," dropping into a large
plunge pool.

Over the next 9.0 miles of road six more parking areas with approach trails will be encountered. Due to the terrain, the only practical way to fish the Linville in the gorge is to backpack down into the
canyon for a day or two. If you choose this approach, there is also
the possibility of encountering one of North Carolina's most celebrated
and haunting phenomenons. For years visitors have reported encountering the Brown Mountain Lights at the Linville Gorge. These lumi-

nescent orbs are said to hover above the chasm and as yet have never been adequately explained.

The final section of the Linville River that is of interest to fly casters seeking trout is the tailwater below Lake James. This reservoir is formed by dams on both the Catawba and Linville rivers in south Burke County. When the waters rose in the impoundment, they spilled through a gap between the river valleys forming a single lake. Today, no water is released from the Catawba River Dam, leaving the river-bed completely dry except for the trickle provided by feeder streams below the lake. All the releases from Lake James go through the powerhouse of Linville Dam, with about one mile of the tailwater being public trout water.

From the first bridge on SR 1223 below the dam, down to the river's junction with Muddy Creek (where the combined flow once again becomes the Catawba), the Linville is big water. The large pool just below the first SR 1223 bridge does have a public fishing pier on the south shore and some shoals are present just downstream. In spite of these, the river is big water, better suited to float-fishing in a canoe or float tube. The best take-out point for a float is at the second bridge across the river on SR 1223. This part of the Linville is open under hatchery-supported regulations and receives a substantial stocking of 10,000 fish spread from March to August.

Access to the tailwater of the Linville is available by traveling east from Marion on US 70 to South Powerhouse Road (SR 1223). Turn north and stay on this paved road until it crosses the river just below the dam.

CAMP CREEK
USGS Linville Falls • DeLorme 33

This small, gently flowing stream in the southeastern edge of Avery County is the only tributary of the Linville River that provides any appreciable public fishing. Although quite heavily foliated along its banks, it is possible to find room for tight fly-casting.

The stream receives no stockings of trout, but contains a population of wild browns. Regular North Carolina wild-stream regulations apply, even though the stream is on Blue Ridge Parkway lands. Access to Camp Creek is from the Blue Ridge Parkway between mile posts 315 and 317, north of the town of Linville Falls.

WILSON CREEK

USGS Chestnut Mountain, Collettsville,
Grandfather Mountain • DeLorme 33

Wilson Creek is the principal tributary of the Johns River and contains the bulk of the trout waters found in the river's drainage. From its headwater on the south slope of Grandfather Mountain in eastern Avery County, Wilson Creek grows from a tiny brooklet to truly big water before reaching the lower end of its trout water in Caldwell County.

Along this course Wilson Creek flows through two separate areas that have public access. These sections of water offer very different opportunities to fly casters. The portion located farthest downstream consists of roughly two and a quarter miles of big water flowing through the Wilson Creek Gorge on Forest Service land, plus another mile and a half upstream that crosses a mixture of private and public lands. The downstream limit of this stretch is the dam in the Brown Mountain Beach Campground, with the upstream boundary at the mouth of Phillips Branch, just short of the second bridge over the creek above the campground. All of this lower part is located in Caldwell County.

Through here Wilson Creek is characterized by huge deep pools, broken by short shoals or mild ripples. The creek is open to fishing under hatchery-supported regulations and the stream is amply supplied with stockers. The annual plantings of fish run to 11,000 trout of all species. Because of the slow currents found in the deep pools, the water is noted for holding some large brown trout.

Access to the creek in the gorge is moderately difficult. Ralph Winchester Road (gravel) parallels the creek through the gorge, always in sight of the water, up to the junction with NC 90. On the other hand, the road is far up on the canyon side, high above the stream. There are adequate parking areas through the gorge, but anglers must climb down steep trails to the water.

Above Wilson Creek Gorge the road runs at creekside, but many tracts of private land are mixed with public access. There is also a shortage of places to park along the road, even in the public sections.

To reach lower Wilson Creek, take NC 181 to the northwest from Morganton. Turn right onto Brown Mountain Beach Road. At Ralph Winchester Road (SR 1328) turn left and proceed to Wilson Creek Gorge.

Upstream of Phillips Branch, Wilson Creek is entirely on private land all the way to the northern edge of Caldwell County and for a short way into Avery County. Then it is once again on Forest Service property in the Pisgah Game Lands, all the way to its headwater near the Blue Ridge Parkway.

This upper part of Wilson Creek is quite different from the lower portions in the gorge. The terrain surrounding the stream is remote, rugged, and quite scenic. In this area Wilson is a small- to medium-size flow, with more of a cascading mountain-brook character. This is also wild-trout country, with no stockings taking place. Both rainbow and brown trout are found in this part of the stream. Fishing is allowed with single-hook, artificial lures only, with catch-and-release mandated. Except for the area around the FS 192 crossing in the stream's headwaters, Wilson Creek offers enough room for fly-casting along its upper course.

There are a couple of ways to reach the fishable portions of Wilson Creek's wild-trout water, but all involve hikes of 0.5 to up to 3.0 miles. FT 258 parallels the creek all the way through the game lands from the FS 192 crossing downstream.

Unfortunately, the downstream end of the trail is not marked on FS 45 where it comes out and there is no noticeable trailhead. Using this trail upstream requires several miles of walking to get down to where Wilson Creek affords room for casting.

Another entry point is FT 257, which approaches the creek from the east, originating at a trailhead on FS 45. Again, the trailhead, which is six miles southwest of the junction of FS 45 and US 221, is not well marked. Presently only a post on the road shoulder indicates the beginning of the trail and the only parking is also on the shoulder of the road.

This trail drops sharply for a quarter mile down to Cary Flat Branch, a wild-trout stream feeding Wilson Creek, but too small for fly-casting, then climbs and follows the ridge on the other side of the branch. At 0.75 mile from the trailhead Cary Flat Branch is again crossed, just 25 yards upstream of its mouth on Buck Timber Creek. The last couple of hundred yards to this crossing are very steeply downhill. After this crossing of the branch, an old logging road is encountered, which the path follows down to Buck Timber Creek.

At this point the old road and FT 257 cross both creeks (Buck Timber is another wild-trout stream, but also very small), then follow Buck Timber for 0.25 mile down to Wilson Creek and the intersection with FT 258. At this junction Wilson Creek is a small, tumbling, but fishable stream.

The final access point for upper Wilson Creek is off FS 45 at 9.7 miles south of the road junction with US 221. The trailhead is difficult to locate, but FT 264 offers a short 0.5-mile hike down to the creek.

Finding upper Wilson Creek can be tricky since some maps of the area show FS 45 as SR 1514. Regardless of its designation, the gravel road runs in an arc to the northwest of the creek, roughly paralleling the flow of the stream. The road intersects with another gravel road (designated NC 90, SR 1511, or FS 981, depending on the map being used) at the crossroads of Edgemont.

LOST COVE CREEK
USGS Grandfather Mountain • DeLorme 33

Lost Cove Creek is a major tributary of Wilson Creek that rises beneath Sassafras Knob and Ned Mountain in Avery County. The stream meanders down a valley to the southwest of Wilson Creek with the two watersheds separated by Yancey Ridge.

There are three situations that set Lost Cove Creek apart from the other surrounding waters in this area. First, even in its upper reaches it has a relatively gentle flow, especially considering its elevation. Secondly, the stream is managed under catch-and-release, single-hook, fly-fishing-only regulations. Finally, it is legendary for the big brown trout that inhabit its pools.

Lost Cove is only a small to medium flow throughout its drainage, but many of the pools are large and open enough for easy casting. These waters are also crystal clear, making the already wary brown trout even tougher opponents. Virtually all of the fish encountered are browns.

The only place where there is any road access to Lost Cove is at its mouth on Wilson Creek, and this land is in private hands. Above this point the creek is remote, flowing through a steep, narrow valley.

Although several trails enter the Lost Cove Creek valley, most entail quite long and rugged hikes. The only one appropriate for use on a day trip to the creek is FT 263. Called the Hunt Fish Falls Trail, this path begins on FS 464, east of the intersection of that road and NC 90. The trail is only 0.5 mile long, but is extremely steep. While easy to descend, the ascent back out is a strenuous one. There is one stretch of the path, however, near its midpoint that allows for catching one's breath as the trail meanders through a small cove.

Where the trail meets Lost Cove Creek, Hunt Fish Falls drops over a series of 10-foot cascades and rock slides, broken by several large pools. A small brook joins the creek, plunging down a 100-foot rock wall beside the path, adding to the spectacular scenery. Some truly huge boulders jut up on both sides of the creek through here, as well.

To reach Lost Cove Creek, follow the directions for lower Wilson Creek, but continue up Ralph Winchester Road until it dead-ends into NC 90. Turn left on this gravel road and proceed to the intersection with FS 464. Another left turn and a 3.0-mile drive leads to the Hunt Fish Falls Trail head.

GRAGG PRONG
USGS Grandfather Mountain • DeLorme 33

This small creek is a feeder stream of Lost Cove Creek and is located to the east of the larger flow. Although bushy, there are some portions open enough for casting with a fly rod. There are patches of private land in both the lower and headwater portions of the creek, leaving only about a mile of public access on game lands in its midsection.

Gragg Prong is open under hatchery-supported fishing rules. The stream receives only 600 stocked trout, which are planted in March through May.

Access to Gragg Prong is via FS 981, which crosses the creek near the middle of the public access. There are a number of primitive campsites located at this crossing. For a short distance upstream FS 981 follows the stream, while FS 192 runs up the other side. Downstream of the crossing, access is on footpaths. The FS 981 bridge is located 4.0 miles northwest of the gravel road's intersection with NC 90.

ROCKHOUSE CREEK
USGS Grandfather Mountain • DeLorme 33

Flowing just to the east of Lost Cove Creek, Rockhouse Creek feeds into that larger stream near the crossroads of Edgemont. The name of this stream, which is in Avery County, can cause some confusion, since a creek of the same name is located in northeast Caldwell County. Additionally, both of the flows are wild-trout streams.

The Rockhouse Creek in the Lost Cove watershed is a small stream that tumbles down a rocky course beside FS 981. This part of the creek is very tightly foliated, but offers some casting possibilities as it goes through a series of drops and potholes. At the upper limit of this stretch

FS 981 crosses the creek and no longer parallels it upstream. The creek above the bridge is too small for comfortable casting. Land near the mouth of the creek is on private property and is posted, leaving about one-half mile of water that can be fly-fished by the public.

Virtually all of the fish encountered on Rockhouse are small rainbows in the 6- to 8-inch range. An occasional brown trout also turns up in the lower end of the creek.

To reach Rockhouse Creek, take NC 90 to the settlement of Edgemont and turn west on FS 981. After several hundred yards of posted land the creek will appear on the left of the road.

THORPE CREEK
USGS *Chestnut Mountain* • *DeLorme 33*

Thorpe Creek merits mention only because of its location near Wilson Creek and the fact that it runs through the middle of the Forest Service's Mortimer Campground. The campground is located on NC 90 just east of Edgemont on the northern edge of Caldwell County.

Although Thorpe is a very small stream, it is stocked for one mile through the campground, up to the falls above the road. Because of the cleared banks in the campground, it is possible to cast in spite of the size of the creek. It also has a number of in-stream structures that have been installed to provide more holding water for fish.

Thorpe only receives 100 stockers, which are released in March. Obviously, due to the number of people using the campground, it can be difficult to fish the creek.

NORTH HARPER CREEK
USGS *Chestnut Mountain* • *DeLorme 33*

North Harper Creek is a feeder stream that runs into Wilson Creek just north of Phillips Branch. Rising on the east side of Headquarters Mountain, North Harper flows across Avery County into Caldwell County before joining the larger stream.

For virtually all of its journey downstream, North Harper is a wilderness creek, and never attains more than small size. It is a wild-trout stream that very much resembles a smaller version of Lost Cove Creek. Local anglers report that in earlier years this creek also produced some quite large brown trout, until state biologists treated the stream with rotenone to get rid of the overabundance of chubs, which the locals contended the browns fed on. This treatment also got rid of the trout. Now that the stream has been restocked, it produces mostly small rainbows and an occasional brown trout.

Open under wild-trout regulations, North Harper offers difficult casting conditions. South Harper Creek, which feeds into the north branch, is also a wild-trout stream, but is too small to be of interest to fly casters.

North Harper Creek can be reached by foot travel from its headwaters via FT 266 which parallels the flow downstream. The trailhead for this path is just south of the FS 58 bridge over the creek.

The creek can also be reached over FT 260 from Ralph Winchester Road. This trail runs up North Harper Creek to its junction with South Harper, where the trail intersects FT 266. From this same junction, FT 267 runs upstream on South Harper Creek, eventually connecting with the end of FS 58.

FS 58 can be reached at its intersection with FS 464 to the west of that latter road's junction with NC 90. At a point 3.5 miles west of the FS 464 and NC 90 intersection, a trail runs south off FS 464 down to North Harper. On maps this is marked as FT 239, but the sign at the trailhead indicates FT 266A. This path joins the creek at its midsection.

One other trail approaches North Harper from FS 464. The Persimmon Ridge Trail (FT 270) is 0.75 mile long, with the final 200-yard approach to the creek being steeply downhill. This trail is 2.25 miles west of FS 90.

UPPER CREEK

USGS Chestnut Mountain • DeLorme 33

This medium to small stream is another that can cause some confusion because of its name. There is also an Upper Creek located in Yancey County that is part of the Nolichucky River system. Adding to the problem is that the Upper Creek in Burke County in the Catawba system does not appear in the trout fishing regulations' list of public water.

Upper Creek is open enough for fly-casting along its course through the Pisgah Game Lands of the Daniel Boone Wildlife Management Area. Once the creek exits the public lands, it runs south to empty into the Warrior Fork, which in turn enters the Catawba River.

The trout in Upper Creek are the usual mix found in wild streams.

Rainbows are predominant, with most fish running fairly small and an occasional brown trout showing up. Wild-trout regulations are enforced on Upper Creek.

To find Upper Creek, take NC 181 north from Morganton to FS 982 and turn right. At the FS 982 bridge over Upper Creek, FS 197 runs off to the left to parallel the creek for 1.5 miles to a gate. The Forest Road then continues upstream as a foot trail. From the bridge, FS 982 follows the stream down its course for 0.25 mile before leaving the creek. At that point, FS 986 crosses the creek and continues downstream. This latter road is gated, offering only foot travel.

STEELE CREEK
USGS Chestnut Mountain • DeLorme 33

This stream feeds into Upper Creek, but their confluence is near the intersection of NC 181 and Brown Mountain Beach Road, off the Pisgah Game Lands and the Daniel Boone WMA. Like its sister stream, Steele is not listed among North Carolina's public trout waters.

Of small size on public lands, the signs along the stream indicate the flow is open to fishing under wild-trout regulations. It is difficult fishing, however, since the rocky, tumbling stream offers little casting room.

A portion of FS 2128 runs along Steele Creek for 2.0 miles, then the road turns into FT 237 and provides foot access upstream. FS 2128 runs west off NC 181 just south of the intersection of that highway with FS 982.

JACOB FORK
USGS Casar • DeLorme 55

Jacob Fork is a medium to small flow located in South Mountain State Park in southern Burke County. After leaving the park it eventually runs into the South Fork of the Catawba River. The first two miles of water upstream to the mouth of Shinney Creek in the state park are composed of stocked waters open under delayed-harvest regulations.

On this section of the stream, 3600 trout are stocked in March through August. Unlike the usual mix of trout stocked in North Carolina, the planting on Jacob Fork is equally split between brook, brown, and rainbow trout.

Fishing is limited from March 1 to the first weekend in June to the use of single-hook, artificial lures, and no fish may be harvested. Beginning in June the stream reverts to regular hatchery-supported regulations of no bait or size limits and a creel limit of seven fish per day.

Fishing is excellent in the delayed-harvest section of Jacob Fork up through June, but the fish are quickly thinned out when the regulations change. The stream gets light pressure in the spring, but heavy usage when the harvest begins. Due to a lack of parking on the lower end of the creek, the best access is at the park's picnic area.

Above the mouth of Shinney Creek, Jacob Fork is open under wild-trout fishing rules. Some stockers will move up into this part of the stream, but wild rainbows are most prevalent. By the time the High Shoals area is reached on Jacob Fork, only wild fish are present. Although a lot of hikers use the trail up to High Shoals, fishing pressure is quite light.

Nettles Branch is a small feeder stream that enters Jacob Fork from the west above High Shoals. It is open under wild-trout regulations as well, but is quite small, offering little casting room.

Access to Jacob Fork is via South Mountain Park Road which runs west off Old NC 18. There is a sign for the park at this intersection. The entrance road dead-ends at the picnic area, but a trail follows the creek for 0.5 mile up to Shinney Creek, then continues on up to High Shoals. Primitive campsites are available upstream along Jacob Fork, on a reservation-only basis. Check at the park information center for details on obtaining a campsite.

SHINNEY CREEK
USGS Casar • DeLorme 55

Largest of the headwater tributaries of Jacob Fork, Shinney Creek offers very meager fly-casting opportunities. Its lower reaches will hold a number of stockers that have moved up from the delayed-harvest section, although Shinney receives no plantings itself.

Only about 100 yards of this small flow are open enough to fly-fish. At the upper end of this section is a large pool that will often hold a number of stockers year-round, plus some wild fish.

Shinney is open under regular, state wild-trout regulations. A trail follows Shinney Creek upstream from Jacob Fork, and some reserved primitive campsites are on the creek.

17

Cheoah River System

Mention the Cheoah River and only those who are very well versed in North Carolina geography are likely to know anything about the waterway. It is even less probable that the average trout angler in the Old North State will be familiar with this river. The flow begins at the foot of the dam at Santeetlah Lake in Graham County. From there it flows northwesterly to empty into the Little Tennessee River at Cheoah Reservoir.

Actually, to say that the river "flows" is a bit misleading. Water from Santeetlah Lake is run cross-country through a pipeline to the Santeetlah Power House, located on the shore of Cheoah Reservoir. Thus, no water is released directly into the Cheoah River downstream of Santeetlah Lake. All of the water in the river comes from feeder streams that empty into the Cheoah below the dam.

Along its 12- to 15-mile course down to the Little Tennessee, the Cheoah's rocky, steeply descending bed holds pools that seem reluctant to give up any water to flow downstream. What should be a tumbling, racing torrent is only a string of calm, crystalline pools. Although some trout may drop down into the river from time to time, the NCWRC does not consider the Cheoah to be trout water.

There are, however, a number of streams feeding into Santeetlah Lake that contain trout, as well as one that feeds directly into the Cheoah downstream. All of these are located entirely within Graham County. While most of the creeks are quite small or are on private property, the watershed does contain a few public streams. A couple of them, Big Snowbird and Santeetlah creeks, rate with the very best in southern Appalachia. Other public waters in the Cheoah drainage

145

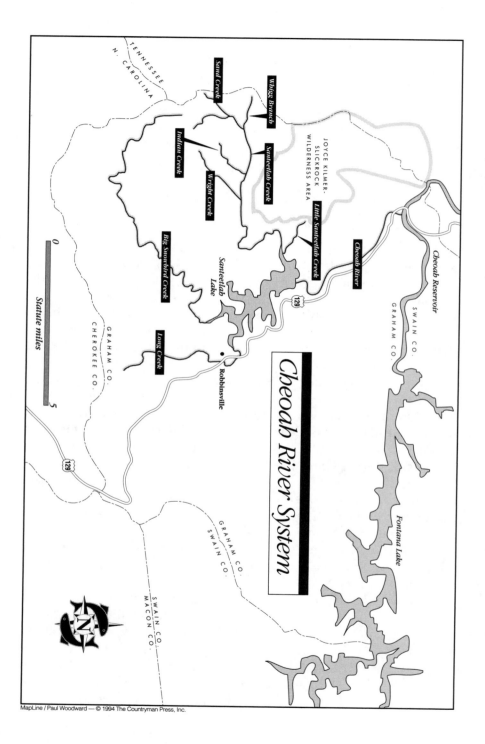

Cheoah River System

Sand Creek
Whigg Branch
Indian Creek
Santeetlah Creek
Wright Creek
Little Santeetlah Creek
Cheoah River
Big Snowbird Creek
Long Creek
Santeetlah Lake
Robbinsville

JOYCE KILMER-
SLICKROCK
WILDERNESS AREA

Cheoah Reservoir
Fontana Lake

N. CAROLINA
TENNESSEE
N. CAROLINA
GRAHAM CO.
SWAIN CO.
GRAHAM CO.
CHEROKEE CO.
GRAHAM CO.
SWAIN CO.
GRAHAM CO.
SWAIN CO.
SWAIN CO.
MACON CO.

129
129

0
5
Statute miles

MapLine / Paul Woodward — © 1994 The Countryman Press, Inc.

are found on Long Creek and Little Santeetlah Creek.

The streams feeding into Santeetlah Lake that the NCWRC considers public, but which offer little actual access or no fly-fishing room, are Talula, South Fork Squalla, Squalla, Little Buffalo (also known as Huffman), West Buffalo, Mountain, and Franks creeks. Yellow Creek feeds the Cheoah from the east, joining the river below Santeetlah Dam. All of these creeks are stocked trout streams.

LONG CREEK
USGS Robbinsville • DeLorme 50

When you check the North Carolina fishing regulations for the list of public trout streams, Long Creek may or may not be found. It is one of those mystery creeks that tends to drop from the list, but reappear later. Even in the years that it vanishes, however, the NCWRC stocking records indicate that it is receiving planted trout.

Long Creek rises on the north slopes of the Snowbird Mountains in the Nantahala Game Lands almost directly south of the town of Robbinsville. Although four miles of the creek, stretching almost into the town, are stocked each year, the only part of interest to the fly caster is the first mile of water above the game-land boundary. In this section, up to the first bridge on the national forest land, the stream is small, bushy, and tight. While not easily fished, it does provide some casting possibilities.

Long Creek receives one stocking of trout each year, all of which are fingerlings. The planting is composed of 500 rainbow and 500 brown trout. The browns are produced from half-wild stocks at the hatchery.

Access to Long Creek is via Long Creek Road from its intersection with Upper Atocah Road at the south edge of Robbinsville. The intersection is just west of US 129 which runs directly through the town.

BIG SNOWBIRD CREEK
USGS Santeetlah Creek • DeLorme 50

Although Big Snowbird's reputation as a trout stream is based on being one of the very best wild, native brook trout streams in the southeastern U.S., it offers a variety of other appealing assets. Flowing eastward between Sassafras Ridge on the south and Deerlick Ridge to the north, Big Snowbird runs the gamut from being a small brook trout stream, to a medium-size wild rainbow and brown trout fishery, and finally a medium to large stocked trout stream. Regardless of which section you tackle, the stream is impressive.

From the point where Big Snowbird empties into the upper end of Santeetlah Lake upstream to where it first exits the national forest property managed as Nantahala Game Lands, the creek is big water managed as a hatchery-supported fishery. Through here it crosses a mixture of public and private lands. Access to much of this water is difficult since the paralleling road often meanders away from the stream. At some places the creek is on public lands, but private holdings separate it from the road.

Once the edge of the national forest lands is reached, there are another five and a half miles of water upstream that are stocked. Big Snowbird is only a medium-size flow in this section. Throughout its length, 14,000 trout are stocked from March through August. The heaviest stockings take place in March and April. These lower portions of the creek are also noted for producing some large brown trout in the 15- to 22-inch range. The larger pools, on the game land portion of the creek that is stocked, are the best bets for these brutes.

At the upper end of the stocked water, the road along the stream ends at a point known as Junction. The name comes from this being the location of an old railway junction. From this site upstream the creek is open under wild-trout regulations and features a mixture of browns and rainbows. There are three major waterfalls on the main branch of Big Snowbird, with the first being Big Falls, then Middle Falls, and lastly Upper Falls. These act as barriers to separate the native brook trout waters from the rest of the creek. It requires a minimum hike of five miles to reach the best brookie water, where an encounter with a 10- to 13-inch native fish is possible.

Access to Big Snowbird Creek is over Big Snowbird Road (also marked SR 1120 or FS 75), which parallels the stream from the intersection with Little Snowbird Road up to Junction. These roads are directly west of Robbinsville. Where the road ends at Junction, Big Snowbird Trail begins and follows the stream virtually to its headwaters. There is a parking area at Junction, as well as plenty of pull-offs along the road through the game lands.

The wild-trout section of Santeetlah Creek is noted for its brightly colored brown trout and offers plenty of room for fly-casting.

SANTEETLAH CREEK

USGS Santeetlah Creek • DeLorme 50

For some fly casters, Santeetlah Creek is the epitome of southern Applachian brown trout water. The wild browns found in the creek are noted for their brilliant colors and fighting spirit. Yet, the creek provides several other fishing opportunities besides those for brown trout.

Rising in the western edge of Graham County between Haw Knob on the west and Hooper Bald to the east, Santeetlah Creek first flows directly to the north, then turns east to flow into Santeetlah Lake. Throughout this course, the stream is of small to medium width. Virtually the entire creek is located on Nantahala Game Lands within the national forest of the same name.

In spite of the creek's reputation as a brown trout haven, there is no shortage of wild rainbows in the upper portion of Santeetlah. In fact, on one trip I made to the creek with a couple of angling companions in the spring, a day and a half of drifting dry flies through the runs of the upper creek produced a total of 72 rainbows, but only 20 browns.

Another facet of Santeetlah fishing is that it is not known for very good summer angling. Once the weather heats up, the fishing, especially with dry flies, drops off markedly. This upstream part of Santeetlah Creek is open to fishing under wild-trout regulations.

There are a number of small feeders emptying into the wild-trout portion of Santeetlah that offer some casting room near their mouths. From the headwaters of the main creek and moving downstream, these are Sand Creek and Whigg Branch entering from the north side, while Indian and Wright creeks join from the south. Small wild rainbows are the most likely fish encountered on these tributaries, which are also open under wild-trout rules.

Once below the confluence of Wright Creek, Santeetlah is regulated as a hatchery-supported stream down to the lake. A total of 7300 trout are released into this lower portion of the creek.

Access to Santeetlah Creek is available on FS 81, which parallels the creek from the bridge over the stream up to Whigg Branch. The first 4.0 miles above the bridge are on the hatchery-supported portion of the stream. At the junction with Whigg Branch, FS 81C forks to the south to continue following Santeetlah, which is now a small stream.

Camping is allowed along the creek, with a number of primitive sites available. Below the FS 81 bridge Santeetlah meanders away from the road, with this lower mile or two open to foot access only. Finally, just before entering Santeetlah Lake, the creek runs along Kilmer Road and through the Forest Service campgrounds at Rattlers Ford and Horse Cove.

LITTLE SANTEETLAH CREEK
USGS Santeetlah Creek • DeLorme 50

Little Santeetlah is a small feeder stream of Santeetlah Creek. It rises in the Joyce Kilmer/Slickrock Wilderness Area, flowing down a valley that parallels its larger namesake creek lying to the south.

Open as a wild-trout stream with corresponding regulations in effect, Little Santeetlah offers very tight casting conditions. The predominant fish in the stream are small rainbows, with an occasional brown trout appearing.

To reach Little Santeetlah, FS 416 runs west off Kilmer Road to the Joyce Kilmer Memorial that is located at streamside. This forest road runs along the creek bank for 0.5 mile to the memorial parking area. Above this point FT 55 continues to follow the creek upstream into the wilderness area.

18

French Broad River System

The French Broad River basin is another of North Carolina's stellar systems that offer a vast array of trout waters, both in number and quality. From its headwaters near the South Carolina border in Transylvania County, along its course northward through Henderson, Buncombe, and Madison counties to the Tennessee border, the French Broad is constantly receiving the clear, cold flows from trout-stream tributaries.

Once the West Fork, Middle Fork, East Fork, and North Fork of the river are united near the town of Rosman, the French Broad is big water along its entire course. Even the main river contains trout in this area, and, as it moves north, it picks up the waters of nationally renowned wild-trout streams and hatchery-supported waters. Throughout much of this swath it cuts across western North Carolina, the French Broad is also well known as a canoeing destination.

As with the other watersheds in the Old North State, some of the streams listed by the NCWRC as public trout water do not meet the criteria needed to merit discussion here. In fact, over 20 creeks and rivers fail the standard in the French Broad basin.

In Transylvania County, the Middle Fork and East Fork of the French Broad River, plus Laurel Creek, are either too small for fly-casting or are predominantly on private land. Cane Creek, which crosses the Henderson-Buncombe county border, also falls in this category. Moving northward, Bent, Reems, Dillingham, Carter, Mineral, Corner Rock, and Stony creeks, plus the Swannanoa and Ivey (also known as Big Ivey Creek) rivers all fail to meet the criteria. In Madison County, Big Laurel, Shelton Laurel, Big, Spillcorn, Little, Shutin, Mill, and Puncheon creeks, as well as Meadow Fork and

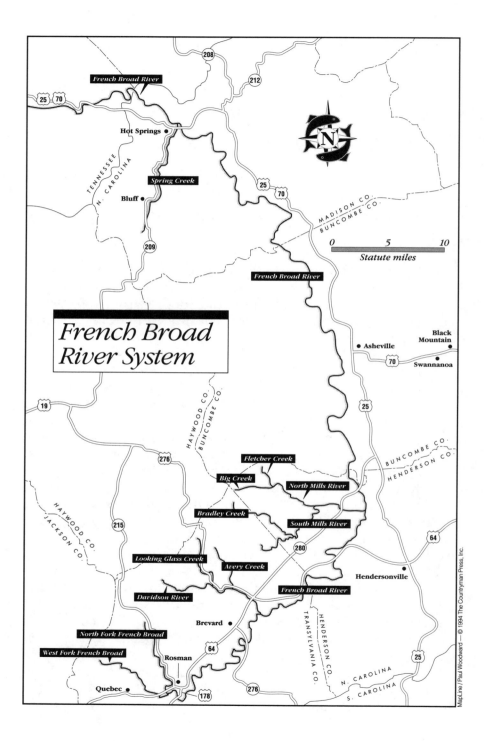

French Broad
River System

Statute miles

Roaring Fork, are not fly-fishing destinations. Of those listed above, all are hatchery-supported waters, with the exception of Carter Creek, which is open under wild-stream, catch-and-release, artificial-lure-only regulations.

Having eliminated such a long list of streams from the public fly-fishing list along the French Broad, one might fear that there is little left to entertain the caster. Such an assumption is far from the truth! Again starting in Transylvania County and working north along the French Broad basin, the North Fork, West Fork, and main body of the French Broad River offer public trout fishing. Also in this county are the Davidson River, Looking Glass Creek, and Avery Creek. Additionally, the South Mills River and Bradley Creek both span the Transylvania-Henderson county border.

In Henderson County the list continues to grow with Big and Fletcher creeks, as well as the North Mills River.

Finally, in Madison County, Spring Creek completes the inventory of public trout water in the French Broad watershed.

WEST FORK FRENCH BROAD RIVER
USGS Lake Toxaway, Reid • DeLorme 52

The West Fork of the French Broad rises on the western edge of Transylvania County to the northwest of the Tennessee Valley Divide beneath Shelton Pisgah Mountain. The headwaters lie just at the boundary between the Nantahala National Forest to the west and the Pisgah National Forest on the east. After tumbling over Dismal Falls, the stream runs eastward to join the North Fork in forming the French Broad just east of Rosman.

The only portion of the West Fork that really provides public access begins where the river crosses a segment of Pisgah Game Lands on Forest Service property to the north of US 64. Through here the stream is of medium size, with adequate room for fly-casting, and is paralleled by SR 1309 (Silverstein Road). In all there is slightly over one mile of water at roadside, plus another two miles downstream accessible via a footpath. The trail downriver begins at the SR 1309 bridge. There are also sections of private property on the river where it nears US 64.

The West Fork is open to fishing as a hatchery-supported stream. A total of 1500 trout are released in the stream from March to July.

The fishable section of the West Fork can be most easily reached by turning north onto Silverstein Road from US 64. The intersection is located in the village of Quebec.

NORTH FORK FRENCH BROAD RIVER
USGS Rosman • DeLorme 52

Although the North Fork has a long course running south through the eastern edge of Transylvania County, only about two miles of the stream in the headwaters provide public fishing. Small and rocky, the creek is open enough for limited casting.

Open under wild-trout regulations, the North Fork receives no stockings of trout. Access to the stream is via FS 140, which parallels the creek for two miles upstream of NC 215. At the third bridge on this part of the creek, the road leaves the stream. Although there is trail access further upstream, the creek is too small for fly-fishing.

There are a couple of primitive campsites at streamside just above the third bridge where road access ends.

FRENCH BROAD RIVER
USGS Rosman • DeLorme 52, 53

The main stream of the French Broad River begins just west of Rosman where the West Fork and North Fork join. From there it is a big river, often deep and providing plenty of room for fly-casts.

The problem with the next 22 miles of the French Broad, down to the end of trout water at the US 276 bridge near Brevard, is that virtually all of the shoreline is in private hands. The only practical way to fish this section is by floating the river. Since the French Broad is a popular canoeing stream, there are a number of possibilities for put-in and take-out points.

Access is possible at the junction of the West Fork and North Fork, or at the city park in Rosman. Another four bridges cross the stream before the French Broad reaches US 276.

Open under hatchery-supported regulations, the French Broad receives stockings totaling 4500 fish between March and August. This is a strictly put-and-take fishery, since it is unlikely that any reproduction takes place in this part of the river.

DAVIDSON RIVER

USGS Shining Rock, Pisgah Forest • DeLorme 52, 53

The Davidson River is one of the best-known trout waters in North Carolina and regionally it ranks with the most-renowned fisheries in the southern Appalachian Mountains. It is a stream that was named by *Trout* magazine (the national publication of Trout Unlimited) as one of the top 100 trout streams in the United States. That, of course, puts it in some pretty heady company.

The Davidson River rises in the northwest quadrant of Transylvania County, to the east of Sassafras Knob. The river then runs east, passing just north of the town of Brevard, to empty into the French Broad. Along this route, the Davidson is only a small- to medium-size stream in the public fishing areas.

Below the edge of Pisgah National Forest lands, just upstream of the US 64 bridge, the river is mostly on private property, offering virtually no public access. Upstream on public land the river is easily accessible off US 276 to the mouth of Looking Glass Creek. From there FS 475 stays at streamside for almost the entire distance until the Davidson is no longer large enough for fly-casting. Also located on FS 475 at 1.5 miles above Looking Glass Creek is the Pisgah National Fish Hatchery. At the hatchery, FS 475 changes from paved to gravel road.

Much of the reputation of the Davidson River is based on the segment from the headwaters down to the mouth of Avery Creek. This part of the river is open to fishing as catch-and-release, fly-fishing-only water, containing only wild trout. Due to the publicity the river receives and its rather easy access, the Davidson gets much heavier fishing pressure than similarly regulated waters. In all there are eight and a half miles of castable water in this part of the river.

Thanks to the catch-and-release rules that turn the Davidson into a virtual trophy-trout stream, big fish are not rare on the stream. They are, however, very educated fish, having seen all manner of flies offered to them.

One possibility for beating the crowd is to fish the portion of the river that runs through a short gorge just above the fish hatchery. Since it requires a bit of a climb down from FS 475 to the water, this stretch gets a little less pressure.

While it is the wild-trout area of the Davidson River that attracts the greatest attention, most anglers would be surprised to learn that the portion of the river from Avery Creek downstream to the end of trout water is the second most heavily stocked stream in North Carolina. From March through August this section receives 20,500 planted fish and is open under hatchery-supported rules. There are roughly two miles of stream on the national forest land in the area that are stocked.

Access is good to the Davidson from US 276 and FS 475 all along the river, with plenty of spaces to park. The Forest Service's Davidson River Campground is located one mile upstream of the edge of the public property on US 276. In the area above the fish hatchery on FS 475 there are some primitive campsites as well. One other option for camping near the Davidson is the Lost Cove Campground, located on Lost Cove Creek in the river's headwaters. This is also a Forest Service campground.

To find the national forest section of the Davidson River, take US 276 to the northwest from the town of Brevard. The river will be on the southwest side of the highway.

LOOKING GLASS CREEK
USGS Shining Rock • DeLorme 53

This stream is a major tributary of the Davidson River in the mid-section of the river's watershed. Flowing almost directly south from its beginning around Green Knob on the Blue Ridge Parkway, Looking Glass Creek is paralleled along its entire course by US 276. There are five miles of fishable water, all of which are easily accessible from the highway.

This small stream is open to fishing under wild-trout regulations and is teeming with small rainbows, and an occasional brown trout. There has been a considerable amount of in-stream structure work done on the creek. In 1992 a three-year, experimental, supplemental feeding program on the creek came to an end. The NCWRC, the U.S. Fish and Wildlife Service, and Trout Unlimited cooperated to hang automatic fish feeders over some pools to see if trout size and number increased. Fishing trips to the creek after the program ended produced plenty of small trout, but the feeding seems to have had no noticeable effect on the size of the rainbows.

Although fishing pressure is usually quite light on Looking Glass, two sections of the creek still will be crowded during warm weather. Looking Glass Falls is located about a quarter mile upstream of the creek's mouth on the Davidson. This roughly 50-foot waterfall attracts a lot of attention from sightseers, making parking spots difficult to find.

Not far upstream from the falls is the Sliding Rock Recreation Area. Here a natural 100-foot water slide down the slick, algae-covered rocks attracts hordes of adventurers in warm weather. Stairs to the creek, a handrail for climbing the rocks, dressing and rest rooms, and an observation deck have been installed by the Forest Service at creekside. These are very convenient for water sports, but render the creek unfishable through here during warmer months.

There are plenty of parking areas and picnic grounds all along Looking Glass Creek, but no camping is allowed.

AVERY CREEK
USGS Shining Rock • DeLorme 53

Avery Creek is not a primary fly-fishing destination due to its small size and tight casting conditions. It does, however, offer some small-stream fishing as a diversion if the crowds get too heavy on the Davidson River.

Flowing down from Buckwheat Knob, Avery empties into the Davidson two miles upstream from the edge of the Pisgah National Forest along US 276. The creek is open under wild-trout regulations, and sports a population of predominantly small rainbows. Rainbows up to 15 inches have been reportedly taken from this small creek, however. The fishable waters extend upstream on Avery to the fourth bridge across the creek, which is roughly a mile and three-quarters above the mouth.

Access to Avery Creek is via FS 477 (White Pines Road) which follows the creek. White Pines Campground is located at the fourth bridge on the road. This Forest Service site is a favorite with horse-back riders since the campsites have stable facilities. There are also some primitive camping clearings further up the creek.

SOUTH MILLS RIVER
USGS Pisgah Forest • DeLorme 53

The South Mills is yet another of North Carolina's trout fisheries that ranked in *Trout* magazine's list of the United States' top 100 streams. Again, it is a reputation well deserved. Rising in northern Transylvania County, the South Mills River flows east under US 276 near the Cradle of Forestry in America historic site. This site is where scientific forestry was first practiced in this country, when George Vanderbilt of the Biltmore Estate hired Gifford Pinchot to manage surrounding woodlands in 1892. Eventually, it was also the site of the first forestry school in the United States.

Once across US 276 the South Mills turns south at an old gauging station in the shadows of Funneltop Mountain to tumble over High Falls. Turning west the river crosses into Henderson County and flows off the Pisgah Game Lands of the Pisgah National Forest at a point between Buttermilk Mountain to the north and Forge Mountain on the south. Eventually, the South Mills joins the North Mills to form the main stream of the Mills River.

The entire course of the South Mills is open to fishing under wild-trout regulations, but the last few miles along South Mills River Road near the junction with the North Mills are on private, posted property that allows no public access. The headwaters of the river are quite difficult to reach, with the only road access at the old gauging station at the end of FS 476.

At the water gauge, which stands like a tall stone chimney at streamside, the South Mills is a medium-size creek. Upstream the river becomes small and tight, with the only access from fishermen's paths up the shore. Downstream, FS 476 continues, but is closed to vehicle traffic, allowing only foot travel. The path stays on the river except in the vicinity of High Falls. Just below this waterfall, FS 476 intersects FT 133 which follows the river all the way to the lower boundary of the Forest Service land.

One other point of access exists in the lower portion of the river. Just east of the Henderson County line, FS 297 runs north toward the river, ending in a parking area that leaves a short hike down to the stream.

Throughout its course below the gauging station, the South Mills River is a string of deep, clear pools that are linked by tumbling shoal areas. The trout in the river are rainbows and browns, with fish of up to 20 inches turning up in the less-fished and inaccessible stretches. Most of the big trout taken are browns, for unlike most designated wild-trout streams, the South Mills receives a once-yearly stocking of half-wild fingerling browns. These plantings take place in the lower portion of the river on public land, below the mouth of Cantrell Creek in Transylvania County. The average trout in the river, however, are more likely to be 8 to 11 inches, but quite abundant.

While the South Mills resembles most southern Appalachian streams in that it provides only sporadic and unpredictable hatches, it is noted for producing abundant caddis flies during the hot summer months. Either the Elk-Hair or Chuck Caddis patterns in sizes 12 to 16 are good choices in flies.

To reach the gauging station on the South Mills take FS 1206 east from US 276. Turn south onto FS 476 and follow it to the end. There are several primitive campsites at the parking area. Access to the lower river is gained over FS 297 from NC 280 just east of the Henderson-Transylvania county line.

BRADLEY CREEK
USGS Dunsmore Mountain, Pisgah Forest • DeLorme 53

This small- to medium-width stream is one of several in the Mills River drainage that tend to "come and go" with regard to showing up on the list of North Carolina trout waters. What makes them a bit unusual is that these creeks in Transylvania and Henderson counties are wild-trout streams running entirely on game lands. Usually, under these circumstances, the streams undergo no changes of regulations. Indeed, Bradley, plus Big and Fletcher creeks on the North Mills River, has remained under wild-trout designation for a number of years, but still does not always appear on the yearly listings.

Regardless of this lack of constant recognition, Bradley Creek provides three miles of easily accessible water in its upper reaches, plus another equal amount of stream that can be reached via hiking trails. From its head on Little Bald Mountain in extreme north Transylvania County, the creek at first runs south, then turns east to parallel FS 1206 for three miles and crosses into Henderson County. The upper mile of creek along the road is too small and bushy to be of much interest to fly casters, but then opens up enough to allow some casting room. Although near the road, the stream is in a steep-sided valley that requires a climb down from the road to the water. Quite often the water is out of sight of the roadway.

At the lower end of road access the creek turns southwest to flow another three miles down to the South Mills River near the edge of the Pisgah Game Lands. In this section FT 351 follows Bradley Creek downstream, intersecting FT 324, which finishes the job of following the creek to its mouth.

Open under wild-trout regulations, Bradley receives very limited fishing pressure, especially in the section away from FS 1206. Small rainbows are the most often encountered species of trout.

The approach to Bradley Creek from the west is via FS 1206 off US 276 north of the Cradle of Forestry historic site. From the east the creek can be reached by taking North Mills River Road off NC 280. When the North Mills River Road ends at the Forest Service's North Mills River Campground, take FS 1206 west from that point.

NORTH MILLS RIVER
USGS Dunsmore Mountain • DeLorme 53

The smaller of the two forks of the Mills River, the North Mills is a small stream that descends a rather level course through northwest Henderson County. There are about two miles of water from the point that Fletcher and Big creeks join to form the North Mills down to where the river exits Forest Service land.

Open under hatchery-supported fishing regulations, the stream receives stockings of 5500 trout from March to August. Much of the stocking is done on the lower end of the river's course through the game lands at the North Mills River Campground. There, access to the water is easy via FS 1206 and North Mills River Road. Below the game lands, the river is all on private property. Upstream of the campground a footpath follows the river to its head at the junction of Fletcher and Big creeks. Fly-fishing conditions are quite tight on the stream.

BIG AND FLETCHER CREEKS
USGS Dunsmore Mountain • DeLorme 53

Big Creek on the west and Fletcher Creek to the east are the headwater arms of the North Mills River. Originating in northern Henderson County along the Blue Ridge Parkway, both are quite small, difficult to fish, and open under wild-trout regulations. Neither constitutes a fly-casting destination by itself, but combined with the North Mills they provide a variety of water to fill a day astream. Small rainbows are the most commonly hooked fish on these streams.

As noted in the description of Bradley Creek, these two streams have not appeared on the list of North Carolina public trout streams every year.

Access to the streams can be gained at their junction. Take FS 5000 (this road is marked as FS 479 on most maps, but signs on the road now show the FS 5000 designation) north from the North Mills River Campground. At 2.1 miles, turn west onto FS 142 (this road does not appear on all maps of the area). At the end of FS 142 is a parking area. Follow the Hendersonville Reservoir Road Trail (the old road, now blocked) down to the junction of the streams. FT 108 follows Fletcher Creek from that point, while FT 102 heads west along Big Creek.

SPRING CREEK
USGS *Spring Creek* • *DeLorme 30*

Spring Creek is the last trout stream feeding into the French Broad River before it crosses into Tennessee. In all, 10 miles of Spring Creek are stocked and open to fishing under hatchery-supported regulations. From March to June, 5000 fish are planted in the creek.

The portion of the creek upstream of the mouth of Meadow Fork Creek at the crossroads of Bluff is a mixture of both private holdings and some right-of-way access along NC 209. This road is at streamside all the way to the headwaters of the creek. There are several quarter- to half-mile stretches of accessible water through here.

Below Bluff, Spring Creek enters a gorge that is located on Pisgah Game Lands owned by the U.S. Forest Service. Although NC 209 continues to run parallel to the creek, the water is not easily reached along here. The Rocky Bluff Campground and Recreation Area at the foot of the gorge offers the best spot to get on the creek. Foot trails follow the creek up into the gorge from that point. Below Rocky Bluff the creek is again located on private land.

Spring Creek can be reached by traveling south on NC 209 from its junction with US 25/70 in the town of Hot Springs in Madison County.

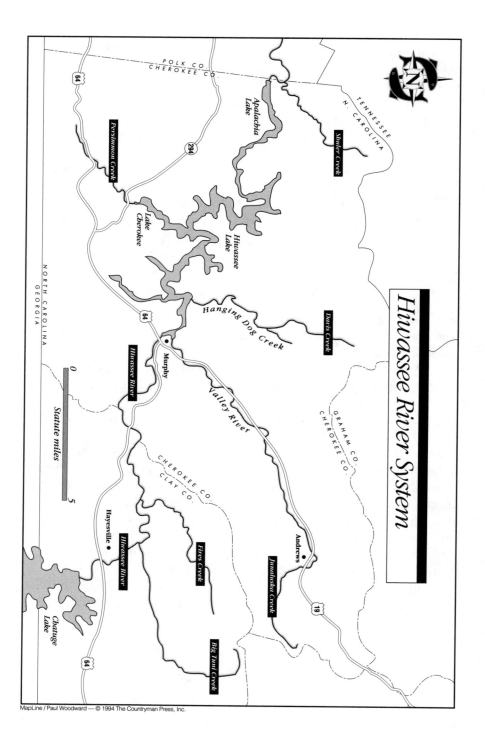

Hiwassee River System

POLK CO
CHEROKEE CO

TENNESSEE
N. CAROLINA

Shuler Creek

Apalachia Lake

Persimmon Creek

Lake Cherokee

Hiwassee Lake

Hanging Dog Creek

Davis Creek

Murphy

Hiwassee River

Valley River

Statute miles
0
5

NORTH CAROLINA
GEORGIA

GRAHAM CO.
CHEROKEE CO.

CHEROKEE CO.
CLAY CO.

Hayesville

Hiwassee River

Fires Creek

Junaluska Creek

Andrews

Chatuge Lake

Big Tuni Creek

19

Hiwassee River System

The Hiwassee River system is the most westerly of the trout waters found in the state of North Carolina. The river begins its journey to the sea deep in the Appalachian Mountains of north Georgia, then crosses into the Tarheel State in the impounded waters of Lake Chatuge in Clay County. From that point it arcs to the northwest through Clay and Cherokee counties to enter Tennessee just downstream of Apalachia Lake.

Anglers who are familiar with the portion of the Hiwassee downstream of Apalachia powerhouse in Tennessee will find the North Carolina portion a disappointment. This part of the river bears little resemblance to the nationally renowned tailwater in the Volunteer State. At no point along its course across the Old North State is the Hiwassee itself trout water. This is due to the relatively low elevation of the Hiwassee's valley. This same problem affects most of the river's tributaries, making all but a few of the streams marginal trout water. As is often the case with streams lying at lower elevations in level, fertile valleys, private farms dominate the surroundings. This, of course, also limits public access to the fishery in this drainage.

The streams in Clay County that the NCWRC lists as public trout water, but which do not meet the criteria for coverage, are Shooting, Tusquitee, Vineyard, and Hothouse creeks. The first two of these fall victim to having too much private land along their banks, while the latter pair are quite small and heavily foliated.

Once across into Cherokee County, the Hiwassee is fed by the Valley River, as well as North Shoal, Bald, Hyatts, Beaver Dam, and Webb creeks. None of these streams offer enough public access to merit being described as fly-fishing destinations.

On the other hand, Cherokee County does contain Junaluska,

Davis, Persimmon, and Shuler creeks, which provide varying amounts of public access to fishable trout water. Additionally, upstream in Clay County, Fires and Big Tuni creeks have fishing possibilities that are attractive and accessible for the fly caster.

Our look at the trout waters of the Hiwassee basin will begin at the Georgia border and work downstream to Apalachia Dam.

BIG TUNI CREEK
USGS Topton, Shooting Creek • DeLorme 50

Big Tuni Creek is a medium to small stream that rises in Tuni Gap in the extreme northern tip of Clay County. From there it runs south, skirting to the east of Tusquitee Bald, to empty into Tusquitee Creek. Although the creek is shown as Big Tuni on most maps, the fishing regulations put out by the state refer to it simply as Tuni Creek.

Also on the maps of the area, access looks rather easy to this flow, since FS 440 runs along virtually all the creek's length. The first half mile upstream from Big Tuni's mouth is on private land, but above there four miles of public water on Forest Service land are fishable.

What the maps do not show is that the road along Big Tuni is often up on the wall of a gorge or even over a ridge from the stream. In many places the walk down to the water is quite strenuous. In others, however, the road does dip down to streamside.

Open to fishing as a hatchery-supported stream, Big Tuni Creek is stocked only once a year. This release is composed of fingerling trout, with the total split equally between brookies and rainbows. Due to this stocking pattern, many small fish are encountered and fishing pressure is rather light.

The Forest Service maintains the Bob Allison Campground on the headwaters of the stream. Access to the campground and creek is via FS 440, which runs north off Woods Road (SR 1307), northeast of Hayesville.

FIRES CREEK
USGS Andrews, Hayesville • DeLorme 50

This medium-size flow is the crown jewel of the Hiwassee River system in North Carolina. With over 10 miles of tumbling, fishable water on Nantahala Game Lands, it offers the only true wild-trout water on public land in the Hiwassee drainage.

Beginning on the western slope of Tusquitee Bald, the creek runs westerly through Clay County, with its valley staying just north of the Tusquitee Mountains. Eventually the creek empties into the Hiwassee to the northeast of the town of Hayesville.

The stream's course is a rough and tumbling one, offering plenty of drops, plunge pools, and deep runs. Casting room is no problem on Fires Creek.

There is one mile of Fires Creek downstream of the National Forest property to the bridge at SR 1300. This part of the creek is the only portion presently mentioned in the NCWRC fishing regulations. It is open as hatchery-supported water and receives 2050 adult trout between March and June. Unfortunately, it is also mostly on private land.

On the other hand, what the regulations do not mention is that the upper 10 miles of Fires, as well as a couple of feeder streams, are open under wild-trout regulations. Little Fires Creek and Long Branch are both quite small brooks, but offer some casting room near their confluences with Fires Creek. Both brown and rainbow trout are present in this watershed, with rainbows being most common.

All of the creek is accessible from FS 340. This gravel track runs 1.7 miles from the edge of the public land up to Fires Creek Picnic Area. There is one patch of private land just downstream of the picnic grounds.

An impressive waterfall is in the picnic area where a small tributary tumbles down into Fires Creek from the north. Above the picnic area Fires Creek is down in a gorge for the next three and a quarter miles and is difficult to reach from the road. A foot trail at creekside running upstream from the picnic ground offers the best access to the gorge.

Above the gorge the road rejoins the creek. At 6.8 miles above the edge of public land a primitive camping area is located on the creek. There are a few other campsites along the stream, but they are not very common. The hills on either side of Fires Creek are fairly steep, leaving little level space.

Above the point where FS 340 passes the junction with FS 340C, the road becomes very rough and the creek again enters a gorge. The creek is small upstream, but is still open enough to fly-cast. Due to the several gorges, Fires Creek appears to get rather light fishing pressure along most of the flow.

To reach Fires Creek, take US 64 west from Hayesville. At Bethesda

Church, turn north onto SR 1302. Just across the Hiwassee River, turn right onto SR 1300. FS 340 runs north off this road at Fires Creek.

JUNALUSKA CREEK
USGS Andrews • DeLorme 50

This small stream in Cherokee County descends a rocky, narrow course along Junaluska Road, just southeast of the town of Andrews. About one mile of the creek is located on Forest Service land, beginning three miles from the city limits and running upstream to the FS 440 bridge over the flow. Access from the road is quite easy.

Junaluska does not offer much casting room, but does have some potholes and pockets that can be reached. A total of 2800 trout are stocked in the creek during March to June, but these are released along the entire six miles of the stream, most of which are private. Fishing is allowed under hatchery-supported regulations.

To reach Junaluska Creek, take Junaluska Road (SR 1505) to the southeast out of Andrews to the national forest boundary.

DAVIS CREEK
USGS McDaniel Bald • DeLorme 50

Davis Creek rises in western Cherokee County beneath Freeman Knob. Although the headwaters are on public land, they are also very small, bushy, and unsuitable for fly-casting.

As the stream continues down the valley it is paralleled by FS 420. Along this course it crosses both Forest Service and private lands. Two of the stretches of public property are each roughly a half mile long and easily reached from the road. They provide some very tight fishing conditions. Davis Creek runs into Hanging Dog Creek, which empties into Hiwassee Lake.

Davis Creek and its feeder stream Bald Creek receive stockings of 3500 trout from March to August. Fishing is open under hatchery-supported rules. Davis Creek appears to get plenty of fishing attention from local anglers.

To find Davis Creek, take Brown Road north from the town of Murphy to Beaver Dam Road and turn right. Stay on this road until it intersects with Davis Creek Road (FS 420) and turn right again.

PERSIMMON CREEK
USGS Persimmon Creek • DeLorme 30

The next trout stream feeding into the Hiwassee that provides any public fishing is Persimmon Creek. Flowing for nine miles from south to north down a flat valley surrounded by farm land, the creek empties into Cherokee Lake. This lake is an appendage of Hiwassee Lake, but separated from that larger body of water by Persimmon Dam.

The creek does not offer much of a public fishery, even though it receives 1100 stocked fish in March and April. The only part of the stream that is open to the public is the first half mile upstream of the lake. Through here Persimmon Creek is a small stream on Forest Service land, with room for limited casting. Fishing is regulated by hatchery-supported rules.

To reach the public part of Persimmon Creek, take US 64 west from Murphy. Turn north onto NC 294, which will cross Persimmon at its mouth and then parallel the creek across the public land.

SHULER CREEK
USGS Unaka • DeLorme 30

The final trout water feeding the Hiwassee before the river crosses into Tennessee is Shuler Creek. This medium to small creek is a lowland stream for two miles upstream of its mouth on the Hiwassee, as it flows through both Forest Service land and private tracts.

Further upstream there is more grade to the valley and the creek is a bit more rough-and-tumble. It is possible to fly-cast on the stream for eight and a quarter miles up to the intersection of FS 50 and SR 1328. Along this route FS 50 parallels the creek, but is not always in sight of the water.

Shuler Creek receives only one stocking of trout each year, which consists of 1000 rainbows and 5000 browns from half-wild breeding stock. All of these fish are fingerlings when released. Hatchery-supported fishing regulations must be observed on Shuler Creek.

Shuler Creek can be reached by taking SR 1314 north from Hiwassee Village at the dam on Hiwassee Lake. At the crossroads of Violet, turn left onto SR 1323. This road dead-ends into SR 1322 (FS 50) at Shuler Creek.

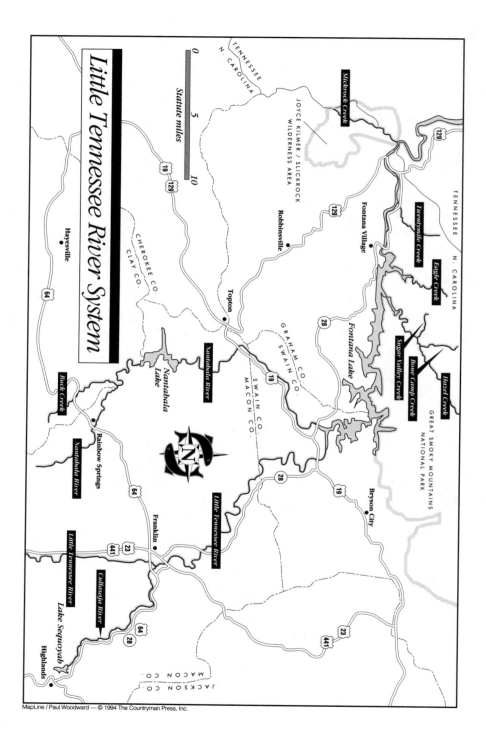

Little Tennessee River System

Statute miles

0   5   10

Slickrock Creek

TENNESSEE
N. CAROLINA

JOYCE KILMER / SLICKROCK
WILDERNESS AREA

129

19
129

64

Hayesville

CHEROKEE CO.
CLAY CO.

Robbinsville

129

Fontana Village

Twentymile Creek

Eagle Creek

TENNESSEE
N. CAROLINA

Topton

28

Fontana Lake

Sugar Valley Creek

Bone Camp Creek

Hazel Creek

GREAT SMOKY MOUNTAINS
NATIONAL PARK

Nantahala Lake

Nantahala River

GRAHAM CO.
SWAIN CO.

19

Buck Creek

Rainbow Springs

Nantahala River

SWAIN CO.
MACON CO.

N

64

28

19

Bryson City

Franklin

64

23
441

Little Tennessee River

28

Little Tennessee River

Cullasaja River

64

28

23

441

Lake Sequoyah

JACKSON CO.
MACON CO.

Highlands

20

Little Tennessee River System

The Little Tennessee River system has much in common with the Hiwassee system. As in that drainage, the Little T is formed in the north Georgia highlands, flows north to cut across western North Carolina and finally enters the state of Tennessee.

Although the Little Tennessee has attained legendary status in southern trout-fishing lore, at no point in the Tarheel State is it considered trout water. The river's reputation rests on the once fabulous brown trout angling that existed on the Tennessee portion of the river. Unfortunately, that resource was drowned by the rising waters of Tellico Lake in the late 1970s.

Like the Hiwassee to the west, the Little T flows at low elevations as it journeys across Macon and Graham counties to exit the state just south of the Great Smoky Mountains National Park. Unlike the Hiwassee, the Little Tennessee's feeder streams offer a wide variety of opportunities to the fly-fisherman. These trout waters in the Little T basin extend beyond the two counties that the river runs through. Besides Macon and Graham, some of the river's tributaries are located in Clay and Swain counties as well.

The trout streams of the Little Tennessee watershed found in Macon County are the Cullasaja River and the upper reaches of the Nantahala River. The Nantahala also crosses into Swain County where Hazel, Eagle, and Twentymile creeks are also found. The last three of these are on lands in the Great Smoky Mountains National Park. The only Little T feeder stream located in Clay County is Buck Creek, while Graham County holds Slickrock Creek.

In addition to these streams that provide public access and enough

169

size for fly-casting, there are others in the basin that do not fit that profile. The ones that the NCWRC lists as public trout water, but do not fit the criteria for coverage, are Cartoogechaye, Ellijay, Roaring Fork, Tessentee, and Burningtown creeks in Macon County, plus Panther, Sawyer, and Stecoah creeks in Graham County. In Swain County, Alarka Creek fails the test of adequate public access.

CULLASAJA RIVER
USGS Highlands, Scaly Mountain,
Corbin Knob • DeLorme 51, 70

The Cullasaja River is the major tributary of the Little Tennessee in Macon County. The public access on this big-water stream begins at the foot of Lake Sequoyah in the town of Highlands. From there it runs to the northwest through national forest lands, plunging through the Cullasaja River Gorge for seven miles. Once out of the gorge the river courses through private property to its mouth in Franklin.

Besides containing a respectable volume of water, the Cullasaja is steeply graded as it rushes, brawling, down a boulder-strewn bed. Although constantly in sight of US 64, the river is down in the gorge at several places and very difficult to reach. The precipitous drop of the river makes it a favorite with sightseers who enjoy viewing waterfalls.

The first fall in the Cullasaja Gorge area is one of the most photographed in the South. A small feeder stream drops over a jutting ledge of rock to form Bridal Veil Falls. The waters of the creek then flow under US 64 into the Cullasaja. A spur of the highway has been built that allows vehicles to drive under the rock shelf behind the plunging waters.

Just downstream of Bridal Veil, the main river drops over Dry Falls into a large plunge pool at the foot of the 60- to 70-foot cascade. Near the end of the gorge, the river leaps over the edge of a 200-foot drop at Cullasaja Falls. Needless to say, extreme care should be exercised anytime one ventures into the gorge, but especially in the vicinity of any of these waterfalls.

Open under hatchery-supported fishing rules, the Cullasaja receives 7500 stocked trout from March to August. These fish, however, are not all released in the gorge, but are planted along the entire 13 miles of water from Highlands to just upstream of Franklin. There is plenty of room for fly-casting on all portions of the Cullasaja.

Access to the Cullasaja River is off US 64, which follows the stream all the way along its trout waters. The portion of the river from Dry Falls up to Lake Sequoyah is quite difficult to reach from the road, as is the last half mile of the gorge below Cullasaja Falls. There is a four-mile stretch between these areas that provides easier approaches to the river. Parking spaces are not overly abundant along US 64, but there is a bridge and Forest Service campground near the midpoint of the gorge. Van Hook Glade Campground is on the north side of US 64 and the river.

NANTAHALA RIVER
USGS Rainbow Springs, Topton, Hewitt,
Wesser • DeLorme 51

The Nantahala River is one of the best-known streams of any size in western North Carolina. Renowned for its variety of trout-fishing possibilities, its exciting white-water boating, and its mystical beauty, this river probably attracts more visitors than any other in the region. To attempt to describe the river is a real challenge and could undoubtedly fill an entire volume of its own.

In flowing across Macon and Swain counties to its junction with the Little Tennessee River in Fontana Lake, the Nantahala passes through several segments of land in the Nantahala National Forest. The wide variety of its fishing opportunities along this course prompted *Trout* magazine to include it on their list of the top 100 trout streams in the United States.

The Nantahala begins its trek to the sea on the eastern slope of Standing Indian Mountain in the Nantahala Mountains of southern Macon County. The river is given birth by the joining of a host of small feeder streams with names like Big Indian, Little Indian, Bearpen, Curtis, and Kimsey creeks. The small tributaries are all trout streams, some even containing the native brook trout. They are not, however, capable of handling much fishing pressure and are the domain of the backcountry angler who cares to put out the effort to explore them.

The practical fly-fishing area of the Nantahala begins in the vicinity of Mooney Falls. In this headwater section the river is small, bushy, usually out of sight of the paralleling Forest Service road, and at times down in a gorge. Four miles downriver from Mooney Falls is the Forest Service's Kimsey Creek Campground, while the Standing Indian Campground is an additional two miles further downstream. Below the Standing Indian facility there is one more mile of water down to the edge of the national forest property. Along the river's entire length from Standing Indian up to Mooney Falls, FS 67 follows the stream as a gravel road. From Standing Indian Campground down to US 64 the road is paved.

This upper portion of the Nantahala and all of its feeder streams are open under wild-trout fishing regulations. Most of the fish hooked in the river are small rainbows, but a brown trout can turn up.

In the Standing Indian to Kimsey Creek area the river is of small to medium size, and has a number of clearings at streamside. Although these were obviously used for camping in the past, they are now off limits to that activity.

To reach the upper end of the Nantahala River take US 64 to just north of the crossroads of Rainbow Springs. Turn east on FS 67, which will lead to the Standing Indian and Kimsey Creek campgrounds.

Once across US 64 to the north, the Nantahala takes on a different character. Long clear runs are interspersed with deep pockets along this medium to large stream. Unfortunately for the average angler, virtually all of the water from US 64 down to Nantahala Lake is controlled by the Rainbow Springs Club and posted.

The next section of the Nantahala that is open to the public begins at the foot of Nantahala Dam. The stream is drastically different at this point from when it entered the lake. Only a tiny flow of water comes through the spillway of the dam, with the rest of the river diverted through a pipeline down to the powerhouse at the head of Nantahala Gorge. This leaves over seven miles of the river dependent on its feeder streams for water. In effect, the river starts over from scratch.

The river from the dam down to the Forest Service's Appletree Campground, where the river again enters national forest land, is sluggish, extremely marginal habitat, and sometimes virtually dry. Although paralleled by SR 1401, the area is of little interest to anglers.

From Appletree Campground there are three and a half miles of water downstream that are small to medium in width and flow. They provide only marginal trout habitat, although stocked by the NCWRC with 3000 trout from March to June. Fishing is regulated under hatchery-supported rules from Nantahala Dam down to the mouth of White Oak Creek. Access is easy along this part of the river, since FS 308 runs at streamside.

Below the mouth of White Oak Creek, the Nantahala's fishing regulations undergo yet another change. The next three and three-quarter miles are open as a delayed-harvest trout stream. From the first of March through the first of June no trout may be harvested on this portion of the Nantahala and only artificial lures may be used, but the rest of the year hatchery-supported regulations apply.

Although still rather marginal trout habitat, the river receives very heavy plantings of fish. One unusual aspect of the stocking is that equal numbers of brook, rainbow, and brown trout are released into the stream. The stockings are "front loaded" as well. In March, April, and May over 3000 fish are added to the river each month, but when the harvest period begins, only 1000 to 1500 are stocked monthly. The stockings, which total 13,300 fish, run from March through August.

After White Oak Creek adds its flow (which drops over a scenic waterfall into the Nantahala) to the river, the stream is of medium size all the way down to the powerhouse. Often rough, rocky, and tumbling along this portion, the Nantahala provides adequate room for fly-casting.

Trout in the delayed-harvest section run from 8 to 11 inches, but larger trout are also encountered. There is a resident carryover population of browns that reach 20 inches or better. Casting for trout on this part of the Nantahala can be spectacular before the harvest period begins. Every pool and run will have several fish and they normally respond well to dry flies. Adams patterns in regular or female styles produce very well along here.

Once the river is opened for harvest, the bait casters pound it unmercifully, particularly on the first weekend. A conversation with a NCWRC ranger on this stream revealed that a creel survey counted more than 1000 trout taken on the opening weekend of 1993. After a couple of weeks of this pressure, many of the pools have been fished out, leaving the shoal water as the most productive. A surprising number of brook trout will be found in shallow runs under the overhanging tufts of grass once the harvest begins. This is probably due to these riffles being overlooked in favor of the enticing deeper pools.

The delayed-harvest portion of the Nantahala can be reached by turning west off US 19 at the head of the Nantahala Gorge onto Ball Road (SR 1310). The delayed-harvest water begins upstream of the powerhouse, with the road continuing at streamside up to White Oak Creek.

The final section of trout water on the Nantahala is composed of eight miles of river running through the Nantahala Gorge, just after it crosses into Swain County. This is the part of the river that is nationally known for its white-water rapids, which attract canoers, kayakers, and rafters from all over the eastern U.S. As a result of this boating activity, the excellent fishing on this stretch gets underutilized.

Once the nutrient-laden waters of Nantahala Lake surge out of the pipeline at the powerhouse to replenish the river, the Nantahala is a big-water flow. This description, of course, only applies when water is being released from the lake. At other periods the gorge portion of the river is a medium-size stream that meanders along the river's bed. The added flow from the powerhouse turns the river into a turbulent, rushing stream that rates from difficult to impossible to wade during high water.

During the warm months, the only time that low water is encountered is in the early morning hours before the powerhouse switches on the generators. Anglers who venture out for this fishing will find the river much easier to wade, but caution is necessary to prevent being caught in a vulnerable situation when the waters rise.

The biggest problem with fishing on the Nantahala once the water does rise, aside from the difficult wading, is the torrent of floaters who cover the river's surface. If you do not mind the company and can avoid hooking the rafts, however, the fish do not seem to notice all the commotion. Undoubtedly, they have become accustomed to the heavy boat traffic. The best places to fish during high water are eddies off the main flow or the side channels behind small islands. These generally have few floaters and less-rapid currents.

The gorge section of the Nantahala is open under hatchery-supported fishing regulations, receiving 6000 stockers in March through August. These fish gain weight and size quickly due to the high quality of the food supply in this tailwater. Most fish encountered are under 12 inches and may be either stocked or stream bred. Abundant holdovers are also found, many of which reach the 16- to 20-inch range. One other facet of the fishing regulations that sets the gorge portion of the Nantahala apart is its designation as the only North Carolina trout water where night fishing is permitted.

Although the sides of the Nantahala Gorge plummet steeply from the surrounding mountains, giving credence to the translation of Nantahala from the Cherokee Indian language to mean "land of the midday sun," access to the river is easy. The river is closely followed through the gorge by US 19, all the way down to the area of Little and Big Wesser falls. There are plenty of turnouts and parking areas all along the river.

To reach the Nantahala Gorge portion of the river, take US 19/129 north from the town of Andrews. Continue on US 19 beyond the village of Topton where US 129 turns northeast. The highway will strike the Nantahala River just north of the village of Beechertown.

BUCK CREEK
USGS Wayah Bald • DeLorme 51

This small stream is the only feeder of the Nantahala River that merits coverage on its own. It is also the only creek in the Little Tennessee watershed in Clay County that is discussed.

Rising on the north side of Chunky Gal Mountain and to the south of Doe Knob, Buck Creek runs to the northwest to empty into the Nantahala River above Nantahala Lake on the Clay-Macon county border. Along this route Buck Creek is a small stream descending a level valley. Although there are areas of the creek that are open enough to fly-cast, there is not a great deal of holding water on the stream. It tends to run wide and shallow, not having much in the way of shoals and pocket water.

At the midpoint of Buck Creek's flow, US 64 crosses the stream. Upstream of this point is one mile of fishable water to the first culvert road crossing. This part of the stream is paralleled by FS 71.

Downstream of US 64 the creek has two and a half miles of access along FS 350A. Although the road follows the creek, it is rarely in sight of the water. Where FS 350A ends, at a gate on private land, is also the boundary of Forest Service property. Below this point the creek is private and posted. Both sections of Buck Creek above and below US 64 are on Nantahala National Forest lands. Primitive campsites are plentiful along both sections of the creek.

Buck Creek is open to fishing as a wild-trout stream with corresponding regulations. The fish population in the creek is dominated by rainbow trout, with most being under 9 inches long.

To reach Buck Creek, take US 64 east from the village of Shooting Creek in Clay County. FS 350A will run to the north just before the highway crosses Buck Creek. The entrance to FS 71 on the south side of US 64 is about 1.0 mile past the creek.

HAZEL CREEK

USGS Silers Bald, Thunderhead Mountain,
Tuskeegee • DeLorme 28, 29

Hazel Creek is one of a triumvirate of celebrated wilderness trout streams lying in the Great Smoky Mountains National Park in Swain County and feeding into Fontana Lake. Hazel and Eagle creeks run into the main body of the reservoir, while Forney Creek feeds the Tuckasegee River arm of the lake. The reason these streams are usually thought of as a group is that they all require extremely long hikes, or boat rides across Fontana, to reach.

Hazel Creek is the most famous trout stream situated in the Smoky Mountains park. Located midway down the north shore of Fontana, Hazel Creek was one of the last areas added to the Great Smoky Mountains NP. Prior to the park's acquisition of the watershed a booming mining community existed there, producing copper ore. As many as 2000 people once inhabited the valley.

Another facet of Hazel Creek history is its association with legendary southern outdoorsman Horace Kephart, who wrote several of his books while living on the stream's headwaters.

The rich tradition surrounding Hazel Creek has served to increase its popularity to the point that it now receives heavy visitation—at least for a wilderness stream. Most of these visitors arrive by boat from Fontana Marina or from the public boat ramp directly across the lake at Cable Cove Campground.

Hazel Creek is a medium to large stream in its lower elevations and for several miles upstream. In spite of reports that the trout fishing has declined in recent decades, Hazel still has plenty of wild rainbows of up to 11 or 12 inches. It also produces several brown trout each season in the 8- to 10-pound range. Indeed, Hazel Creek is noted for its fine brown trout fishery, especially in the lower reaches of the stream. Standard Great Smoky Mountains NP fishing regulations apply on Hazel Creek and all of its tributaries.

Upstream of its mouth, Hazel Creek is fishable for 15 miles as it tumbles down from Silers Bald. This creek is a major stream at a higher elevation than any other in the park. It is also one of the few large creeks where native brookies still turn up in the headwaters of the main stream.

Additionally, at four and four and a half miles upstream from Fontana, first Sugar Valley Creek and then Bone Camp Creek enter

The valley of Hazel Creek was one of the last areas added to the Great Smoky Mountains National Park. Its trout fishing has gained an almost legendary reputation among southern fly casters.

Hazel from the west. Both of these are large enough for fly-casting and offer some good rainbow trout fishing. Sugar Valley Creek is followed upstream by Jenkins Ridge Trail, while Bone Valley Trail follows Bone Camp Creek for 1.5 miles.

Near its mouth Hazel Creek flows over relatively level terrain. As one moves upstream, however, waterfalls and shoals are encountered with increasing frequency. The size of the plunge pools gives the impression that the creek is getting larger as you ascend it.

The entire main stem of Hazel Creek is paralleled by Hazel Creek Trail. Near the lake it is actually a well-maintained gravel road used by Park Service vehicles that are ferried across the lake. Also in this vicinity are a couple of houses, a stable, and fenced pasture used by park rangers and their horses. Just upstream of these structures are the ruins of buildings dating from the copper mining era.

To reach Hazel Creek by land requires hikes in the 12- to 15-mile range, regardless of whether you start at Fontana Village, Clingmans Dome, or Nolan Creek. Unless you particularly want to do these treks, boating across Fontana is a better option. If you bring your own boat, Cable Cove Campground's boat ramp is your best bet. It is at the end of Cable Cove Road off NC 28. If you are boatless, you can arrange a round-trip ride across at the Fontana Marina on NC 28 for a reasonable price. For information on this service call (704) 498-2211, or write to Fontana Village, Fontana, NC 28733.

EAGLE CREEK

USGS Thunderhead Mountain, Cades Cove,
Fontana Dam • DeLorme 28

Located just to the west of Hazel Creek, Eagle Creek is a small flow that offers a diminutive version of the fishing on Hazel Creek. Accessible only via a 5.5-mile hike from Fontana Village or a short boat ride across the lake, it too suffers from excessive visitation.

At its mouth the creek is relatively level and shallow, but soon changes to a rough-and-tumble stream as you progress upstream. The surrounding terrain is steep and the woodlands are beautiful. On a fishing trip to Eagle Creek a couple of summers ago, it was brought home forcefully just how powerful is the spell that this valley can cast over a person.

I was introducing professional bass-fishing guide Bill Vanderford to Smoky Mountains backcountry trout fishing with a long weekend of day trips across Fontana to the wilderness streams. While we were fishing up Eagle Creek, a couple of men in their midforties accompanied by a teenaged boy passed us going upstream on the nearby trail. They were all very heavily laden with camping equipment.

Later Bill and I climbed out of the creek at one of the bridges where the trail crossed. Here we found two gentlemen resting who, when we struck up a conversation, mentioned being in their eighties and that they had been fishing Eagle Creek for over half a century. The group laden with camping gear we had seen earlier were their sons-in-law and a grandson who had come along to carry the equipment up to a campsite for them. Meanwhile the octogenarian fishing partners were making their way up the trail at their own pace, reliving past exploits as they went.

Eagle Creek is a wilderness stream that attracts a following of devoted anglers who cross Fontana Lake by boat to test its waters.

It is no wonder that Eagle Creek can call its faithful back. The fishing is very good for rainbow trout, although the average fish is small. Trout of 7 to 8 inches abound, with larger ones appearing occasionally. Brown trout are present but not plentiful in the creek. Fishing regulations on Eagle Creek adhere to standard Great Smoky Mountains NP rules.

To reach Eagle Creek by land entails a 5.5-mile hike on the Eagle Creek Trail from Fontana Village at Fontana Dam. By water the approach is easier, since the creek is almost directly across from Fontana Marina.

TWENTYMILE CREEK
USGS Cades Cove, Fontana Dam • DeLorme 28

Yet another stream that flows off the south slope of the Great Smoky Mountains NP, Twentymile Creek enters the Little Tennessee in the waters of Cheoah Reservoir, downstream of Fontana Lake. Unlike

Eagle and Hazel creeks, there is road access to Twentymile.

Unfortunately, at least in the lower portion of the stream, Twentymile has little in common with the wilderness creeks near it. Access is at the Twentymile Ranger Station, where very limited parking is available behind the ranger station. Also behind this building are the stable and horse lot, which the stream runs through. It is not a very pretty sight, since horses show little respect for trout water!

Twentymile Creek is a small stream, and, in spite of first impressions near its mouth, it is a good rainbow trout fishery. The fish, however, run on the small side, averaging less than 8 inches. Catching a brown trout from Twentymile rates as a rare occurrence. As with all park streams, no stocking is done, and fishing is allowed under regular park regulations.

To reach Twentymile Creek, take NC 28 to the west across Fontana Dam from Fontana Village. The entrance to the ranger station is on the right at the bridge over Twentymile Creek. From the ranger station, Twentymile Trail offers foot access to the creek upstream in the national park.

SLICKROCK CREEK
USGS Tapoco • DeLorme 28

Slickrock Creek is a medium- to small-size stream that enters the Calderwood Lake portion of the Little Tennessee River. For roughly two and a half miles upstream from its mouth, Slickrock forms the state boundary between Tennessee and North Carolina. Flowing to the northeast in a corridor between the Unicoi Mountains on the northwest and Hangover Lead to the southeast, Slickrock is a quality trout stream.

There is no road access to any portion of Slickrock Creek as it knifes its way through the 17,000-acre Joyce Kilmer-Slickrock Wilderness Area. This preserve straddles the state border, insulating the stream from all anglers except those willing to travel by foot. For obvious reasons only light fishing pressure is usually found on Slickrock Creek.

Those anglers who do make the trek into Slickrock are drawn by the chance to tangle with some of the most beautifully colored, feisty, wild brown trout found in southern Appalachia. The best area for these naturally reproducing jewels begins at the first waterfall upstream of Calderwood Lake. This 12- to 15-foot cascade is about a mile from the creek's mouth.

The deep runs and plunge pools of the portion along the state border provide plenty of room for fly-casting to these prized fish. Once the creek bears off into North Carolina it gets smaller, but still offers several miles of castable water. Throughout its length brown trout are the predominant species with a few rainbows showing up near the mouth of the creek and some brook trout in the headwaters.

Slickrock Creek is open to fishing year-round on both sides of the state border and is managed under a reciprocal agreement between North Carolina and Tennessee. A fishing license from either state is sufficient to fish the part of the creek forming the border, but only a North Carolina permit is honored upstream of that point.

The daily creel limit on Slickrock is four trout, regardless of species. The minimum size limit for brook trout is 7 inches, while it is 10 inches on brown and rainbow trout. Angling is limited to single-hook, artificial lures.

Access to Slickrock Creek is not easy from any direction. For the lower stretch of the creek, FT 42 (Slickrock Creek or Ike Branch trail depending on which maps you consult) provides access. It begins at the US 129 bridge across Calderwood, just below the Cheoah Dam. The trail runs beside the lake downstream to the mouth of Slickrock Creek where it turns to follow that stream over the bed of an old logging railroad. To get to the best angling the walk will be about 2.5 miles.

The other alternative is to approach the midsection of Slickrock from Big Fat Gap to the southeast of the creek. Slickrock Creek Road, a single-lane gravel track, runs off US 129 to climb a tortuous path of 7.2 miles up to the parking area in the gap.

From the gap, FT 41 (Forest Service and other maps show this as Big Flat Trail, but the sign at the trailhead says Big Fat Trail) descends for 2.0 miles to the creek. The sign at the trailhead shows a rating of Most Difficult for this path. Another trail (FT 400; Windy Gap Trail) also begins at the parking area and carries a rating of More Difficult. Make sure you get on FT 41, for FT 400 descends to connect with FT 44 which will then meander back into FT 41. In other words, if you start out on the wrong trail, you will eventually get where you wanted to go, but the walk will be much longer. Entering the Slickrock Creek valley from this direction, the entire approach over roads and trails is in North Carolina.

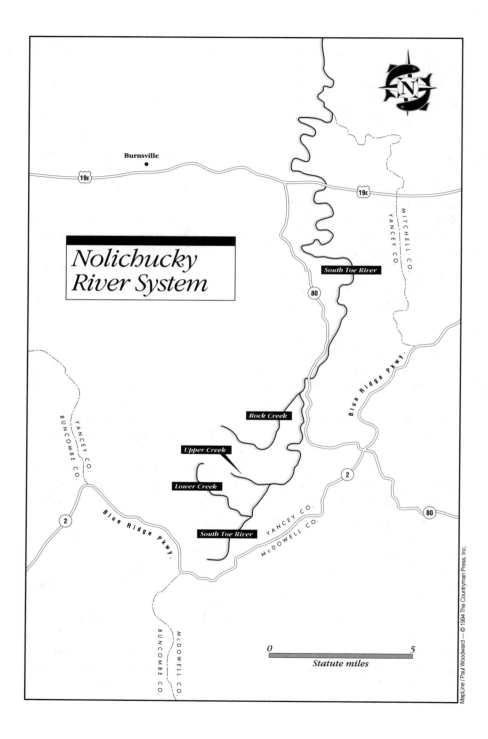

Nolichucky
River System

Burnsville

South Toe River

Rock Creek

Upper Creek

Lower Creek

South Toe River

Blue Ridge Pkwy.

MITCHELL CO.
YANCEY CO.

YANCEY CO.
BUNCOMBE CO.

YANCEY CO.
McDOWELL CO.

McDOWELL CO.
BUNCOMBE CO.

0   5
Statute miles

21

Nolichucky River System

The Nolichucky River forms in west-central North Carolina drain-ing the counties of Yancey, Mitchell, and Avery. The three main tribu-taries of the river are the North Toe, South Toe, and Cane rivers. When they have all joined to create the Nolichucky, it begins life as a large river, but it is also almost out of North Carolina. The junction of the North Toe and Cane on the Yancey-Mitchell county line, al-most directly north of Burnsville in Yancey County, marks the offi-cial beginning of the Nolichucky.

The main river contains no trout waters in North Carolina, and within a few miles crosses over into Unicoi County, Tennessee. The river is another of the Tarheel State's watersheds that looks much better on paper as trout water than in reality. According to the NCWRC fishing regulations, the Cane, South Toe, and North Toe rivers have a total of 26 wild- and stocked-trout streams in their drain-ages. When the number is reduced to those that have appreciable public access and are large enough to permit fly-fishing, however, the list plummets to only four.

Among the streams winnowed out are the main courses of the North Toe and Cane rivers. The Cane is the smaller of these two. As it drains the western half of Yancey County, it and all of its tributaries having trout habitat manage to meander all around the public lands of the Pisgah National Forest in the area. Unfortunately, none of them ever find their way onto Forest Service land. Thus, Elk Wallow, Bald Mountain, and Price are stocked streams in the watershed that do not provide adequate access to merit discussion. Lickskillet Creek also falls in this category, but it is classified as a wild-trout stream.

The watershed of the North Toe River covers portions of Avery,

Mitchell, and Yancey counties, but none of its trout-bearing feeders are located in Yancey. This river also manages to cover this long course without ever crossing any publicly owned lands in the national forest. Its stocked feeder streams that fail to meet the standard for coverage in Mitchell County are Cane, Grassy, and Big Rock creeks, plus the East Fork of Grassy Creek. In Avery County, Squirrel, Plumtree, and Roaring Fork fall in the same category.

The North Toe also has a number of wild-trout streams that are quite small or not publicly accessible. In Mitchell County they are Green, Little Rock, and Wiles creeks, while Avery County contains Cranberry, Horse, Cow Camp, Kentucky, and Jones creeks.

This leaves the South Toe River and its tributaries in southern Yancey County as the only truly public fly-fishing water in the Nolichucky system. The South Toe and four feeders make up this drainage, and only Middle Creek is so small that it is not a fly-fishing possibility. The South Toe River, Rock, Upper, and Lower creeks make up this fishery.

SOUTH TOE RIVER
USGS Montreat, Old Fort, Celo • DeLorme 32

The South Toe River draws water from a number of small rivulets coursing down the southeast face of Mount Mitchell, the tallest peak east of the Rocky Mountains. The mountain stands 6684 feet above sea level, which gives it an elevation differential of 3600 feet above the valley of the South Toe. On the other side of the valley, to the southeast, lies Lost Cove Ridge and Big Laurel Mountain. All of the South Toe's course is located in Yancey County.

From its twin wellheads of Pinnacle and Hemphill springs on Bald Knob Ridge, the South Toe becomes a fishable stream by the time it reaches FS 472. This gravel road then parallels the river for 5.5 miles to the northwest to the edge of the Pisgah Game Lands. Along this route the stream is a rocky, tumbling stream of small to medium size that is open enough to fly-fish.

The portion of the South Toe on game lands is open as a wild-trout stream. The exception to this is the one and a third miles of water from the concrete bridge above the Forest Service's Black Mountain Campground down to the edge of the game lands. This stretch is open under catch-and-release, fly-fishing-only regulations. Obviously, the trout through here run larger than in other sections of the river, and get less fishing pressure.

Below the game lands, down to the mouth of Clear Creek, there are over three miles of water on the South Toe open to fishing as a wild-trout stream. Once below Clear Creek, however, another 11 miles of the river is open to angling under hatchery-supported rules. This last stretch receives 16,000 stockers from March to August. Fortunately, the river is well posted with the diamond-shaped NCWRC signs indicating the various regulations.

Access to the lower stocked part of the South Toe is available off Halls Chapel Road (SR 1169), but there is a patchwork of private, posted tracts and right-of-way access along the roadside. Further upstream Celo Clinic Road and NC 80 both have stretches that provide access to the river. Through these parts of the river up to the game lands, the river is big water, offering plenty of room to cast a fly.

At the point that NC 80 bears away from the river to the east, FS 472 begins to follow the flow upstream. There are three Forest Service campgrounds on the South Toe in the game lands. Briar Bottom, Black Mountain, and Carolina Hemlock are all good locations to headquarter for a few days of exploring the stream. Also on the Forest Service land at streamside is the Lost Cove Picnic Area.

To get to the South Toe River, take NC 80 south off US 19E between the towns of Burnsville to the west and Spruce Pine on the east.

UPPER CREEK
USGS Old Fort • DeLorme 32

This very small stream is a tributary of the South Toe that flows off Mount Mitchell. Sandwiched between Buncombe Horse Range Ridge to the southwest and Grassy Knob Ridge to the northeast, Upper Creek is crystal clear as it tumbles along its rocky bed.

Open as a wild-trout stream, with catch-and-release, artificial-lure-only restrictions, this creek offers very little casting room. The majority of trout encountered are likely to be small rainbows in the area around the creek's mouth.

The only access to Upper Creek is via foot travel along a trail running upstream from the bridge on FS 472.

LOWER CREEK
USGS Old Fort • DeLorme 32

Lower Creek is a carbon copy of Upper Creek, as it runs down a parallel course to its sister stream. The two watersheds are divided by Grassy Knob Ridge.

The water, stream, and fishing conditions are just like those on Upper Creek, and both flows share the same fishing regulations.

Access is also by foot travel from the FS 472 bridge crossing of this creek.

ROCK CREEK
USGS Celo • DeLorme 32

The final feeder stream of the South Toe to be covered is Rock Creek. It is slightly larger than either Upper or Lower creeks, but still only qualifies as a small stream. It is, however, a bit more open than those tightly foliated creeks, as it slips down its tumbling, rock-strewn course.

Another wild-trout stream, Rock Creek is open under standard wild-stream regulations and is more accessible than the other South Toe tributaries.

To reach the creek take Colvert Creek Road to the west off NC 80 just north of the Carolina Hemlock Campground. Turn south (left) onto Aunt Julie Road (SR 1159). When this road makes a 90-degree turn to the east and crosses Rock Creek, FS 5521 will branch off to follow the creek upstream on the east side of the creek.

For almost 1.0 mile the gravel road will continue up the creek, with vacation cabins visible on the opposite shore. The stream, however, is on Forest Service land. At the end of the road, a trail affords further access to the stream.

22

Pigeon River System

The Pigeon River watershed is a bit unusual among North Carolina's major river systems in that it is fairly extensive, yet it is contained in and drains only one county. Rising in a number of forks and prongs in southern Haywood County, the Pigeon River is born near the crossroads of Woodrow at the junction of the East and West forks of the river. From there it continues to flow northward and through the town of Canton.

The main stream of the Pigeon River is a large flow, but is not recognized trout water. Several of its headwater tributaries do contain trout habitat. As the Pigeon runs further north it collects the waters of more than a half-dozen trout streams in upper Haywood County. Two of these are Big and Cataloochee creeks, which drain the extreme eastern edge of the Great Smoky Mountains National Park.

Eventually the Pigeon River crosses the state border into Tennessee near the village of Waterville. Through most of its course in the northern half of Haywood County, the river is followed by I-40, which is important in gaining access to several of the trout streams in the drainage.

There are only two trout streams in the Pigeon River system that the NCWRC designates as public trout water, but do not provide enough access to merit discussion. These are Jonathan Creek and its major tributary, Hemphill Creek. Jonathan Creek is a sizable flow and quite visible as it runs through the popular tourist area of Maggie Valley. It also receives large monthly stockings of trout that total 15,000 fish each year.

Unfortunately, so much of Jonathan's shore is on private tracts that the creek is difficult to reach. This same scenario holds true for Hemphill Creek, which lies to the north of Maggie Valley, with the only difference being that Hemphill is not as heavily stocked.

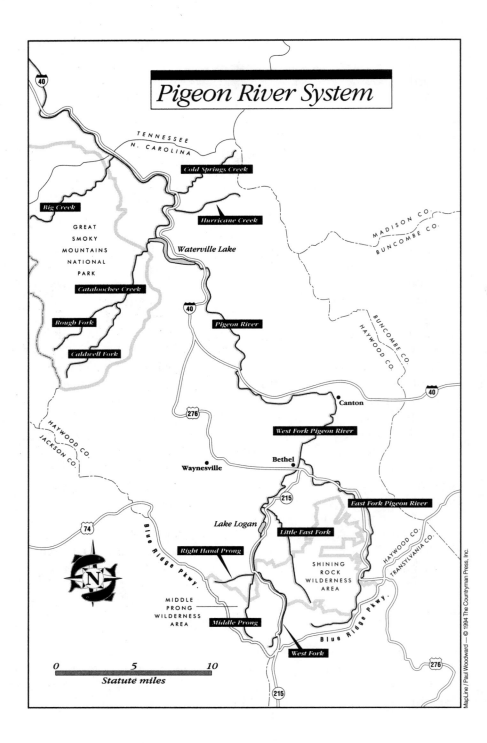

Pigeon River System

TENNESSEE
N. CAROLINA

Cold Springs Creek

Big Creek

Hurricane Creek

MADISON CO.

BUNCOMBE CO.

GREAT
SMOKY
MOUNTAINS
NATIONAL
PARK

Waterville Lake

Cataloochee Creek

Rough Fork

Pigeon River

BUNCOMBE CO.

HAYWOOD CO.

Caldwell Fork

Canton

276

HAYWOOD CO.

JACKSON CO.

West Fork Pigeon River

Bethel

Waynesville

215

74

East Fork Pigeon River

Lake Logan

Little East Fork

Right Hand Prong

Blue Ridge Pkwy.

SHINING
ROCK
WILDERNESS
AREA

HAYWOOD CO.

TRANSYLVANIA CO.

MIDDLE
PRONG
WILDERNESS
AREA

Middle Prong

West Fork

Blue Ridge Pkwy.

276

0   5   10

Statute miles

215

MapLine / Paul Woodward — © 1994 The Countryman Press, Inc.

The streams of the Pigeon River watershed will be covered starting with the branches of the stream's headwaters, then moving downstream toward Tennessee. The streams in the headwaters of the Pigeon that will be discussed are the East Fork, Little East Fork, West Fork, Middle Prong West Fork, and Right Hand Prong West Fork of the river.

In the northern half of Haywood County the streams that compose the Pigeon River trout fishery are Hurricane, Cold Springs, Cataloochee, and Big creeks.

EAST FORK PIGEON RIVER
USGS Shining Rock • DeLorme 52

The East Fork of the Pigeon River flows in an arc across southern Haywood County, with US 276 almost continuously at streamside. Along this course it is a large- to medium-size stream. Although portions of the water look quite tempting, the NCWRC lists none of this accessible portion of the river as public trout water. It is near the point where the highway turns eastward and leaves the stream that the public trout water begins.

From the edge of the Pisgah Game Lands upstream, the East Fork is a medium to small creek, but still offers almost six miles of public water. The part of the creek upstream of US 276 is in the Shining Rock Wilderness Area and the only access is by foot travel on the Big East Fork Trail (FT 357) that parallels the stream. The trailhead and parking lot are on US 276 at the bridge over the East Fork.

The East Fork is open to fishing according to standard wild-trout regulations. Small rainbow trout are most prevalent, but browns are also present.

To reach the East Fork, take US 276 to the southeast from the village of Bethel to the Big East Fork Recreation Area. The parking lot will be on the right side of the road at the bridge over the stream.

LITTLE EAST FORK PIGEON RIVER
USGS Sam Knob • DeLorme 52

Located to the west of the East Fork, this small stream offers a couple of miles of public water for fishing. It is also in the Shining Rock Wilderness Area, above the Boy Scouts' Camp Daniel Boone. The camp is located at the end of Little East Fork Road.

This stream has very tight casting conditions, as well as requiring approach by foot travel. For these reasons it is not a primary fly-casting destination. The Little East Fork is open under wild-trout rules, with small rainbows providing the bulk of the action.

Little East Fork Road runs east off NC 215 just north of Lake Logan. A parking area is provided beside Camp Daniel Boone at the trailhead of the Little East Fork Trail (FT 107), which follows the creek to near its headwaters.

WEST FORK PIGEON RIVER
USGS Sam Knob • DeLorme 52

The West Fork of the Pigeon is the only branch of the river that receives any stocked trout. It is a medium-size flow on the public property of the Pisgah Game Lands, as it descends from Tanesee Gap on the Blue Ridge Parkway.

Although the river is stocked all the way down to Lake Logan, the portion from the mouth of the Middle Prong downstream has too much private property to be of interest. The upper part of the river is all on public land and closely followed by NC 215.

Hatchery-supported fishing regulations apply, and the stream receives a total of 5050 trout from March to August. One oddity of the stocking is that only brown trout are released into the river above the High Arch Bridge.

The West Fork can be reached by taking NC 215 south from the village of Bethel, or north from the Blue Ridge Parkway at the Transylvania County line.

MIDDLE PRONG WEST FORK PIGEON RIVER
USGS Sam Knob • DeLorme 52

In the case of this stream, the name is almost as long as the creek itself. The Middle Prong is a small stream originating at Sweetwater Spring near Parker Knob just off the Blue Ridge Parkway. From there it flows north through the Middle Prong Wilderness Area, to join the West Fork at the Sunburst Recreation Area on NC 215.

The Middle Prong is another wild-trout stream, loaded with small rainbows, and offering some limited casting possibilities. Although the creek is five miles long, it becomes too small to fish only a mile or two upstream of the recreation area.

Access to the stream is via FS 97, which is a gravel track that follows the creek for 0.25 mile. It then becomes a trail offering only foot access. FS 97 is not presently marked with a sign, but is immediately adjacent to the Sunburst Picnic Area. There are plenty of sites for primitive camping along FS 97.

RIGHT HAND PRONG
WEST FORK PIGEON RIVER
USGS Sam Knob • DeLorme 52

As we discuss this river system, it seems that the names get longer— and the streams get smaller. The Right Hand Prong is quite small, and would not be worth mentioning, except for its location.

This creek flows west to east from Richland Balsam on the Blue Ridge Parkway down to join the Middle Prong just before that stream empties into the West Fork. The last hundred yards or so of the Right Hand Prong are in the primitive camping area along FS 97. In fact, the Forest Service road fords the creek.

Open to fishing as a wild-trout stream, it is worth checking out while exploring the other streams of the upper Pigeon drainage. Expect to find small rainbows hiding in the crystal-clear pools of the Right Hand Prong.

CATALOOCHEE CREEK
USGS Luftee Knob, Bunches Bald, Dellwood, Cove
Creek Gap • DeLorme 30, 52

Cataloochee Creek is one of the major watersheds of the extreme eastern end of the Great Smoky Mountains National Park in northern Haywood County. From its headwaters near Cataloochee Balsam, the creek's twin forks of Rough and Caldwell flow down to join and form the main stem of Cataloochee Creek. This junction of the forks takes place at the Park Service's Cataloochee Campground.

Cataloochee Creek's location off the beaten path in a relatively seldom-visited part of the national park leads to light fishing pressure. From the confluence of the two upper forks, the stream is medium to large in size until it leaves the park. Around the campground it is also rather broad and shallow, providing level, pastoral stretches. The fact that it is much less steeply inclined than most Great Smoky streams means it does not provide many deep areas of holding water.

For these reasons, some fly casters have reported only minimal success and interest in this stream. There are, however, a number of others who trek up the Rough Fork of Cataloochee and, if pressed, will admit to encountering excellent fishing for wild rainbows above the end of vehicle access. Here the descent of the stream is steeper and pocket water more common.

Standard Great Smoky Mountains Park fishing regulations apply on Cataloochee. Rainbows are the predominant fish in the stream, with some browns in the lower area as well.

There is also a stretch of one mile of Cataloochee that crosses Pisgah Game Lands after it leaves the national park. This part of the creek is big water, and quite remote. It is managed by the NCWRC as wild-trout water down to the point at which it empties into Waterville Lake. The only way to approach this part of the creek is over a foot trail from the east off White Oak Road on the south side of the lake.

Access to Cataloochee Creek, Rough Fork, and Caldwell Fork is via the paved approach road to the Cataloochee Campground. This road extends up the Rough Fork as far as the auto-access horse camp at Palmer Creek. An unpaved road then follows the stream for a short way, before giving way to the Rough Fork Trail. Caldwell Fork is paralleled upstream from the vicinity of the Cataloochee Campground by the Caldwell Fork Trail.

The main stem of Cataloochee Creek is accessible at the campground and further downstream along SR 1397, which is a gravel road running from the edge of the national park at Cove Creek Gap to the Tennessee state line at Davenport Gap on the Appalachian Trail.

HURRICANE CREEK
USGS Cove Creek Gap • DeLorme 30

Hurricane Creek lies in northern Haywood County and feeds directly into the Pigeon River from the east, just downstream of Waterville Lake. The creek is small, situated in rugged terrain, difficult to find and to reach.

Almost the entire course of the creek is located on Pisgah Game

Lands, with only a couple of blocks of private property along the shore. Of this distance, only about one mile allows any fly-fishing room, and the first half of this is above the stream's mouth and down in a steep gorge below the adjacent Forest Service road.

Although Hurricane Creek is open to angling under hatchery-supported regulations, it does not receive stockings every year. Undoubtedly, this has something to do with the difficult access that leads to light fishing pressure.

In fact, getting to this creek can be downright dangerous. It is paralleled by FS 233, a very rough dirt road. This dirt pig path is entered directly from I-40's northbound lane! The junction is located on a downhill slope of the interstate, and can easily be missed unless one is very alert. Of course, if you do not know where the turnoff is located and you are traveling slow to look for it, you may get run down from behind by an 18-wheeler. The turn onto FS 233 is located 6.0 miles north of Exit 15 on I-40 northbound.

COLD SPRINGS CREEK
USGS Cove Creek Gap • DeLorme 30

The next tributary of the Pigeon River that contains public trout water as one moves north down the drainage is Cold Springs Creek. It is very similar to Hurricane Creek in size and location. Emptying directly into the eastern side of the Pigeon, Cold Springs flows for three miles through Forest Service property.

Stocked with 3600 trout each year from March to July, this brook is subject to hatchery-supported regulations. Only about a mile of the creek upstream of I-40 offers any fly-fishing possibilities.

Again mirroring the Hurricane Creek situation, FS 148 which follows Cold Springs exits directly from the interstate highway. It is, however, a more easily seen and safer exit. The forest road is also in better shape than the one along Hurricane Creek.

BIG CREEK
USGS Luftee Knob, Waterville • DeLorme 30

This medium-size stream is the second major drainage on the eastern rim of the Great Smoky Mountains National Park. The creek forms along the old railroad grade in extreme western Haywood County near the Tennessee border. From there the creek flows to the northeast, exiting the park and feeding into the Pigeon River at the Waterville Power Substation.

Big Creek's streambed is filled with large boulders in the national park, interspersed with big, deep pools. The water in the creek is extremely clear even by Smoky Mountains' standards, indicating a lack of nutrients in the flow. This condition also makes stalking trout difficult on this stream.

Some anglers rate Big Creek as being only a fair trout-fishing destination when compared with other park waters. Of course, that is much like calling a college basketball team the worst one in the NCAA's Final Four championship tournament. Only championship-caliber teams get that far—just as Great Smoky Mountains streams are all extremely high-caliber trout habitat.

The trout in Big Creek are very similar to what is found in the lower reaches of Cataloochee Creek, which also drains this end of the national park. Small rainbows are most prevalent, but Big Creek is noted for holding more large brown trout than its sister flow. In the lower portion of Big Creek, brown trout are numerous as well as often being big.

Once Big Creek leaves the Great Smoky Mountains NP it crosses a short tract of private land. From there it flows for a half mile along Waterville Road through property owned by the Forest Service and by Carolina Light and Power Company. Most of this down to the Pigeon River at the Waterville powerhouse is open to fishing under NCWRC wild-trout rules.

Access to Big Creek in the national park is available off the approach road to the Big Creek Campground. This approach road runs west from SR 1397 at the edge of the park, south of Davenport Gap. Due to Big Creek's proximity to I-40, it gets heavier visitation than other streams on this end of the park.

23

Savannah River System

To anyone familiar with the geography of the southern Applachian region, finding the Savannah River system listed under North Carolina should come as quite a shock. While it is true that the Savannah and its feeder streams the Chattooga and Tugaloo rivers form the boundary between Georgia and South Carolina, only the extreme headwaters of the Chattooga reach into the Tarheel State.

Listing the Savannah in the section on North Carolina is more one of convenience than anything else. There are four streams located in the deep southwest area of the state in Macon, Jackson, and Transylvania counties that provide public trout waters, then cross the state line into either Georgia or South Carolina. These feed into the Chattooga or Keowee rivers. Rather than adding two very short chapters for these, the common denominator of the watersheds is that they eventually both empty into the waters of Lake Hartwell on the Savannah River.

For that reason, rather than providing a description of the complete river system, suffice it to say that Big Creek in Macon County, which feeds the Chattooga in Georgia; the Whitewater River on the Jackson-Transylvania county line; plus the Thompson and Horsepasture rivers in Transylvania County will be covered. These last three all run into South Carolina and the Keowee River.

The streams will be discussed beginning on the western end of this drainage and moving eastward.

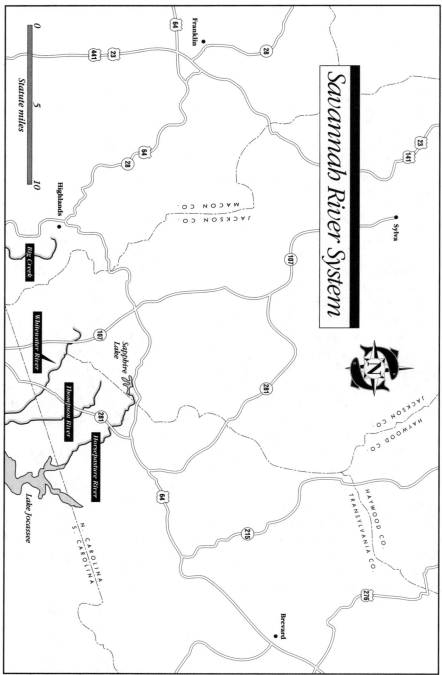

Savannah River System

Statute miles
0
5
10

Franklin

Sylva

Highlands

Big Creek

Whitewater River

Thompson River

Horsepasture River

Lake Jocassee

Sapphire Lake

N. CAROLINA
S. CAROLINA

JACKSON CO.
MACON CO.

JACKSON CO.
HAYWOOD CO.

HAYWOOD CO.
TRANSYLVANIA CO.

Brevard

MapLine / Paul Woodward — © 1994 The Countryman Press, Inc.

BIG CREEK
USGS Highlands • DeLorme 70

In spite of its name, Big Creek is only a small stream in North Carolina. It rises just to the southeast of the town of Highlands in the shadow of Rich Mountain, then flows directly south to plunge over Big Creek Falls and into Georgia.

Although the fishing conditions are tight, fly-casting is possible on the roughly two miles of stream that are on Forest Service land. The creek is stocked with adult trout and open to fishing under hatchery-supported rules from the base of the falls to the Georgia border. The land along the creek for the first mile below the falls is private, then the stream enters the federally owned woodlands. The downstream end of Forest Service property is at the second bridge over the creek below the falls.

Access to Big Creek is available off Walking Stick Road, which follows the creek from the falls to the end of public lands. Along this stretch the creek is rarely visible from the road, but is down in a little gorge off the western shoulder of the roadway. The upstream end of the public access area is 1.3 miles south of the junction of Walking Stick and Horse Cove roads. To find Big Creek, take Horse Cove Road east from Highlands and turn south onto Walking Stick Road.

WHITEWATER RIVER
USGS Cashiers • DeLorme 70

The most unique feature of this medium to large stream on the Jackson-Transylvania county border is that it has two of the tallest waterfalls in the eastern United States on its course. Lower Whitewater Falls is the smaller of these and is just across the border in South Carolina, but Upper Whitewater Falls is in North Carolina and drops over 400 feet.

Managed as a wild-trout stream in North Carolina, the Whitewater receives no stocked fish. The portion of the stream below the falls down to the South Carolina border, however, gets some migrations of fingerling rainbows and browns that move up from stockings in South Carolina. One look at the Upper Falls and it is obvious that none of these stockers get above the cascade. Most of the trout on the Tarheel State portion of the Whitewater are rainbows, with some browns. Standard wild-trout regulations apply to the fishing on this river.

From the South Carolina border up to the bridge at NC 281 the land along the river is owned by Duke Power Company and managed as the Toxaway Game Lands. On the other side of the highway the river is on Forest Service property managed as part of the Nantahala Game Lands. All of these, of course, are open to public use. The upper limit of the public access is just below the mouth of Silver Run Creek.

Both sections above and below NC 281 are rather remote, with footpaths providing the means of entry. A road runs off NC 281 just north of the state boundary that leads to the Overlook Trail for Upper Whitewater Falls. The Foothills Trail is intersected by the Overlook Trail. The Foothills Trail then drops almost straight down the gorge to the river below the cascade. It is a good entry point, but a killer to climb out. A better option is to enter here, fish down to the state line, then hike out at the Bad Creek Project in South Carolina (see the Whitewater River in section four).

Upstream of NC 281 the river has footpaths paralleling the stream bed. Both sections of the Whitewater are large enough to permit easy fly-casting.

THOMPSON RIVER
USGS Reid • DeLorme 70

The Thompson River is a small- to medium-size stream that begins just south of Bearpen Mountain in Transylvania County. From there it arcs to the southeast to pass under NC 281 and flow into South Carolina. Along this route it crosses a portion of Forest Service property in the Nantahala Game Lands to the north of the highway, while all of the stream in North Carolina that is south of NC 281 is on the Toxaway Game Lands.

The Thompson River is open under hatchery-supported fishing regulations in North Carolina, although no stockings have been done recently. South Carolina fisheries managers, however, do stock fingerling rainbow and brown trout in the river annually. These fish, of course, pay very little attention to state boundaries. The Thompson has been noted for years as primarily a brown trout stream.

In spite of this long course on public land, the Thompson is still one of the most remote and difficult-to-reach trout streams in ex-

Lower Whitewater Falls, across the border in South Carolina, provides a spectacular finish for the Whitewater River's course. The waters of Lake Jocassee back up virtually to the foot of the cascade.

treme southwestern North Carolina. Other than the crossing at NC 281, which has no parking area available, the only other practical way to reach the river is by the Foothills Trail. The best place to get on the trail is at the Bad Creek Project in South Carolina (see the Thompson River in section four). The hike from that point is more than three miles and moderately strenuous, but when you reach the river you will be in North Carolina.

The NC 281 crossing of the Thompson River is not easily recognized. The stream goes through a culvert and the river is not visible

A hike of several miles along the Foothills Trail is required to reach the Thompson River in North Carolina.

from the road, thus it is easily missed. The crossing is 1.9 miles west of the NC 281 bridge over the Horsepasture River.

HORSEPASTURE RIVER
USGS Reid • DeLorme 70

The most easterly of the Savannah River feeders in North Carolina that has public trout waters, the Horsepasture River originates in Jackson County and flows through Sapphire Lake and Sapphire Valley to enter Transylvania County. The river is recognized as public trout water below the Jackson County line, but the first real public access is below the NC 281 bridge where it first crosses some Nantahala Game Land property and then Duke Power's Toxaway Game Land holdings.

Along this course the stream is medium to large in size, offering plenty of room for casting. It is managed under hatchery-supported rules, but like the Thompson, has not been stocked recently. Expect to encounter both brown and rainbow trout on this stream.

The Horsepasture is almost as remote as the Thompson. There is some trail access around the NC 281 crossing, plus the Foothills Trail crosses the river down near its mouth. To reach the Horsepasture entails very long hikes of up to 10 miles from either direction on the Foothills. One other option is to come upstream on Lake Jocassee from South Carolina by boat, to reach the mouth of the Horsepasture, which lies in North Carolina.

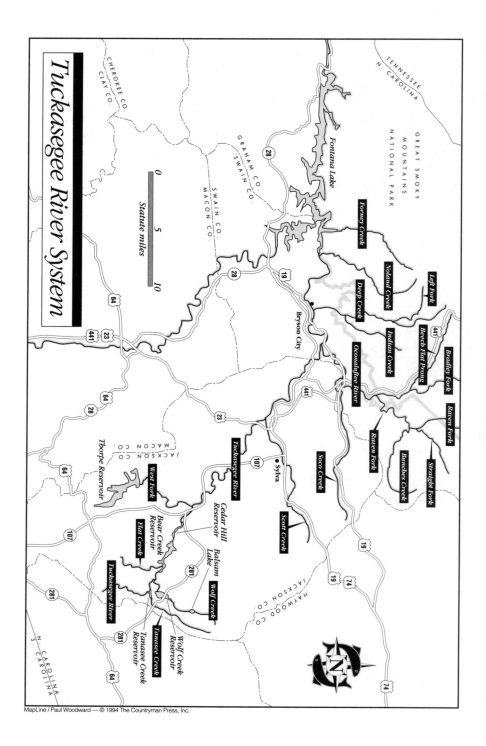

Tuckasegee River System

MapLine / Paul Woodward — © 1994 The Countryman Press, Inc.

24

Tuckasegee River System

The Tuckasegee River system is one of the most important to trout anglers of any of the watersheds in the Old North State. It contains a wide variety of streams, some of the best-known ones in southern Appalachia, as well as some very high-quality creeks that have largely avoided the spotlight.

The Tuckasegee rises on the northwest flank of Toxaway Mountain in the extreme southern tip of Jackson County. From there it courses north to be impounded in a string of lakes beginning with Tanasee Creek Reservoir, then Bear Creek Reservoir and Cedar Hill Reservoir. The part of the river below Tanasee Creek Reservoir is dry, with the river waters diverted through a pipeline to the power station at the head of Bear Creek Reservoir. In this headwater section, only one of the listed public trout streams does not fit the criteria for our discussion. Gage Creek is a wild-trout stream feeding into Wolf Creek, but it is very small and offers no casting room. At the foot of the last of the dams forming these lakes, the Tuckasegee finally appears as a free-flowing river.

From this beginning the Tuckasegee runs north through Jackson County, through a relatively lower-elevation portion of the watershed. Through here it picks up the waters of several streams recognized by the NCWRC as trout water. These stocked creeks, however, are primarily on private land. For that reason the stocked waters of Green's, Cullowhee, and Savannah creeks will not be discussed. Caney Fork Creek is in this same section, but is a wild-trout stream flowing almost exclusively on private property.

As the Tuckasegee flows past the town of Sylva it picks up the waters of the Scott Creek drainage from the northwest. Both Buff

Creek and the North Fork of Scott Creek are tiny tributaries in this watershed that are quite tiny flows not suited for fly-fishing.

Once north of Sylva the Tuckasegee turns to the west and enters Swain County heading for its junction with the Little Tennessee River in Fontana Lake. Along this westward course the river skirts the Bryson City–Great Smoky Mountains National Park area, picking up the flow of a number of trout streams from the vicinity. There is only one trout stream on this portion of the Tuckasegee's valley that does not qualify for coverage. Connelly Creek is a stocked stream, but so much of it is on private holdings that it is virtually off limits to most anglers.

One unique feature of the Tuckasegee system is the Qualla Cherokee Indian Reservation's Fish & Game Management Enterprise waters. The Eastern Band of Cherokee Indians manages the streams on their reservation as a business, complete with fishing permits, a fish hatchery, and regular stocking program. Located just south of the Great Smoky Mountains NP around the tourist town of Cherokee, parts of the Oconaluftee, Raven Fork, and Straight Fork rivers, as well as Soco and Bunches creeks, are on the reservation and open to fishing. These waters are stocked with 250,000 trout each year, including a number of trophy-size fish.

Open to anglers from the last Saturday in March to the last day in February each year, the reservation has a creel limit of 10 fish per angler and all trout caught must be kept. A special Enterprise Waters permit must be purchased to fish on the reservation, but a regular North Carolina fishing license is not required. Anglers under 12 years old can fish for free if accompanied by an adult with a permit. One-day, three-day, five-day, and season permits are sold at most stores on the reservation. Streams are stocked on either Tuesday or Wednesday each week, with the creeks receiving fish closed to angling on stocking days.

TUCKASEGEE RIVER
USGS Big Ridge, Reid, Sylva South • DeLorme 52

The main stream of the Tuckasegee River provides two distinct angling opportunities to fishermen. In its headwaters above Tanasee Creek Reservoir the stream is small in size, and open to fishing under wild-trout, catch-and-release, single-hook, artificial-lure-only regulations.

In this part of the river, small rainbows are most numerous with some browns as well. Upstream where the river is just forming from mountain brooks and springs, some brook trout can be found.

The problem with this part of the river—which lies on Nantahala Game Lands managed by the NCWRC, but not on Forest Service property—is the difficult access. Posted private lands bar entrance from NC 281 at the downstream end, while reaching it from the upper end requires hiking in from Cold Mountain on the Transylvania County border from the southeast. The trailheads near the end of Cold Mountain Road (Cole Mountain on some maps) above Lake Toxaway are not well marked and space to park off the road is limited. Cold Mountain Road runs west off NC 281 on the eastern side of Lake Toxaway in Transylvania County.

The better-known and more-accessible portion of the Tuckasegee River is found downstream of the junction of the river with its West Fork. From this point the river is big water with plenty of room to let out some fly line. Open to fishing under hatchery-supported rules, the Tuckasegee's main claim to fame along here is that it produced a North Carolina state-record brown trout. The 15-pound behemoth was tops in the state for a number of years before being bested. The river gets annual stockings of 12,000 trout released between the mouth of the West Fork and the bridge on Valley Road in the village of Wilmont, some 20 miles downstream.

Again, access is a bit of a problem on this part of the Tuckasegee. Much of the shoreline is in private hands, with some of it posted. The river is so big, however, that it is better suited to float-fishing anyway.

Possibilities for entering the water with a canoe or Belly Boat are found at the NC 281 bridge at the junction with the West Fork, the NC 107 bridge at the mouth of Caney Fork Creek, and at a number of spots along Wayehutta Road down to its junction with Old NC 107. Wayehutta Road runs along the northeast shore of the river and even offers access to several wadeable shoal areas.

Near the point at which Wayehutta Road bears off to follow the creek of that same name away from the Tuckasegee, a small dam blocks the waters of the river, but there is a portage path for detouring around it. On downstream, Old NC 107 runs at streamside, but offers very minimal access to the water.

Another portion of the river with some shoal access is located directly south of the town of Sylva on North River Road. To reach this road take NC 116 to the west off NC 107 north of the village of Cullowhee. At about 1.0 mile North River Road runs to the north to parallel the river for a couple of miles to Dillsboro.

Be aware that another small dam is located on the Tuckasegee at Dillsboro. This one lies near the junction of North River Road and US 441/23. It is a more difficult portage, demanding extra caution in approaching it. Below this dam, down to Wilmont, public access to the Tuckasegee is virtually nonexistent.

TANASEE CREEK
USGS Reid • DeLorme 52

This small stream runs along the western foot of Tanasee Ridge, which forms the boundary between Jackson and Transylvania counties. At its confluence with the Tuckasegee, the river is impounded in the Tanasee Creek Reservoir.

To the east of the creek, the stream's lower valley is lined with a spectacular row of stone cliffs on the side of Wolf Mountain. The first mile of the creek above the reservoir is followed by FS 4660 (Wolf Mountain Road). This gravel road provides good access to the creek up to the bridge at the junction with Tanasee Gap Road. Tanasee Creek is open to fishing as a wild-trout stream, with small rainbows being the most often hooked fish.

Above the bridge the road leaves the creek, which is beginning to get quite small at this point. Although FS 4660 eventually meets FS 4655 (Charley Creek Road), which crosses Tanasee in its headwaters, the creek is too small to be of interest that far up. The drive up to that point, however, affords the opportunity to see more Scotch pine Christmas trees than can be easily imagined. The mountains are covered with Christmas-tree farms.

Access is available to Tanasee Creek via Wolf Mountain Road, which runs north off NC 281 at the head of Tanasee Creek Reservoir.

WOLF CREEK
USGS Sam Knob • DeLorme 52

Wolf Creek is another of the small feeder streams of the Tuckasegee in southern Jackson County. Rising between Parker Knob and Gage Ridge the creek descends to the west of Wolf Mountain, which separates its valley from that of Tanasee Creek on the east.

Along its course, Wolf Creek passes through two man-made lakes. The first is Balsam Lake, which has the Forest Service's Balsam Lake Recreation Area located on its shores. Further downstream and just above the creek's mouth on the Tuckasegee is Wolf Creek Reservoir.

Access to the headwaters of the stream is available where FS 4655 (Charley Creek Road) crosses the stream. At this point the creek is quite small, but can be fished under extremely tight conditions for a little way upstream. Downstream the road is near streamside for 0.5 mile down to Balsam Lake. Below the lake the road leaves the stream. The only access to this part of Wolf Creek is on FS 4654 which runs east off Charley Creek Road. Although the maps show it as a road, it is not maintained, is overgrown, and suited for foot travel only. There is no upstream access from the head of Wolf Creek Reservoir.

Wild-trout-fishing regulations apply on Wolf Creek, with small rainbow trout making up the mainstay of the fishery. Since 4200 brook, rainbow, and brown trout are stocked in Balsam Lake, it is not unusual to find some of these have gotten into the portions of the creek both above and below the lake.

FLAT CREEK
USGS Big Ridge • DeLorme 52

This small stream feeds into the waters of Bear Creek Reservoir on the south shore, having flowed down through the Nantahala Game Lands of the Roy Taylor Forest. The creek is so small and remote that it is hardly worth mentioning in connection with fly-fishing. A couple of extenuating circumstances, however, have put it in the discussion.

Small, rocky, and bushy, Flat Creek is open to fishing as a catch-and-release, single-hook, artificial-lure-only stream. It is also home to a population of native southern Appalachian brook trout. Finally, it is one of the few such streams that it is possible to reach in a car.

Although maps of the area show that Rock Bridge Road runs west off NC 281 at the Tuckasegee River and dead-ends into a series of Forest Service trails, the road actually goes all the way to Flat Creek. It is a tortuous, rough, 4.0-mile road, but one that even most passenger cars are capable of handling.

The road ends at a primitive campsite and ford across the creek. The road beyond this point is no longer passable. From here, where the stream is extremely small, foot trails go both up- and downstream.

WEST FORK TUCKASEGEE RIVER
USGS Glennville • DeLorme 52

The West Fork of the Tuckasegee River is a medium-size flow from the dam at Thorpe Reservoir down to its mouth on the Tuckasegee. Through this area, the river is stocked with trout from the mouth of Shoal Creek down to the head of Little Lake Glennville. NC 107 follows the stream along this entire 3.0-mile route. The West Fork is planted with stockers through here, with standard North Carolina hatchery-supported regulations in effect. It is worth noting that Little Lake Glennville is stocked with trout as well, and produced the North Carolina state-record rainbow trout in 1989. Terry L. Gregory was the lucky angler who took the 16-pound, 5-ounce trout.

For the first two and a quarter miles downstream of Shoal Creek the river is down in a bit of a gorge, and there is very little parking space available along NC 107. The best bet to find a place to leave a car is at the mouth of Trout Creek, about halfway down the run. The final three-quarter mile of water above Little Glennville offers much easier access from the road.

SCOTT CREEK
USGS Hazelwood, Sylva North • DeLorme 52

Scott Creek differs very dramatically from the small wild-trout streams of the Tuckasegee's headwaters area. In fact, this medium-size stream is an urban/suburban fishery as it flows through both the outlying fringes and the very heart of the town of Sylva.

Scott Creek is stocked with 8000 trout from March through August, with the plantings taking place from the mouth of Jones Creek down to the junction with the Tuckasegee. Fishing is allowed under hatchery-supported rules. Although there is a good bit of private land along this stretch, there are also several places that afford appreciable public access. Several of these are at parks and bridge crossings in downtown Sylva.

Further out, three-quarters of a mile of Scott is at roadside off Skyline Drive to the north of town, with easy access. Above this section is another mile of water flowing through a steep gorge that is very rocky and scenic. Skyline Drive continues to run along one side of the creek, while the tracks of the Smoky Mountains Railroad run up the other. At the upper end of the gorge the creek is on private land.

One other point of public access can be found along Robinson Store Road and the rail line, just south of the road's junction with US 23/74 at the crossroads of Willits. This half-mile run is immediately downstream of the mouth of Jones Creek. The creek is quite small, but runs through a level valley with some parts open enough for limited casting.

OCONALUFTEE RIVER

USGS Clingmans Dome, Smokemont,
Whittier • DeLorme 29

The Oconaluftee River is a major tributary that drains the eastern end of the Great Smoky Mountains National Park. It is also one of the most-renowned trout fishing streams located in North Carolina. Part of that reputation lies in its being the most accessible and visible of the major streams in the national park.

The name Oconaluftee comes from the word in the Cherokee language that means "place by the river." This place by the river attracted the attention of early white settlers, with Dr. Joseph Dobson moving in to occupy 50 acres along the river in 1790. He was the first recorded settler in the vicinity of the Great Smokies.

Today the "Luftee," as some of its fans call it, still attracts visitors. These modern travelers generally come for the superb trout fishing available on the river and its tributaries. The river's main stream is formed deep in the Smoky Mountains where its Beech Flats and Kephart prongs join. From there it flows as a medium-size stream beside US 441 down to the edge of the national park. Parking areas are abundant along the highway and even in the portion where the river is down the hillside from the road, well-maintained walking trails make the water easy to reach. Of course, it is not as easy to get back to the road since some of these trails descend steeply.

The Luftee is open to angling under general park regulations, and is spacious enough to permit fly-fishing all along its length. There is even enough room for some casting on the Beech Flat Prong, which is at roadside above the junction that forms the river. Both rainbow and brown trout are present in the Oconaluftee, with some large browns of over 18 inches reported. On the other hand, rainbows are most numerous, while a brook trout would be a rare catch on the river.

The Park Service's Smokemont Campground is located on the river at the mouth of the Bradley Fork. The park's visitors center on US 441 is also located on the riverbank further downstream.

With the addition of the waters from the Bradley Fork and then the Raven Fork, just as the river leaves the Great Smoky Mountains NP, the stream becomes a big flow. It also crosses directly onto the Qualla Reservation to become Cherokee Enterprise waters.

The transformation of the river is not limited to size, for the fishing on the Oconaluftee changes drastically too. Although trout reproduce in the lower part of the stream on the reservation, the river also receives massive stockings of trout from the tribal hatchery on the Straight Fork. Many stockings include some fish that are already of trophy size, plus there are always holdovers in the river that grow large. The deep, slow part of the river just below the town of Cherokee is noted for producing these big trout, particularly browns.

Fishing on the reservation adheres to tribal regulations, with the Oconaluftee closed to fishing on Tuesdays each week when it is being stocked.

BRADLEY FORK

USGS Mount Guyot • DeLorme 29

The Bradley Fork is the largest of the Oconaluftee's tributaries that feed it in the Great Smoky Mountains NP. Formed from a number of brooks running down from Laurel Top on the Appalachian Trail to the east of the Oconaluftee, Bradley Fork eventually empties into that river at the Smokemont Campground. In fact, Bradley Fork flows through the middle of the campground, which is the most popular in the national park. At the point the two flows join they are about of equal size.

Fishing on the Bradley Fork is open under standard park regulations, with good numbers of rainbows present throughout the stream. Browns are more prevalent in the lower reach around Smokemont.

During the warm months, the stream will be crowded with tubers and waders around the campground, and fishing is only possible beginning at the waterfall at the upper end of the campsites. Probably because of the large number of campers (most are not anglers) the area just above the campground does not appear to get much fishing pressure and rainbows of 10 to 11 inches are fairly common.

Access to the upper reaches of the Bradley Fork is by foot travel on the Bradley Fork Trail. Due to the walk in, fishing pressure is light.

RAVEN FORK
USGS Smokemont • DeLorme 29

Moving downstream the next fishable tributary of the Oconaluftee is the Raven Fork. Almost the entire length of this stream is located on the Cherokee Reservation. Above the reservation, the Raven Fork is quite small and inaccessible in the national park. Open as Enterprise Waters on the reservation, the Raven Fork can be fished from the mouth of the Straight Fork downstream to where it empties into the Oconaluftee. A medium-size stream from the Straight Fork downstream, it has attained the size of a big flow by the time it reaches its mouth.

Raven Fork is stocked with trout from the tribal hatchery on Wednesdays. It is closed to fishing on stocking days. As on the Oconaluftee, the stockings are of massive proportions and include some already hefty trout. In fact, this river has produced the current North Carolina state records for both brook trout and brown trout. In 1980 George Marshall Jr. hooked and landed a brookie that tipped the scales at 7 pounds, 7 ounces. A decade later in 1990 Thomas H. Meeks III took a 15-pound, 13-ounce brown from these same waters.

About a quarter mile of the river is on national park lands just upstream of its mouth on the Oconaluftee. This part of the stream has stockers that have moved downstream, and has easy access off Big Cove Road just east of US 441.

STRAIGHT FORK
USGS Bunches Bald • DeLorme 52

This is a small- to medium-size stream that languishes virtually un-known near the Great Smoky Mountains National Park. For most folks, the only connection between trout and the Straight Fork is the fact that the Cherokee Indians have their tribal hatchery on the creek. The hatchery is situated just at the northeast edge of the reservation lands, and the short stretch of the Straight Fork downstream of it to the Raven Fork is closed to fishing.

For that reason, not many anglers venture above the hatchery and onto the national park lands. Here the stream is beginning to get small, but has some castable pools and runs. Small rainbows are the predominant fish in the creek.

Access to the Straight Fork on national park lands is available off Big Cove Road all the way up to the horse camp at Round Bottom.

BUNCHES CREEK
USGS Bunches Bald • DeLorme 52

This small stream is a feeder of the Raven Fork, with all of its fishable waters lying on the Cherokee Reservation. It joins the Raven Fork just downstream of the Straight Fork, entering from the east.

Bunches Creek Road is an extremely rough track running off Big Cove Road to parallel Bunches Creek. The stream is open to fishing as Enterprise Waters up to the second bridge on the road. Stocking takes place and the creek is closed to fishing on Wednesdays.

SOCO CREEK
USGS Sylva North, Whittier • DeLorme 29, 52

This is another small stream with fishable waters located entirely on the Cherokee Reservation. Soco Creek runs on an east-to-west course paralleling US 19 across the Indian lands to empty into the Oconaluftee just below Cherokee.

Although quite tight, some of the creek has open shoreline along US 19 that permits casting room. The fishing is regulated under Enterprise Water rules, with stockings taking place on Tuesdays. The stream is closed to fishing on those days.

Access is available at roadside to much of Soco from US 19 and Old Soco Road to the east of the town of Cherokee.

DEEP CREEK
USGS Clingmans Dome, Bryson City • DeLorme 29

Deep Creek is the next tributary of the Tuckasegee River downstream from the Oconaluftee River. Deep Creek originates high in the Smokies near Newfound Gap. It then tumbles down the mountains, picking up more volume from each feeder stream it passes. The two largest and most important of these are the Left Fork of Deep Creek and Indian Creek.

Finally, the stream runs through the Deep Creek Campground and out of the national park. There are a couple of miles of water below the park down to the Tuckasegee. This stretch is stocked by the NCWRC, but offers very minimal public access.

The portion of Deep Creek in the Great Smoky Mountains NP is now noted as one of the best brown trout streams in the Old North State. This has not, however, always been the case. The change from predominant rainbow trout water to a brown trout stream has taken the better part of two decades to occur. Today, large brown trout of up to 20 inches are found even far up into the headwaters on Deep Creek. Biologists now estimate the stream's trout population to be equally divided between the browns and rainbows.

Local anglers consider the best area for fishing on Deep Creek to be the portion about two and a half miles upstream from the park boundary beginning at an area called Bumgardner Bend, and continuing on up for about two miles to the Bryson Place. Long, slick pools are mixed with shoals and pocket water through the entire stretch.

Deep Creek is open to fishing under Great Smoky Mountains park regulations. The only drawback to fishing this stream is found on the first half mile or so upstream from the park boundary. During the spring and summer this part of the creek is full of tubers. There are even a couple of tube livery businesses located just outside the park along Deep Creek Road. Channels of rocks have been built in the stream to direct the flow for better floating. Obviously, this is an area to avoid. Fortunately, from the mouth of Indian Creek upstream tubes are not allowed.

On my first trip to Deep Creek one summer Friday morning, I found myself trekking up the trail along the creek with dozens of folks in bathing suits carrying inner tubes of all descriptions. Already the stream was so full of floaters that it was useless to attempt a cast.

Having continued walking up the creek to the first pool above Indian Creek, I finally began to fish. My second cast with a Royal Wulff provoked a vicious rise, which turned into a sizzling run upstream toward the head of the pool. After a couple of minutes of playing the fish I netted a beautiful 14-inch brown. Not bad for a first fish from a mountain stream, and I was still within sight of the floating masses as they embarked downstream!

Access to Deep Creek above the campground of the same name is via the Deep Creek Trail. This footpath stays on the stream almost to its headwaters, with the trail finally peeling off to meet US 441 below Newfound Gap. The Deep Creek Campground is located at the end of Deep Creek Road, which runs north out of the town of Bryson City.

LEFT FORK DEEP CREEK
USGS *Clingmans Dome* • *DeLorme 29*

This headwater tributary of Deep Creek lies west of the main stream, having its origins on the slope of Mount Collins. Although a small stream, its periodic tendency to flood has kept the creek channel open enough to permit fairly easy fly-casting.

As is the case on any of Deep Creek's feeders, rainbows will be more prevalent than on the main creek, but brown trout are present even here. Open under regular park fishing rules, angling pressure is light to nonexistent here. Part of the reason is the rugged nature of the area. It is so off the beaten path that the Cherokee Chief Tsali used it as a favorite hideout from the U.S. Army in the early nineteenth century.

Today the area is not much more civilized than it was in those days. Although the Fork Ridge Trail parallels the creek upstream from its mouth, it stays far up on the ridge to the northwest. To reach the Left Fork, follow the Deep Creek Trail up to the mouth of the creek. The mouth of the Left Fork is not clearly visible from the trail, so it is easy to miss unless you are alert. The hike is in excess of four miles.

INDIAN CREEK
USGS *Bryson City* • *DeLorme 29*

This small feeder stream of Deep Creek is located just at the head of the tubing water on the main stream. Although the fishing is tight, there is room to cast, especially below Indian Creek Falls, which lies just upstream of the mouth.

Indian Creek's reputation as a trout stream rests on its overabundance of wild rainbows. The stream is heavily populated by fish from 6 to 10 inches in length. Fishing is allowed under standard Smoky Mountains rules.

Access to Indian Creek is via Deep Creek Trail to the mouth of the creek. From that point a foot trail ascends Indian Creek.

NOLAND CREEK
USGS *Clingmans Dome, Noland Creek* • *DeLorme 29*

Located to the west of Deep Creek Valley and separated from that watershed by the Noland Divide, Noland Creek is a medium-size flow through much of this length. Descending from the heights of Clingmans Dome, Noland eventually empties into the Tuckasegee River arm of Fontana Lake.

Great Smoky Mountains NP fishing regulations apply to the creek, which is located entirely within the park. Rainbow trout are the predominant inhabitants of the stream, but fishing the lower stretches of the creek can turn up a few browns. The fly-fishing is noted to be at its best on this stream in the late summer months.

In spite of being on the north side of Fontana, road access is still available to Noland Creek. This is thanks to the Smoky Mountains' "road to nowhere." Originally planned as a road through the park on the north side of the lake, Fontana Road has never been a favorite of the Park Service, although local folks very much wanted it. The paved road got as far as Noland Creek where it dead-ends, hopefully never to get any further.

Although Noland gets relatively light fishing pressure, there are times when the parking spaces at the bridge over the creek are filled. This is because the parking lot is filled with vehicles pulling horse trailers. This is a very popular jump-off point for riders on the wilderness trails north of Fontana Lake.

Fontana Road runs north out of Bryson City, then turns west to parallel the north side of the Tuckasegee to Noland Creek. At the bridge over the creek, foot trails lead down to the stream.

FORNEY CREEK
USGS *Silers Bald, Noland Creek* • *DeLorme 29*

Dropping down from the southwest face of Clingmans Dome, Forney Creek has a more steeply graded valley than the other streams on the north side of Fontana Lake. It is also one of the lesser-known flows draining this part of the Great Smoky Mountains National Park.

Overshadowed by better-publicized creeks like Eagle or Hazel, and less accessible than Noland Creek, Forney nonetheless merits the effort to get to it. A medium-size flow, it has small pools, but the pocket water tends to be fairly deep. The steep, rocky bed of the creek makes it a bit more difficult to wade as well.

Smoky Mountains Park fishing regulations apply here, with most of the fish encountered being rainbows. There is, however, a good population of brown trout as well. The rainbows run a bit larger on average than the fish in Hazel, Eagle, or Noland. This is partially due to the light fishing pressure imposed by the remote location.

On one fishing trip to the north side of Fontana, outdoor writer, photographer, and fishing guide Bill Vanderford and I were trying to catch an above-average rainbow for some photographs. We had fished both Hazel and Eagle creeks, which yielded nothing over 10 inches to our efforts. Finally we made the run over to Forney Creek.

Fishing in the lead, I was drifting a Slate Green Caddis pattern through a deep but narrow run when it was taken with gusto. The rainbow quickly took to the air, revealing its length to be in the 14- to 15-inch range. I immediately began yelling for Bill to bring the camera, since I could see him about 50 yards downstream.

The fish made a strong run upstream along the far shore that resulted in having to fight it back across the current before bringing it to the side of the creek I was on. While this was going on, Vanderford had disappeared from the stream. Wanting the fish to be fresh for the photos, I played it into a calm eddy below me and, since it seemed to want to rest, I let it hold there while I again yelled for the errant cameraman.

Finally Bill appeared from the shoreline woods beside me, at which point I led the trout toward me and watched in horror as the hook pulled loose just inches short of the net. When I regained my powers of speech, I asked Bill why he had taken so long to negotiate the short distance, and especially why he had detoured off into the forest. He replied that his intended route directly up the shore had brought him face to face with a rather belligerent timber rattler that did not seem to want to give up its sunning rock at streamside. Yielding the field to the serpent, Bill had crashed into thick undergrowth that had snagged and tangled with every bit of fishing and photography gear he was carrying. All of this is, of course, just another way of saying Forney

Forney Creek offers the best backcountry fishing on the north side of Fontana Lake in the Great Smoky Mountains National Park.

Creek has some quality fish, as well as explaining why the big one got away as usual.

The most practical way to reach Forney Creek by land is on the several trails leading from the end of Fontana Road at Noland Creek over Tunnel Ridge to the mouth of the creek. These are rather strenuous and long for any but experienced and dedicated backpackers.

Even reaching Forney by boat across Fontana Lake can be difficult. One jump-off point is at the Tsali Campground and boat ramp on the Little Tennessee River arm of Fontana. Unfortunately, making the correct turn east to get into the Tuckasegee River from there can be tricky. There are a number of islands and long points at the intersection of the rivers that can lead to many wild-goose chases for the uninitiated.

Another, probably better option is the boat ramp at the end of Roundhill Road (SR 1313) at Evans Knob on the Tuckasegee arm of Fontana. This ramp lies to the east of Forney Creek. Regardless of which ramp you choose, it is a good idea to take a map of the lake in the boat with you.

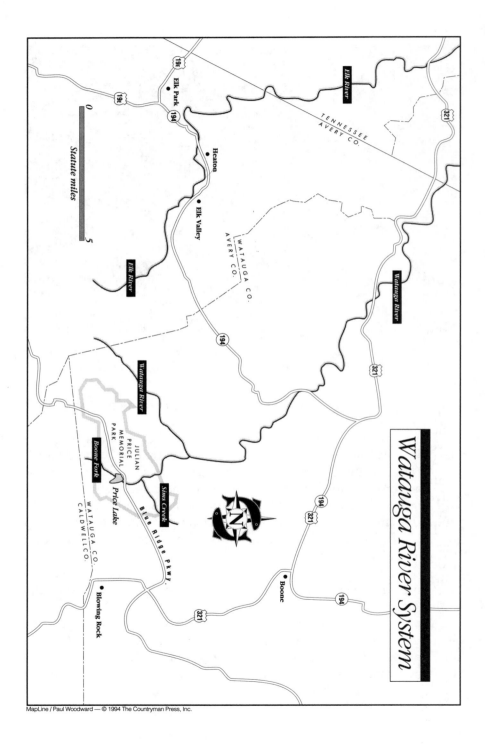

Watauga River System

25

Watauga River System

The Watauga River system is yet another of the watersheds in the northwest corner of the Old North State that is shared with Tennessee. Starting its course on Peak Mountain on the Avery-Watauga county line, the river flows to the northeast toward the town of Boone, then turns abruptly to the northwest at the village of Grandfather View. From there it runs along the western edge of Watauga County to cross into Johnson County, Tennessee.

Along this entire route the Watauga is trout habitat, with most of it designated as public water. A closer look at the river reveals that very little of it can actually be fished. Only a few points of right-of-way access are possible off US 321 in the northern part of the county. The US 321 bridge over the river, where it is a big flow, does offer several hundred yards of wide-open casting room.

All of the tributaries of the Watauga that are listed as public trout water are located in Watauga County, with the exception of the Elk River, which is in Avery County. Of these streams only the Elk and Boone Fork offer enough access to merit coverage.

The streams that are too small or predominantly on private land are Beech, Cove, Crab Orchard, and Laurel creeks, which are all stocked streams. Dutch Creek has both stocked and wild portions, but neither offers a true fly-fishing destination.

BOONE FORK
USGS Boone • DeLorme 13

From its wellhead just south of the Blue Ridge Parkway in southern Watauga County, the Boone Fork is quickly impounded in Price Lake

Below the US 321 bridge, the main stream of the Watauga River offers some wide-open waters that attract fly casters.

within the Julian Price Memorial Park on the parkway lands. Above the lake, both the Boone Fork and Cold Prong (which also enters the lake) hold trout but are too small to fly-fish. When it emerges from the spillway of the lake the Boone Fork is a small stream flowing through a pastoral cove in the park's picnic area.

Although quite bushy, it could be fly-fished under certain conditions. During warm months those conditions would consist of the park rangers running all of the wading and splashing children out of the creek. In this heavily used area, trout can still be seen in some of the pockets and pools when they have not been recently spooked.

The same description as above can also be applied to Sims Creek, which is a tiny feeder that enters Boone Fork among the picnic tables. It would ordinarily be too small to mention, except that its banks have been cleared through here, making it possible to approach it for fishing—assuming you hit the shore when no one is having a picnic there.

After Boone Fork leaves the picnic grounds, it picks up both volume and velocity. Fortunately, the velocity comes in spurts, as the stream drops through steep shoals into long deep pools. This stretch looks like excellent brown trout water—and it is! Almost exclusively populated with browns, the fly-fishing on this stream is legendary.

Browns of up to 20 inches have been taken from the stream. On the Blue Ridge Parkway lands, the Boone Fork is open to single-hook fly-fishing only, with catch-and-release rules in effect.

Below the picnic area there are about two miles of stream in the park, with most of it paralleled by the Boone Fork Loop Trail. The hike along this path is moderately strenuous, but it still provides rather easy access. Where the loop trail leaves the creek, it runs up tiny Bee Tree Creek to the west. This very small feeder is alive with trout in the 7- to 9-inch range. Be aware, however, that the creek is presently closed to all fishing due to research being conducted on it.

Once off the Julian Price Park, Boone Fork is managed by the NCWRC under the same set of fishing regulations for one mile down to the Watauga River. There is practically no public access below the park.

The Julian Price Memorial Park is located to the east of the intersection of US 321 and the Blue Ridge Parkway at Blowing Rock. The park is between mile markers 296 and 297 on the parkway.

ELK RIVER
USGS Elk Park • DeLorme 12, 13

The Elk River forms near the village of Norwood Hollow in eastern Avery County, then cuts through Banner Elk to eventually cross into Carter County, Tennessee. Once into the Volunteer State the Elk joins the Watauga River in forming Watauga Lake.

Along virtually all of its course through northern Avery County the river is on private land with only a few spots of public access along NC 194. This upper portion of the river gets a token stocking of 500 adult trout planted from March to July. The points of access are quite obvious due to the well-worn parking pull-offs along NC 194.

Once the Elk crosses under SR 1306 (Elk River Road) near the Tennessee border it is again stocked as a public trout stream. The first mile of water is paralleled by SR 1306, offering some access, but also a lot of private tracts. At the parking area for the Elk River Falls (shown as Big Falls on some maps) the river enters a parcel of Forest Service land that extends downstream to the state border.

The waterfall is only about 100 yards downstream from the parking area. Above the cascade the stream is only of medium size, flowing slow and clear. After plunging over the 80-foot waterfall into a big and deep pool, the river begins to speed up. The reason that I know the plunge pool at the bottom of the falls is deep comes from a rather dramatic proof of that fact.

On one visit I was working my way into a position to make a few casts into this huge pool. Just before I was ready to cast, a loud bellow came from the lip of the falls and I looked up to see a kamikaze swimmer leap from the cliff and come plunging down to the pool in front of me. After what seemed an eternity he popped back to the surface and swam to the foot of the pool to bask in the sun on the rocks. Needless to say this is not a recommended way to get to the pool, and it practically scared the waders off me!

This lower mile of the river down to the Tennessee line is stocked with 1500 trout from March to August. The entire length of the Elk River is open to fishing under hatchery-supported regulations.

To reach the upper Elk River, take NC 194 to the northeast from the village of Elk Park. Watch for the public access points between the villages of Heaton and Elk Valley.

For the lower Elk River, take Elk River Road to the northeast out of Elk Park. Follow the road until it dead-ends in the parking area at Elk River Falls. FS 190 continues down the river but is blocked by a locked gate. Streamside trails also follow the river down into the Forest Service land.

26

Yadkin River System

The Yadkin River has an extremely long drainage area when compared to other rivers in western North Carolina that have trout waters in their watershed. Rising on the Yadkin Game Lands in northern Caldwell County, the river flows south to the village of Happy Valley, then turns sharply back to the northeast. Crossing into Wilkes County the river passes through the W. Kerr Scott Reservoir and the town of Wilkesboro before leaving the county to become the north-south boundary between Surry and Yadkin counties. The river nears the Forsyth County border before it collects the waters of its most easterly trout-bearing tributary.

Like other rivers of the Appalachian foothill country of the west-central part of the state, the Yadkin has a number of feeder streams that are rather marginal as trout habitat. They are quite often found on private land as well, since these lower elevations are often still farmland. What sets the Yadkin's watershed apart, however, is the presence of Stone Mountain State Park and the Thurmond Chatham Game Lands in Wilkes County, as well as a portion of the Blue Ridge Parkway along the northern border of that county. These sections of public domain provide the Yadkin drainage with some truly public trout fishing.

The main stream of the Yadkin provides no trout fishing at any point along its course. On the other hand, feeder streams in five counties do contain trout. Three wild-trout streams are located in northern Caldwell County on the Yadkin Game Lands, but all of these are very small on the public property and offer no fly-casting room. These are Buffalo and Rockhouse (not to be confused with the stream of the same name located in Avery County) creeks, plus Joe Fork.

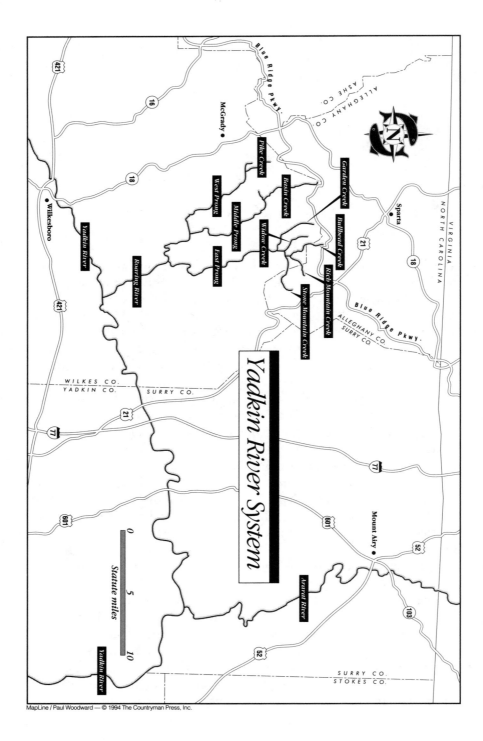

Yadkin River System

MapLine / Paul Woodward — © 1994 The Countryman Press, Inc.

Another very small wild-trout stream that rises in Alleghany County, but crosses into Surry County to eventually add its waters to the Yadkin, is Ramey Creek. Elk Creek also crosses a county line on its way to the Yadkin, but it is a stocked trout stream. This creek forms in Watauga County, but meets the river in Wilkes County.

Other stocked trout streams in the Wilkes County part of the Yadkin basin, virtually all found on private land, are the Middle Prong of the Roaring River; North Fork, Middle Fork, South Fork, and North Prong (also known as Darnell Creek) of the Reddies River; South Prong of Lewis Fork; Stony Fork; and Fall Creek. In Surry County, Little Pauls Creek, the Little Fisher River, Merritt Creek, and the Fisher River all also fit the same description.

Two other streams located in Wilkes County are recognized as wild-trout water and have their headwaters in Stone Mountain State Park. In the case of both, however, they are quite small on the public lands and have no easy access. These are Harris and Big Sandy creeks.

In spite of this long list of exclusions, the Yadkin basin still provides a number of quite varied trout fishing opportunities with public access. These will be discussed beginning at the headwaters of the Yadkin and moving downstream.

PIKE CREEK
USGS McGrady • DeLorme 14

A very small stream located in Wilkes County, Pike Creek offers only marginal room for fly-casting. On the other hand it is readily accessible on the Thurmond Chatham Game Lands, located in the northern portion of the county. The creek's waters eventually reach the Yadkin by way of the Roaring River and its West Prong.

With 6267 acres of land owned by Champion International and managed by the NCWRC, the Chatham Game Lands forms an unusually large tract of publicly accessed land for the foothills portion of the state. Its configuration is unusual as well. The game lands are situated to the north of Long Bottom Road, and divided into east and west sections separated by the Blue Ridge Parkway's Doughton Park.

Pike Creek begins beneath Flatrock Knob and flows three miles down to Long Bottom Road. It is quite bushy and tight, but can provide some casting possibilities. The stream is open under hatchery-supported rules and receives 900 adult trout from March to July.

Additionally, quarter-acre Pike Creek Pond is located on the flow and is stocked with another 150 trout between March and May.

To reach Pike Creek, take NC 18 north from the town of North Wilkesboro to the crossroads of McGrady. Turn east onto Long Bottom Road. At the point at which the road crosses Pike Creek, a dirt road will run north up the stream just before the bridge.

BASIN CREEK
USGS Whitehead • DeLorme 14

This small, tumbling stream is located west of Stone Mountain Park, and in the Doughton Park section of the Blue Ridge Parkway lands that split the Thurmond Chatham Game Lands. Rising near Wildcat Rock near the parkway, the stream is quite rocky, steep, and heavily foliated as it descends the park lands.

Open under the Blue Ridge Parkway special fishing regulations, Basin Creek and all of its tributaries can only be fished with single-hook, artificial flies and no fish may be harvested. For this reason, even though the stream is tight, it is worth exploring. Both rainbow and brown trout are present. Once out of Doughton Park, Basin Creek quickly empties into Cook Branch and the Middle Prong of the Roaring River.

The best access to the stream is found at the bridge on Long Bottom Road at the southern edge of Doughton Park. There is an area available for parking at the bridge. A foot trail follows the creek upstream from here. Basin Creek lies to the east of Pike Creek and can be reached by continuing east on Long Bottom Road from that stream.

EAST PRONG ROARING RIVER
USGS Glade Valley • DeLorme 14

The East Prong of the Roaring River is the major stream draining Stone Mountain State Park in northern Wilkes and southern Alleghany counties. Along the portion of the river that contains trout, it never gets any bigger than a medium-size flow.

The river is formed where Stone Mountain and Bullhead creeks join in the park, just west of the Wilkes-Alleghany county boundary. Below this point there are two and a half miles of river down to the edge of the state park. This stretch of water is open to fishing under North Carolina's delayed-harvest rules. Just over 8000 trout are released into the stream from March to August. The fish are almost equally divided between brook, brown, and rainbow trout, with the heaviest stocking taking place in March through May.

Particularly after the harvest period begins in June, the East Prong attracts heavy fishing pressure. During warm months it also is heavily used by waders, swimmers, and tubers.

Below the park, down to the bridge on SR 1943, the river is stocked with another 3500 trout consisting of the usual mixture of 40 percent each of brook and rainbow trout, plus 20 percent browns. This water, however, offers very little public access. The stockings here take place from March to September.

Access to the portion of the East Prong in Stone Mountain State Park is excellent. The John P. Frank Parkway (also listed as Stone Mountain Road on some maps) is a paved and gravel track that follows the stream through the park, offering plenty of streamside parking areas.

Stone Mountain State Park can be reached by traveling to the southeast on US 21 from the town of Sparta. After passing the Blue Ridge Parkway and the crossroads of Roaring Gap, turn west onto Stone Mountain Road, which will lead to the park.

STONE MOUNTAIN CREEK
USGS Glade Valley • DeLorme 15

This small stream is the major headwater of the East Prong of the Roaring River. From its wellhead in southern Alleghany County it crosses into Wilkes County, finally joining Bullhead Creek to form the East Prong.

Although a very small stream, some portions are open enough to offer very limited fly-casting opportunities. These are found along the roughly one mile of water from Bullhead Creek up to the Alleghany County line that is paralleled by Stone Mountain Road. Further upstream it is too small for fishing.

From Bullhead Creek to the Alleghany County line the creek adheres to the delayed-harvest rules found on the East Prong. Above that point it is open under wild-trout regulations.

BULLHEAD CREEK
USGS Glade Valley • DeLorme 14, 15

Bullhead Creek is open to fishing under a complicated set of rules that borrows an idea or two from "proper" English trout fishing. The most significant feature of this fishing is that the main stream and its tributary, Rich Mountain Creek, are divided into eight "beats." Only one angler is allowed on each beat, which is reserved on a first-come, first-served basis. The only exception to this rule is that two anglers on adjoining beats can agree to use them both, as long as no more than one person is on either beat at one time. This arrangement must, however, be cleared with the ranger on duty in advance.

Bullhead and Rich Mountain creeks are located entirely within Stone Mountain State Park, with both having their beginnings in southern Alleghany County below the Blue Ridge Parkway. They both cross over into Wilkes County before becoming big enough for fishing. After receiving the waters of Rich Mountain Creek, Bullhead meets Stone Mountain Creek to form the East Prong of the Roaring River.

All the trout in these creeks are wild, but they do receive supplemental feedings to improve their size. In April through September the feeding takes place on Monday, Wednesday, and Friday, while the scheduled feedings are on Monday and Friday in October to March.

A special fishing permit must be purchased to fish in the Bullhead drainage, at which time a beat will be assigned. The fishing rules on these streams are a bit more stringent than other places in the Old North State. All fishing is on a catch-and-release basis. Only fly rods are permitted, using single-hook, barbless flies. Each angler must have a landing net, and no creels or closed containers are allowed on the streams. All accidentally killed fish must be turned in to the rangers. Finally, the streams are open to fishing from 8:30 A.M. until 5:30 P.M. each day, except that they close at 4:00 P.M. on feeding days.

On Bullhead and Rich Mountain the fishing is outstanding. Trout in the 20-plus-inch category are usually seen, as well as often caught. The fishing is tight on these rocky, tumbling creeks, but for those up for a challenge and a change of pace they cannot be beat.

Stone Mountain Road crosses Bullhead at its mouth on the East Prong. A driveway leads upstream to the ranger station and parking area.

WIDOW CREEK
USGS Glade Valley • DeLorme 14

Another small feeder stream of the East Prong of the Roaring River in Stone Mountain State Park, Widow Creek is open to fishing under wild-trout regulations. Although a tiny flow, its rocky bed leaves room to cast for the first couple of hundred yards upstream of its mouth.

At the head of the fishable area is a popular sliding rock and Widow Creek Falls. Some interesting-looking pools are located through here, but they will be full of bathers and sliders in the spring and summer.

Access is at the parking area off Stone Mountain Road at the mouth of the creek. A footpath leads upstream to the falls.

GARDEN CREEK
USGS Glade Valley • DeLorme 14

Much like Widow Creek, this small brook is open to fishing under wild-trout regulations. It is located to the west of Widow Creek along Stone Mountain Road.

Garden Creek offers so little casting room that it is worth mentioning only as a change of pace to try when fishing the East Prong of the Roaring River in Stone Mountain State Park.

ARARAT RIVER
USGS Mount Airy North • DeLorme 16

There are a number of features that set the Ararat River apart from other trout streams in the Tarheel State. Only the Dan River in Stokes County is located further east than the Ararat, which is in Surry County, just at the Virginia border. It is also the last trout stream to join the Yadkin River, emptying into that flow near the Surry-Forsyth county line.

Located near the town of Mount Airy on which the fictional village of Mayberry was based in the old "Andy Griffith Show," so many local landmarks and businesses are named for characters in that sitcom it is surprising the river is not called Opie's Fishing Hole. The river is of medium size as it skirts the eastern edge of town.

Although the Ararat is a lowland flow, and rather marginal trout habitat, it is stocked and open to fishing as a delayed-harvest stream. A total of only 1650 trout are released into the river from March to June. All of the Ararat is open enough for fly-casting.

Access to the river is provided by a strange hodgepodge of holdings. The bridge on Linville Road (SR 1727) marks the upper limit of trout water, and provides one place to approach the stream. The end of trout water is at the Hamburg Street (SR 1759) bridge on the south edge of town. Between these, access is available where the river runs through Riverside Park in the town, or south of NC 103 at the abandoned landfill off City View Street (SR 1760). Although the site is gated, a trail runs down to the river.

About the only reason a fly caster would be interested in the Ararat River is that it can become tiresome trying to find Barney Fife, Goober, Gomer, and Floyd the barber in the town. At least the river provides a change of pace.

SECTION FOUR

SOUTH CAROLINA

Among the states covered in this book, South Carolina is, undoubtedly, the one least associated with cold-water trout fishing. The vast majority of the state is located in the Piedmont or Atlantic coastal plain, leaving only the northwest corner jutting into the Blue Ridge Mountains. As a result of this configuration, only Greenville, Oconee, and Pickens counties contain natural trout waters. In all, the Palmetto State has 34 cold-water streams that are managed by the South Carolina Wildlife and Marine Resources Division (WMRD) and listed in the brochure that department distributes. These creeks and rivers contain roughly 200 miles of water that support trout.

Unfortunately, some of these creeks flow on private property that is not open to the public, while others are so small they cannot be termed "fly-fishing water." The bulk of the water that is open to public access is located on Forest Service land in the Andrew Pickens Ranger District of the Sumter National Forest, lands owned by the Duke Power Company, state park, or preserve lands.

The public trout waters in the Blue Ridge portion of South Carolina are located in four river systems: the Chattooga, Chauga, Keowee, and Saluda.

In addition to the small creeks and rivers, there are two tailrace trout fisheries in South Carolina. One, the Savannah River below Lake Hartwell in Anderson County, has already been mentioned in the section on Georgia as not fitting the criteria for fly-fishing water. The other, below Lake Murray on the Saluda River in Lexington County, is located in the Piedmont region, far from the Blue Ridge Mountains and out of the coverage area of this book.

Finally, 7500-acre Lake Jocassee in Oconee and Pickens counties provides South Carolinians with a true trophy-trout fishery that produces browns and rainbows of 2 to 6 pounds regularly. Jocassee's fishery, however, is not suited to fly-casting and will not be covered in this discussion.

As in the other waters of southern Appalachia, South Carolina's original trout was the brookie. Since the state's cold-water streams lie on the fringe of trout habitat, human encroachment had already pushed the native fish into remote headwaters before the dawning of the twentieth century. Although the brookie continues to tenaciously struggle for survival in a few isolated locations, today no stream in South Carolina can be identified as a valid fly-fishing destination for native brook trout.

A few hatchery-reared brook trout are released into streams each year, but the state limits these introductions. The emphasis in brook trout management is placed on preserving the remaining wild populations. As a result, brookies are of marginal concern in describing South Carolina's fly-fishing opportunities for trout.

Although both rainbow and brown trout were introduced to South Carolina soon after 1900, it was the early 1950s before the state's WMRD began an extensive program of stocking creeks to provide more fishing opportunities to trout anglers. Today, more than 250,000 catchable-size and up to 100,000 fingerling trout are released into Palmetto State waters from February to October annually.

South Carolina streams are open to trout fishing year-round, with anglers required to have a valid state fishing license. No additional trout stamp or permit is required. In South Carolina, it is necessary to obtain permission from landowners before fishing on their property. A number of the trout streams in the state are located entirely, or partially, on private property.

The daily creel limit is 10 trout per day regardless of species. Portions of Matthews Creek, the Middle Saluda River, Estatoe Creek, and the Whitewater River are designated for fishing with artificial lures only and have a creel limit of seven fish per day. These special-regulation waters are marked with signs along the streams.

To obtain a copy of the "Hunting and Fishing Rules and Regulations" brochure produced annually and available in mid-June, write to the South Carolina Wildlife and Marine Resources Department, c/o Rules and Regulations Brochure, P.O. Box 167, Columbia, SC 29202. The booklet, "Brook, Rainbow & Brown Trout in South Carolina" is also available from the same address for a small fee. This publication includes location maps for all of South Carolina's trout streams on both public and private lands.

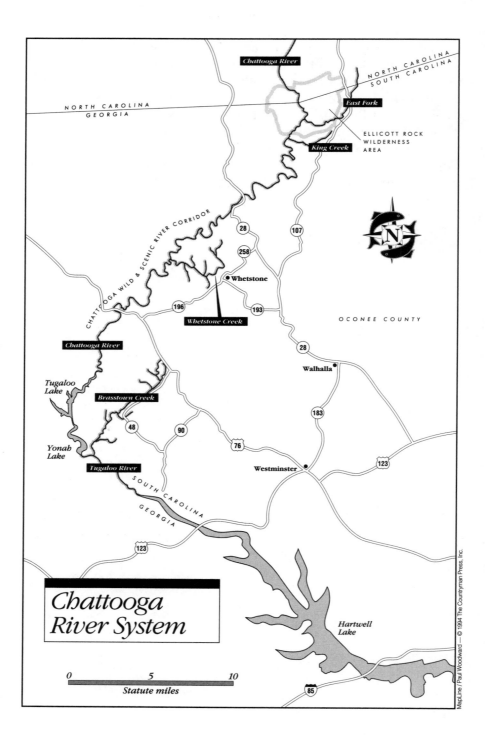

Chattooga River

North Carolina
South Carolina

North Carolina
Georgia

East Fork

Ellicott Rock
Wilderness
Area

King Creek

Chattooga Wild & Scenic River Corridor

28

107

258

Whetstone

196

193

Whetstone Creek

Oconee County

28

Chattooga River

Walhalla

Tugaloo
Lake

Brasstown Creek

183

48

90

76

Yonah
Lake

Tugaloo River

South Carolina
Georgia

Westminster

123

123

Hartwell
Lake

Chattooga
River System

0   5   10

Statute miles

85

MapLine / Paul Woodward — © 1994 The Countryman Press, Inc.

27

Chattooga River System

Undoubtedly the best known and most heavily fished of the South Carolina trout waters, the main stem of the Chattooga has already been covered in the portion of this book dealing with Georgia. Rather than repeating the description, a reminder of the regulations in effect on the river would seem more appropriate.

Anglers holding a license from either South Carolina or Georgia may fish the Chattooga from either shore along the entire length between the two states. In order to fish feeder streams entering from the northeast shore, however, a South Carolina license is necessary. To fish streams entering from the other side a Georgia license is needed. Of course, anyone venturing north of the point where the borders of Georgia, North Carolina, and South Carolina meet on the river must possess a North Carolina license.

South Carolina manages seven streams that feed into the Chattooga as trout streams. Of these, three—Ira Branch, Jacks, and Pigpen creeks—are so small and bushy that they do not constitute fly-fishing destinations. Jacks Creek empties into the East Fork of the Chattooga just downstream of the border with North Carolina, while the other two join the main stem of the Chattooga several miles north of the SC 28 bridge over the main river.

The remaining four creeks in the Chattooga drainage are Brasstown Creek, the East Fork of the Chattooga, King Creek, and Whetstone Creek. The descriptions of these streams start with the most northerly creek and continue down the Chattooga to the south.

235

EAST FORK CHATTOOGA RIVER
USGS Tamassee • SCWFA 95

The East Fork is the major tributary entering the Chattooga from South Carolina that contains trout. It rates as a medium-size creek that averages 25 feet in width along much of its course. The valley it descends is not particularly rugged and the creek sports some sizable pools. Although the fishing is tight in places, fly-casting is possible all the way from the mouth of the creek to the North Carolina border.

The Walhalla National Fish Hatchery and the Forest Service's Chattooga Picnic Area are located on the East Fork, roughly midway along the stream's course through Oconee County. The area around the hatchery gets moderate to heavy angling pressure in the spring through fall, so expect some competition for pools through here. The more remote two-and-a-half-mile stretch between the creek's mouth and the hatchery gets only light fishing pressure. It is, however, paralleled by Forest Service Trail (FT) 31 the entire distance, providing good access.

Upstream of the hatchery to the bridge on SC 107, FT 20, which is part of South Carolina's Foothills Trail, runs along the East Fork. The Foothills Trail does not go directly by the hatchery, but does cross the paved road leading into the Walhalla facility.

The stream gets some moderate to heavy fishing pressure where it runs under SC 107. Still, these deep, narrow pools produce scrappy browns. This area is particularly interesting in the fall when most anglers have put away their rods. Even into December it is possible to take fish on dry flies in these headwater runs.

Although both catchable-size and fingerling brown and rainbow trout are stocked in the East Fork, wild brown trout are also present. The keeper-size planted fish are usually stocked in the vicinity of the Walhalla Hatchery, with the rest of the stream getting predominantly fingerling browns. In the lower reaches of the creek near its mouth or the portion around SC 107, colorful browns in the 8- to 10-inch range most often answer the call of feathered offerings.

The only practical entry point for fishing the lower section of the East Fork is to hike in over the Chattooga River Trail along the main branch of the river from FS 708 at Burrells Ford. The trail is an easy hike of about 1.5 miles.

For the mid-portion of the East Fork, a paved road runs from SC 107 to the Walhalla Hatchery. A parking lot is provided and trails

Deep, calm pools like this one at the junction of the East Fork and main stem of the Chattooga offer excellent brown trout water.

access both up- and downstream stretches of the creek.

The Forest Service's Sloan Bridge Picnic Area is located on the East Fork at the SC 107 crossing and is a good jump-off point for fishing the upper end of the creek. There is about a mile of water between the crossing and the North Carolina border.

KING CREEK
USGS Tamassee • SCWFA 95

King Creek is a small tributary that enters the Chattooga River from the east roughly a quarter mile south of Burrells Ford and FS 708. The creek empties into the river through the Burrells Ford Campground in the Chattooga Wild and Scenic River corridor.

The only access to the stream mouth is by foot along the path that carries the Foothills, Bartram, and Chattooga River trails. King Creek is a small stream, heavily foliated, but open enough to allow fly-casting for at least three-quarter mile upstream to towering, 70-foot King Creek Falls.

When approaching the falls from downstream, anglers find themselves on the shores of a fairly large pool which is located in a virtual grotto. To get above the falls requires backtracking and climbing up the surrounding hills. The effort is hardly worth the trouble for the fly caster, since the creek is small and tight above the cascade. This upper part of the stream can be reached as well, however, by hiking downstream from the point at which the creek's headwaters run under FS 708.

The trout in King Creek are both browns and rainbows. Although there may be some natural reproduction, the bulk of the fish are stocked as fingerlings. There is no stocking of catchable-size trout in the stream. Since these fish are reared in the creek, they act much like wild trout, and generally average from 6 to 8 inches.

Access to Burrells Ford and the approach trail to King Creek is via FS 708 to the west off SC 107 in Oconee County.

WHETSTONE CREEK
USGS Whetstone • SCWFA 94

Whetstone Creek is a medium- to small-size stream that feeds into the Chattooga River in Oconee County between the SC 28 crossing to the north and the US 76 bridge to the south. The portion of the creek downstream from the intersections of FS 721 and FS 722 is on public land in the Sumter National Forest.

Whetstone averages roughly 15 feet in width in its lower sections and is stocked with fingerling brown trout. It is unlikely that any reproduction takes place in the stream since it appears to be only marginal trout water.

The lower section of the creek near the Chattooga is open enough for fly-casting and contains several sizable pools at the foot of waterfalls. Farther up near the edge of the public land the creek is still large enough for fishing, but is heavily foliated and very difficult to fly-fish.

The best access to the lower portion of the creek is found by taking Whetstone Road (paved) west from SC 196. At the point this road changes to gravel it becomes FS 721. Continue on FS 721 until FS 721-A is encountered, intersecting from the left. There is a sign at the intersection identifying FS 721-A. At the end of FS 721-A is a parking area and trailhead. Follow the trail to the Chattooga, then follow the river downstream to the mouth of Whetstone Creek. This is only about a 10- to 15-minute hike.

To reach the upper end of Whetstone on the Forest Service land, turn left off FS 721 just after the point where it turns to gravel. This road is FS 722 and crosses the creek only about 100 yards from the intersection. After crossing the creek, go right at the next two forks (the second one, on the right fork, has a sign: Dead End). Where the national forest boundary markers appear on the right, there is a trail leading to the creek.

BRASSTOWN CREEK
USGS *Tugaloo Lake* • *SCWFA 94*

Brasstown Creek is a medium to small stream that flows through southern Oconee County to empty eventually into the Tugaloo River, which is formed when the Chattooga and Tallulah rivers join in Tugaloo Lake. Most of the upper part of Brasstown parallels SC 48, but is on private land. The portion that is open to public use is at the end of FS 751, which runs west off SC 48.

Brasstown receives stockings of both fingerling and adult rainbow trout. It is a gentle-gradient, lowland creek that is strictly a put-and-take fishery. Brasstown receives heavy fishing pressure during the period when it is stocked.

Access to most of the creek is via a footpath, since FS 751 dead-ends soon after reaching the creek. Due to its marginal waters and heavy bait-fishing pressure, Brasstown is a poor choice as a primary fly-casting destination.

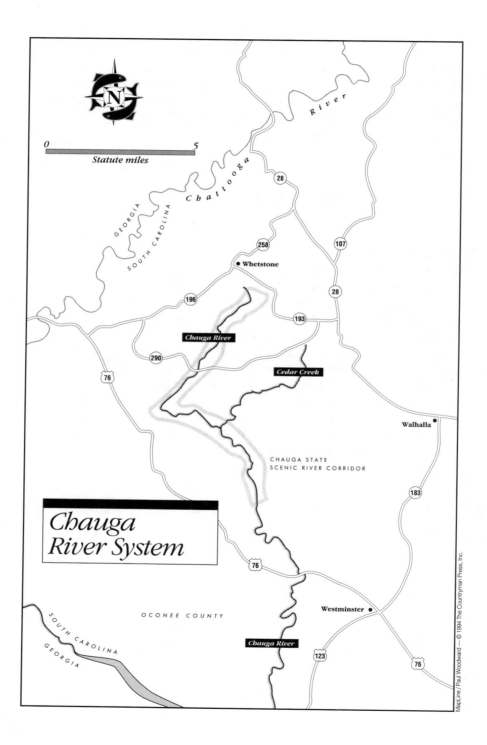

N

0   5
Statute miles

River

GEORGIA

SOUTH CAROLINA

Chattooga

28

258

107

• Whetstone

196

28

193

Chauga River

290

Cedar Creek

76

Walhalla •

CHAUGA STATE
SCENIC RIVER CORRIDOR

183

*Chauga
River System*

76

OCONEE COUNTY

SOUTH CAROLINA

GEORGIA

Chauga River

Westminster •

123

76

28

Chauga River System

The portion of the Chauga River system that contains trout is located entirely in Oconee County. The valley of the Chauga is just to the southeast of the Chattooga River and runs parallel to that waterway.

In all, South Carolina fisheries managers list five streams in the Chauga system as being trout waters. They are the Chauga River, plus Big Stakey, Bone Camp, Cedar, and Hellhole creeks. These last four are, of course, feeder streams of the Chauga.

All of the tributary streams are stocked with fingerling brown trout, with Bone Camp and Hellhole also receiving some fingerling rainbows. None of these feeder waters are stocked with catchable-size fish. They all rate as only poor fly-fishing destinations as well.

In the case of Big Stakey, it is very small and inaccessible by road in the portion on public land. Both Bone Camp and Hellhole creeks are quite small, heavily foliated, and difficult to reach. Cedar Creek is the largest of the feeders, but it is also difficult to reach, except in its extreme headwaters at the Cedar Creek Rifle Range. In the case of all these tributaries of the Chauga River, the habitat in the creeks is only marginal for trout, with no appreciable reproduction taking place.

For these reasons, the Chauga River is the only stream in the system that merits being discussed in relation to fly-fishing.

CHAUGA RIVER
USGS *Whetstone* • *SCWFA 94*

The Chauga River is formed by the joining of Village and East Village creeks in the central region of Oconee County. From that junction until it leaves the Sumter National Forest, the river is a large, often deep flow.

From a point just southwest of SC 28 all of the river's course to the edge of the national forest is through the Chauga River Scenic Area. This corridor is protected by the state of South Carolina due to the natural beauty of the river valley.

The actual trout water on the Chauga extends from its entry onto public land just upstream of Land Bridge Road to the north of SC 193, down to the river's junction with Cedar Creek. Roughly 10 miles of the river are in this fishable area. There is, however, one patch of private property on the northwest shore, just downstream of the SC 193 bridge. Even this stretch of water is accessible to anglers, since a footpath runs along the opposite (and publicly owned) shore.

As mentioned above, the Chauga is big water, averaging 40 feet in width, but often even wider. The key to taking trout on the Chauga is catching it when it is running relatively clear and at normal level. It is an often turbid stream, with water temperatures that are usually warm enough to keep it from being prime trout water.

The Chauga receives stockings of fingerling brown trout, as well as both adult browns and rainbows. There has been some indication in recent years that the browns may actually be reproducing in the river. At any rate, these European immigrants are the attraction that draws most fly-fishermen to the Chauga. Many of the browns are holdovers that have grown husky and added full colors to their sides while maturing in the river.

The Chauga provides plenty of room for casting, is wadeable in many areas, and is not particularly heavily fished. The exception to this last statement can be found at any of the road crossings of the river. After the stocking trucks have paid a visit, these pools are heavily fished by bait casters. If one ventures a few hundred yards up- or downstream though, there is plenty of solitude to be found on the Chauga.

The best access points to the Chauga's trout waters are at the bridges on SC 193, 196, and 290. The lower end of the Chauga can also be reached by hiking one of several trails that run from FS 748 (Spy Rock Road) to the river.

29

Keowee River System

The Keowee River is not a trout stream along its course in South Carolina. In fact, it is not even a river since its entire length in the state is swallowed by the depths of Lake Keowee. In addition, the Keowee's major tributary, the Toxaway, suffers the same fate as it is impounded in Lake Jocassee. Although Jocassee is a noted trout fishery that annually produces the bulk of the trophy-size trout taken in the Palmetto State, it is not a fishery that lends itself to fly-casting.

The streams feeding into Keowee and Jocassee provide the trout angling found in the Keowee system. In all, 13 of these streams are listed by South Carolina fisheries managers as being trout water. Unfortunately, less than half of these meet the criteria to make them true fly-casting destinations.

Oolenoy, Little Canebrake, Little Eastatoe, Reedy, and Rocky Bottom creeks are all tributaries of the Eastatoe River, which feeds into the eastern side of Lake Keowee. They are also almost totally located on private property, leaving very little public access. Additionally, Abner Creek feeds into Big Eastatoe, but is too small and bushy to offer any fly-fishing possibilities.

This leaves the Eastatoe River and Laurel Fork Creek as the only streams entering the Keowee system from Greenville County that merit description.

On the western side of Jocassee, the Thompson and Whitewater rivers, plus Howard and Corbin creeks, will be discussed. Limber Pole Creek, which is a feeder of Howard Creek, is quite small, although it is located on publicly accessible land. Still, due to its cramped size and close foliage, it does not merit description.

With the exception of the Eastatoe River, all of the streams to be

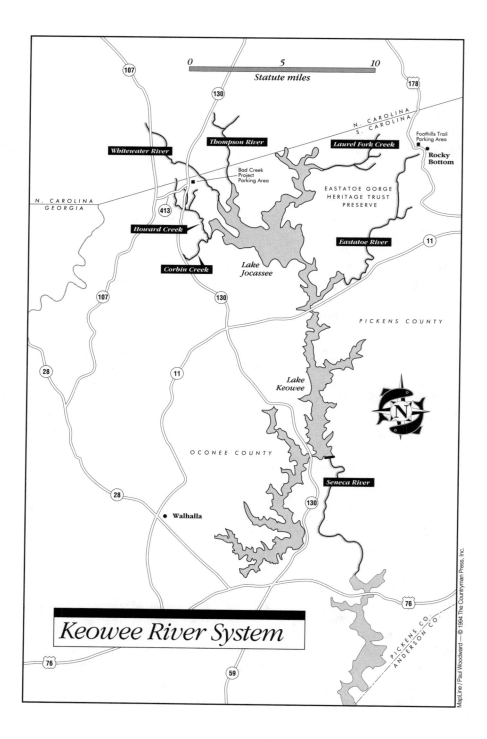

Keowee River System

described are located on lands owned and managed by Duke Power Company. These waters are made available to the public through cooperative agreements between Duke Power and the South Carolina WMRD.

In describing the individual streams, the ones on the east of Keowee basin are covered first traveling north to south, followed by the ones on the western shore in Oconee County.

LAUREL FORK CREEK
USGS Eastatoe Gap, Reid • SCWFA 102, 103

Laurel Fork is one of the more remote and inaccessible of South Carolina's trout streams. It flows westward from its headwaters on the slopes of Flatrock Mountain, located just to the west of US 178. The most distinctive landmarks on the creek are several cascading waterfalls of up to 60 feet. A couple of these are right at the mouth of the creek on Lake Jocassee and known as Laurel Fork Falls. Another falls is about half a mile upstream.

A small stream, averaging only about 10 to 12 feet wide at best, Laurel Fork receives stockings of both fingerling and catchable rainbow trout. There appears to be the possibility of some reproduction of wild fish in its upper reaches as well. Most of the stocking of catchable fish takes place near the mouth of the creek.

Above the upper falls the creek is very cramped for fly-casting, while the waters below the cascade begin to warm to the point that they are rather marginal trout water. For these reasons, most fly casters do not find the difficulty of reaching the creek to be matched by the rewards of fishing it. Laurel Fork is more a bonus to those hiking the Foothills Trail, rather than a reason to venture onto the trail.

Access to the creek is available by boat at the mouth of the stream on Lake Jocassee. The only other way into the creek is by hiking the Foothills Trail from US 178. The parking area for the trail can be reached by traveling 0.9 mile north of the village of Rocky Bottom on US 178 to the bridge over Little Canebrake Creek. Take a left onto the dirt road just past the bridge and drive to the parking area where the road is blocked. The Foothills Trail climbs the hillside opposite the parking lot.

The hike to Laurel Fork is about five miles and is moderately strenuous. Along the way some of the largest virgin hemlock trees (up to five feet in diameter) in the state are encountered. Once the trail reaches the creek they run parallel down to Lake Jocassee. Several wooden bridges cross the creek on the portion below the upper falls.

EASTATOE RIVER
USGS *Eastatoe Gap* • *SCWFA 103*

Also known as Big Eastatoe Creek or simply Eastatoe Creek, this stream is the premier trout water flowing into the east side of Lake Keowee. It is also one of a handful of South Carolina streams managed under special wild-trout regulations. Only artificial lures are allowed and the restricted creel limit on these waters is seven fish per day.

Formed by the junction of Little Canebrake and Rocky Bottom creeks, the Eastatoe flows southwest and is a relatively large stream, averaging about 30 feet in width. It is stocked with both fingerling and catchable-size trout, but also has a reproducing population of wild rainbows. The planted fish, both browns and rainbows, can be found in the lower end of the river near Keowee.

The lower reaches of the river are often turbid and even marginal as trout habitat. They are also almost exclusively in private hands and posted. It is the portion above the end of SC 92, which parallels the lower part of the river, that is of most interest to fly casters. For two and a half miles the river runs though Eastatoe Gorge, which is managed as part of the South Carolina Heritage Trust Program.

Although there is a barrier of private, posted land preventing access from the south, the Heritage Trust lands can be reached by hiking south from US 178. This hike of 2.1 miles is definitely worth the effort. Not only are the 375 acres of the gorge a wonderland of diverse plant life, but they are also home to wild stream-reared rainbow trout. These fish are quite colorful and aggressive, running from 6 to 9 inches in length. Overall, the stream is of medium size through the gorge, with some deep pools and plenty of room for casting.

The hike into the gorge is moderately strenuous and leads to a good primitive camping area at streamside. To reach the trailhead, follow the directions for Laurel Fork Creek to the parking area. Continue on foot down the barricaded road, following the signs for Eastatoe Gorge.

THOMPSON RIVER
USGS Reid • SCWFA 95

The Thompson River is a medium- to large-size stream that flows out of North Carolina and into the western arm of Lake Jocassee in the Palmetto State. Although the river is stocked with both brown and rainbow trout fingerlings, it has enjoyed a reputation mainly as a brown trout fishery.

Most descriptions of the Thompson also include mention of the silting problem that greatly impacted the trout habitat in the river. This silting was the result of highway construction that took place a couple of decades ago. Water clarity on the river is excellent today and visual evidence of the silting, at least on the lower portions of the river, is no longer obvious. Most sources now agree that trout fishing is improving in the Thompson River.

For the most part the river is open enough to fly-fish, as it tumbles down rocky shoals and through deep pools and runs. It is also an excellent place to enjoy some solitude in your fishing. Access is very difficult to the river in South Carolina and the resulting fishing pressure is quite low. The fact that the river is not stocked with catchable-size trout also contributes to this neglect.

The most practical access to the South Carolina portion of this waterway is via boat from Lake Jocassee. Due to the lack of boat ramps on the northern end of the lake, however, even boat access entails a long ride. The shortest route to the river by land requires a three-and-a-half-mile walk along the Foothills Trail from Duke Power's Bad Creek Project, just off SC 130 (also identified as SC 171 on some older maps). The hike is moderately strenuous, and upon reaching the river, you will find yourself in North Carolina, still needing to hike downstream to cross the state boundary.

To reach the Bad Creek Parking area, go 0.75 mile north on SC 130 from its junction with SC 413. The entrance to the complex is at a gate on the right side of the road. The gate is open 24 hours a day, but visitors must sign in and out. There is no limit on the length of time a vehicle can be left in the parking area, making it a good location to begin a weekend of backpacking to the Thompson.

WHITEWATER RIVER
USGS Reid • SCWFA 95

The Whitewater River is a fine wild-trout stream, as well as being one of the top tourist attractions in the mountains of South Carolina. Sightseers flock to the river to view the twin cascades of Upper and Lower Whitewater falls. Each of these drops over 400 feet, making them the tallest in the eastern United States. The Upper Falls is just north of the border between the Carolinas, with the Lower Falls being in South Carolina.

As might be expected due to the presence of the twin waterfalls, the Whitewater flows through the bottom of a precipitous gorge. Like the rest of the streams feeding into this side of Lake Jocassee, the Whitewater River's valley is a wilderness setting with very limited access.

A fairly large stream averaging about 35 feet in width, the Whitewater is stocked only with fingerling rainbow and brown trout. Rainbows are the most plentiful species, with the average fish being in the 8- to 10-inch range. The river is also managed under wild-trout fishing regulations requiring artificial lures and a creel limit of seven fish per day. All along its course in South Carolina there is plenty of room for fly-casting.

Access to the river valley can be gained at the foot of Lower Whitewater Falls by boat from Lake Jocassee, or by foot from Duke Power's Bad Creek Project. Directions to the Bad Creek Parking area are the same as for the Thompson River. From the parking lot it is half a mile by trail to a footbridge over the Whitewater.

There is a primitive camping area at the trail's intersection with the river, as well as an information board with a map of the area's trails. One of these trails leads 1.9 miles to the overlook for the Lower Falls. Be aware that this is not an access point to the river since the platform is very high up on a steep mountainside. Approaching from the lake is the only practical way to fish below the falls.

Above the campground there is one mile of river upstream to the North Carolina border. This border is marked on the trail by a wooden sign noting the end of the portion of the Foothills Trail maintained by Duke Power Company. There are also South Carolina Wildlife Management Area signs on the north face of the trees. There is, however, no marker on the river itself so anglers need to be careful about crossing the line unless they have fishing licenses for both states.

Access to the river below the campground down to the Lower Falls is over fishermen's paths along the shore. As with any waterfall, close approach to the cascade should be avoided. The constantly damp rocks in that vicinity can send a careless angler to an untimely death.

HOWARD CREEK
USGS Tamassee • SCWFA 95

The final feeder stream to Lake Jocassee covered is Howard Creek, along with its two tributaries, Corbin and Limber Pole creeks. Only fingerling rainbow trout are stocked in Howard and Corbin creeks, while Limber Pole receives rainbow and brown fingerlings.

All three of these creeks are small (averaging 8 to 17 feet in width), extremely inaccessible, and offer quite limited fly-casting opportunities. The lower stretch of Howard just before entering the lake is the most promising for the fly-fisherman.

Although the headwaters of both Howard and Limber Pole flow under SC 130, they are mere trickles at this point and there are no trails leading down them toward the lake. Access to all three creeks is best attained by boat from the mouth of Howard Creek on Jocassee.

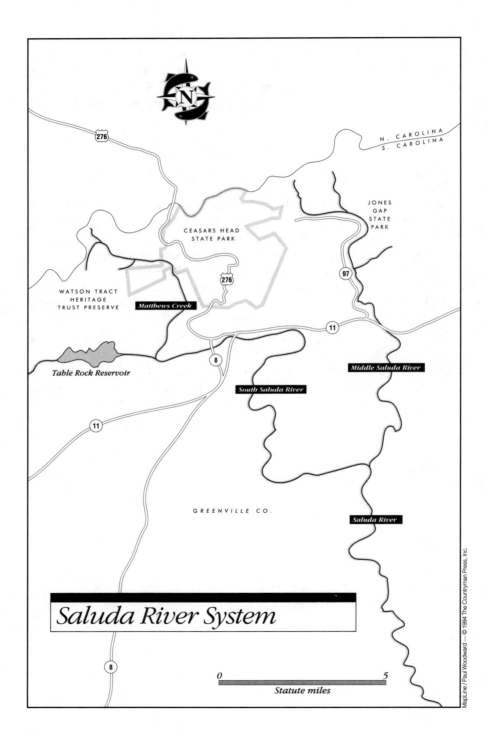

Saluda River System

30

Saluda River System

The most easterly of the river systems in South Carolina that support trout is the Saluda River. The tailrace of the Saluda River below Lake Murray in Lexington County has attracted most of the trout fishing attention on this river system in recent years, but this water is far from the Appalachian highlands and out of the scope of this discussion.

The headwaters of the river along the border with North Carolina are the streams that make up the heart of the Saluda fishery in the mountains. A total of seven Saluda feeder streams are recognized as trout water, with six of these located in Greenville County.

The seventh stream, Crane Creek, is a bit of an oddity. Only marginal trout water, small, and too bushy for fly-casting, it is stocked with brown trout fingerlings. What makes it unusual, however, is its position in Oconee County, far to the west of the other streams. Rising in the same area along SC 107 as tributaries of the Chattooga, Chauga, and Keowee rivers, this stream manages to meander far to the southeast to empty into the Saluda.

Of the remaining streams, the North Saluda River, Gap, and Oil Camp creeks do not merit coverage due to their positions almost entirely on private property. Only a few bridge crossings offer access to each of these.

The remaining three streams that constitute the publicly accessible part of this fishery are Matthews Creek, the Middle Saluda, and the South Saluda rivers. These will be covered by beginning in the west and moving eastward.

MATTHEWS CREEK
USGS Table Rock • SCWFA 60

Matthews Creek rises to the west of US 276 and Caesars Head State Park. This creek flows down a steep, rugged, and isolated valley to empty eventually into the South Saluda River. Although tight, it has some stretches on which fly-casting is possible.

A small stream averaging no more than 15 feet in width throughout its course, it still merits mention due to the quality of the fishing it provides. Managed under wild-trout regulations, only artificial lures are legal on the creek and the creel limit is seven trout per day.

Some stocking of catchable and fingerling trout is done in the lower portions of the creek where it is on private land, but the bulk of the water contains a wild reproducing population of rainbow trout. Also, in its upper reaches around the towering and majestic Raven Cliff Falls, native brook trout occasionally are reported to have been caught.

The areas of the creek open to public fishing are in Caesars Head State Park, and further upstream at Raven Cliff Falls on the Watson Tract of South Carolina Heritage Trust lands.

In spite of the quality of the fishing and excellent scenery on Matthews Creek, fishing pressure is extremely light. This condition is due to the extreme difficulty of getting to the creek.

Access from Ragsdale Road off Table Rock Road (SC 90) at the mouth of the creek is not practical due to private posted lands. The best bet to reach the creek is via a trail off US 276 that approaches the creek from the east. The trailhead is 1.2 miles north of the US 276 junction with SC 8 and strikes the creek near the state park lands. The hike ordinarily takes up to 1½ hours to cover and is strenuous.

One other option for approach to the upper portion of the creek is over the Raven Cliff Falls Trail. The head of this trail is located 1.1 miles north of the entrance to Caesars Head State Park on US 276. The trail is strenuous and runs two miles to an overlook platform for viewing the falls. Unfortunately for anglers, the end of the trail is still far up a gorge wall from the creek. A couple of old logging roads run off the trail to the west before the platform is reached and offer opportunities for the adventurous fisherman to find a way down to the creek.

The Middle Fork of the Saluda River is one of South Carolina's lesser-known trout streams. The section in Jones Gap State Park is excellent fishing water.

SOUTH SALUDA RIVER
USGS Table Rock, Cleveland • SCWFA 60

Although recognized as trout water from its source in Table Rock Reservoir down to just below Blythe Shoals, the public fishery on this river is more restricted. Much of its length along SC 11 and Table Rock Road is on posted private property, leaving only a few short stretches of water open to the public. Due to the river's size (up to 50 feet wide), however, the portion that is open represents enough water to be noted.

The South Saluda is a put-and-take fishery that receives plantings of both browns and rainbows in catchable sizes. Basically a flow composed of slow sections broken occasionally by shoal water, there is plenty of room for fly-casting all along the stream. The portions that are accessible to public fishing are heavily used by bait-fishermen during the spring and summer, but lightly fished the rest of the year.

The best points of access for the South Saluda are around the SC 11 bridge or the SC 8 crossing further upstream.

The grounds of the old Cleveland Fish Hatchery are now a historic site within Jones Gap State Park on the Middle Saluda River. This hatchery pool now contains a number of trout in the 3- to 6-pound range. Sorry, no fishing allowed!

MIDDLE SALUDA RIVER
USGS Standing Stone Mountain • SCWFA 60

The Middle Saluda can lay claim to the title of crown jewel of the Saluda River trout waters. The river is stocked with both fingerling and mature rainbow and brown trout, but also contains wild stream-bred rainbows. Angling is limited to artificial lures and is subject to the restricted creel limit of seven fish per day.

The lower reaches of the Middle Saluda are all on private property, with public access beginning at the edge of Jones Gap State Park. From that point upstream the river is in the Mountain Bridge Wilderness Recreation Area which spans the 5.3-mile distance from Jones Gap up to Caesars Head State Park. The Jones Gap Trail parallels the stream offering access through the wilderness area. Primitive campsites are also located along this trail.

The river, which is as much as 40 feet wide below the park, narrows to only a medium-size stream on the public land. No stocking takes place above the park and wild rainbows make up most of the trout populations. Some large browns show up which have moved upstream from stockings further south on private lands. Fish of up to four and a half pounds have been taken in the park.

The river is a tumbling, rocky stream that has plenty of pocket water interspersed with deeper pools. Fishing pressure can become moderate in the park, but lessens as one moves further upstream into the Mountain Bridge area.

One unique aspect of Jones Gap State Park is the site of the James Harvey Cleveland Fish Hatchery. The hatchery was the first in South Carolina, operating from 1931 to 1963, and is now a historic site. One of the hatchery ponds is now stocked with an impressive array of trout in the 3- to 6-pound range. Unfortunately, these fish are for viewing only—no fishing allowed.

To reach the waters of the Middle Saluda River in Jones Gap State Park take River Falls Road (SC 97) north off SC 11. A parking area is located at the end of the road in the state park.

SECTION FIVE

TENNESSEE

The state of Tennessee has a widespread and extremely varied trout fishery. A total of 51 counties, or half of all those found in the state, provide some type of cold-water fishery that supports trout. These waters range from huge reservoirs to big tailwater rivers, and include seasonal limestone creeks and marginal put-and-take fisheries. There are also tumbling, freestone creeks that are natural trout waters, as well as tiny headwater rivulets that have contained native brook trout for eons.

A great deal of the man-made or marginal trout water in the Volunteer State, however, is located to the west of the Appalachian Mountains on the Cumberland Plateau, along the Highland Rim or feeding into the Buffalo River. On the extreme western edge of trout water in Stewart, Houston, Humphreys, Perry, and Wayne counties, the region is more closely associated with the Mississippi River basin than with southern Appalachia. None of these streams originally contained trout, but were stocked when they were discovered to be cold enough to support the species for at least part of the year.

The only area of Tennessee that provides true mountain trout habitat consists of the 10 counties along the rough eastern border of the state. These counties are east of an imaginary line from Chattanooga northward to Lenoir City, then to the northeast to Johnson City and finally to Bristol at the Virginia border. There can be no argument as to whether this area is part of southern Appalachia. Towering peaks of up to 6000 feet dot the region, while clear, cold, natural trout streams cascade through the coves, hollows, and valleys. The 625,000-acre Cherokee National Forest and 500,000-acre Great Smoky Mountains National Park contain virtually all the public trout fishing waters of the Tennessee Appalachians.

One area that is excluded from this book that might draw some arguments in favor of being part of southern Appalachia is the Big South Fork National River and Recreation Area. This 105,000-acre tract of wilderness on the Tennessee and Kentucky border, between Oneida, Tennessee, and Whitley City, Kentucky, does support some naturally reproducing trout populations and is open to the public. On the other hand, by the time the Cumberland Plateau (on which much of it is situated) has gotten that far south in Kentucky and so far west in Tennessee, it has lost virtually all of its Appalachian Mountain topography.

Since streams in Kentucky that are immediately north of this area are covered, it is admittedly a rather arbitrary line that divides the Big South Fork from the covered areas. A stronger argument could probably be made, however, for having covered fewer of the Kentucky streams, rather than including the Big South Fork.

Other noticeable omissions from the list of covered streams are the tailwaters on the Clinch and South Holston rivers. These might especially raise eyebrows since the Hiwassee and Watauga tailwaters are covered. The reason behind this difference in treatment is that the Hiwassee and Watauga tailwaters both occur just at the edge of the Appalachian Mountains, extending on into the valley to the west. On the other hand, both the Clinch and South Holston, while excellent trout waters, originate at dams in the area between the Appalachians and the Cumberland Plateau.

While the native southern Appalachian brook trout continues to exist in the streams of Tennessee, as is the case in other southern states, it no longer is the primary species. Rainbow trout, first introduced as early as 1880, were stocked in most of the suitable waters of east Tennessee's major watersheds between 1895 and 1910. They now dominate the bulk of those waters. Brown trout were also planted beginning in the 1890s and continue to be present in many streams. The Volunteer State is home to populations of both lake trout and Ohrid (pronounced Oak-rid, these fish are native to Lake Ohrid in the area previously known as Yugoslavia) trout as well. Both of these exotic species have been stocked in Tennessee reservoirs, but do not play a part in the stream fisheries.

Presently, state and federal hatcheries release up to one million mature rainbow trout and half a million fingerlings in the state's waters each year. Approximately another 150,000 catchable-size brown trout are stocked along with 50,000 fingerlings. These plantings take place from mid-March into July annually, with additional stockings of the fingerlings in the fall.

In total, Tennessee boasts 1230 miles of trout creeks and rivers, plus another 245 miles of streams in the Tennessee portion of the Great Smoky Mountains NP. Of these, 230 miles of water are located on the Cumberland Plateau or farther west, out of the scope of this discussion. Only 420 miles of the state-managed waters and all of the Great Smoky streams are composed of primary trout water where the fish can naturally reproduce. Of the state-managed water, 175 miles have sufficient reproduction to maintain the fishery with no supplemental stocking.

Native brook trout have been identified as the dominant species in 52 creeks of the Cherokee NF, totaling 60 stream-miles of the unstocked waters, while rainbows inhabit 95 miles. The remaining 25 miles are home to mainly brown trout. One hundred and twenty miles in the Great Smoky Mountains NP are pure brook trout water, with rainbows dominating in the bulk of the others.

The most disheartening part of these statistics is that a recent study of brook trout found that within the last 12 to 15 years the range of these native fish has contracted by 60 percent in the Cherokee NF streams. Virtually all of the creeks holding brookies today are found at elevations of greater than 2800 feet.

As a result of this mix of stream types and populations, the Tennessee Wildlife Resources Agency (TWRA) uses a three-tier management plan for the state's trout waters. Streams with adequate natural reproduction receive no stocked trout, are open year-round to fishing, and are limited to the use of single-hook, artificial lures. The creel limits and minimum size limits on these streams vary and will be covered in the sections discussing the individual creeks.

The second tier of management is on the streams where reproduction cannot meet the fishing pressure. These creeks receive two to three stockings of catchable trout each year, plus plantings of fingerlings in the fall. They are subject to the statewide creel limit of seven trout, with no minimum size on browns or rainbows. Brook trout have a statewide 6-inch minimum size limit. Both natural and artificial baits are allowed in these waters.

Finally, in streams where the fishing pressure is excessive, weekly stockings of catchable trout take place, and in some cases, special daily permits are required to help offset the cost of these management techniques. While most of these waters adhere to the general state seasons, creel limits, and minimum sizes, some exceptions do exist. These will be covered in the individual stream descriptions.

In the Great Smoky Mountains NP, brook trout can only be taken on a strict catch-and-release basis. Indeed, a large number of park streams where brookies predominate are closed to fishing (signs are posted along these creeks). The creel limit on browns and rainbows in the park is five trout in any combination and fish must be seven inches long. All angling in the park is limited to single-hook, artificial lures or flies.

To fish for trout in Tennessee a valid regular or junior fishing license plus a trout license is required of residents, 13 to 64. Holders of Lifetime Senior Citizen or Sportsman licenses do not need a trout license. Nonresidents aged 13 to 15 years old must possess a junior fishing license, while all other nonresidents must purchase an All Fish license in order to fish for trout. Additional daily permits are required for anyone fishing the Tellico-Citico Trout Area or the Gatlinburg Trout streams.

No special licenses are needed for fishing on the streams of the Great Smoky Mountains NP. In fact, either a Tennessee or a North Carolina license is valid on these waters regardless of which state the stream is located in.

To obtain a copy of the current "Tennessee Fishing Regulations" booklet or the brochure "Trout Fishing in Tennessee," write to the Tennessee Wildlife Resources Agency, Central Office, P.O. Box 40747, Nashville, TN 37204 or call (615) 781-6500.

31

French Broad River System

The French Broad River rises in Transylvania County, North Carolina, eventually crossing into Cocke County, Tennessee, east of the town of Newport. By the time it reaches the Volunteer State, the French Broad is already a large, warm-water flow. Although it does support trout in its headwaters, they are located many miles to the southeast on the North Carolina and South Carolina border. The importance of the French Broad to the Tennessee trouter is not found in the main river, but in the streams that feed into it.

The feeder streams of the French Broad make up a very significant portion of the public trout waters of northeast Tennessee. Among these are the streams flowing out of the portion of the Great Smoky Mountains NP found to the northeast of Gatlinburg, plus Paint Creek, one of the most popular general trout regulation creeks in the state. Two additional streams that are tributaries of the French Broad, but will not be discussed, are Gulf Fork and Brush Creek. In the case of the former, with the exception of bridge crossings, it is entirely on private property. Although Brush Creek flows down the slopes of Meadow Creek Mountain for a mile and a half on national forest lands and is stocked with catchable-size trout, it is very small and so heavily canopied that it is not a fly-casting destination.

After coursing through Douglas Lake to the north of the Smokies and collecting the waters of its trout-holding tributaries, the French Broad joins the Holston River in the suburbs of Knoxville to form the Tennessee River. This review of the French Broad's feeder streams begins at the point at which the river crosses into Tennessee and proceeds downstream.

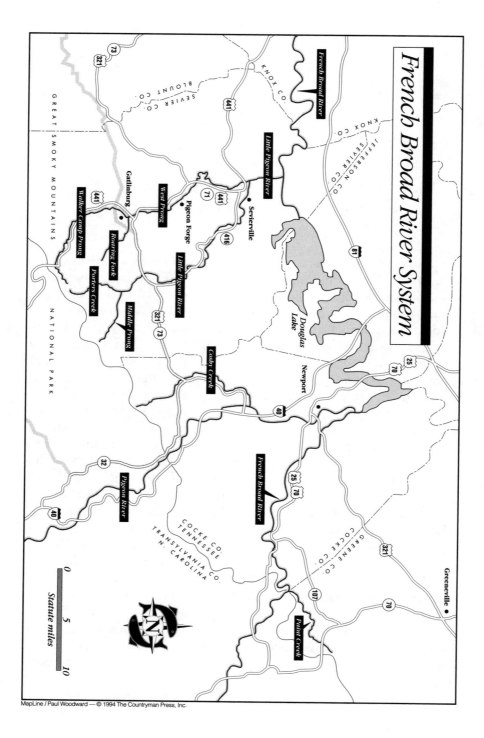

French Broad River System

Statute miles
0   5   10

MapLine / Paul Woodward — © 1994 The Countryman Press, Inc.

PAINT CREEK

USGS Hot Springs, Paint Rock • DeLorme 29

Rising on Green Mountain in the Nolichucky Ranger District of the Cherokee NF in Greene County, Paint Creek flows to the southwest into the French Broad at the Cocke County line. As mentioned above, Paint Creek is one of the most popular east Tennessee trout fisheries. In many families, trips to Paint Creek are second- and even third-generation traditions.

As a result of this popularity, the creek receives heavy fishing pressure throughout the spring and summer months. To support this pressure, the creek is stocked weekly from March through July with stocker rainbows of 8 to 12 inches. Although the water temperatures get marginal for trout in the summer, there appears to be some carryover of fish from season to season, particularly of the brown trout that are also present. It also seems likely that any natural reproduction in the lower portion of the creek is minimal.

Unfortunately for the fly-fisherman, another facet of the tradition on Paint Creek is a heavy emphasis on bait-fishing for the planted fish. Many pools will be staked out by the bait-fishermen, making them unfishable for fly casters.

From its headwaters down to TN 70, Paint Creek is a small stream that alternates in flowing through Forest Service and private lands. For the fly caster, the creek only becomes of interest after it crosses TN 70.

Downstream of TN 70 the creek remains small for a couple of miles to the point at which it passes through the Forest Service's Paint Creek Campground. Along this portion of the creek the only access is via foot travel on FT 10 that parallels the creek from the campground up to TN 70.

Below Paint Creek Campground the creek is of medium size. It is closely paralleled by Paint Creek Road (FS 41) for 5.3 miles, with only a 0.5-mile stretch that lies on private property. The private land is well marked and easily identified. There are a couple of pools designated as swimming holes on the creek. The most popular is at Dudley Falls near the midpoint of the creek. Here the creek tumbles over a sizable waterfall into a large plunge pool. Between the pools such as the one below the falls, Paint Creek also has a good deal of riffle and pocket water.

To locate Paint Creek, travel 13.0 miles south from Greenville on

TN 70. At TN 107 turn west and proceed to the intersection with FS 31. A left turn onto this gravel road will lead to the Paint Creek Campground.

COSBY CREEK
USGS Hartford • DeLorme 45

Cosby Creek is the first of the streams covered that flows through the Great Smoky Mountains NP. Located in the extreme northeast corner of the park in Cocke County, Cosby is a small and rather overlooked stream. Due to its size and location it avoids much of the crowding and fishing pressure experienced on other popular park streams.

Saying Cosby Creek is lightly fished by park standards means that it gets very little pressure even in the peak of vacation seasons. There are so many similar-size streams in the park that offer good fishing (many of which are not as far off the beaten path) that most anglers never get around to trying Cosby Creek.

Bounded by Inadu Knob on the west and Mount Cammerer on the east, the valley of Cosby Creek is quite scenic with the stream's rocky course running down from Cosby Knob beneath hemlocks and through rhododendron thickets. The foliage is open enough, however, to allow for limited fly-casting in the lower stretch of the creek up to the Cosby Campground.

As mentioned earlier, Cosby is a small flow that features mostly rainbow trout in the 6- to 8-inch range. There are, however, fish of 9 to 10 inches and possibly larger in the creek. From the standpoint of the fly caster the creek is of interest only up to the Low Gap Trail crossing, about two and a half miles upstream from the edge of the park. Above that point the stream is brook trout water and closed to angling, as are all of Cosby's feeder streams.

The TWRA stocks the portion of Cosby Creek downstream of the national park, all the way to the creek's mouth on the Pigeon River. The Pigeon, in turn, feeds into the French Broad River at Douglas Lake. Virtually all of the downstream waters on Cosby Creek, however, are located on private land and not available for public fishing.

Access to Cosby Creek in the national park is easy via Cosby Campground Road which parallels the stream as the paved road runs south off TN 32 at the village of Cosby. This road, obviously, leads to the

Cosby Campground, which is one of the park's lesser-used developed camping areas due to its location off the Gatlinburg-to-Cherokee corridor. The campground contains over 200 campsites.

LITTLE PIGEON RIVER
USGS Mount LeConte • DeLorme 45

The Little Pigeon River is a big flow by southeastern trout-water standards, often spanning 70 to 80 feet in its lower section in the Great Smoky Mountains NP. Flowing through an area known as Greenbrier Cove in the northwest part of the park, the river courses between Mount LeConte to the west and Greenbrier Pinnacle to the east.

The river valley was partially logged at the turn of the century and now features a mixture of second-growth and virgin stands of timber. It also retains much of its natural flavor due to the Park Service's decision to limit development in this part of the Smokies.

The Little Pigeon does suffer from something of an identity crisis, however. Although park maps show the Middle Prong of the Little Pigeon as being upstream of the junction with Porters Creek, the whole river is sometimes referred to as the Middle Prong. To add to the confusion the older name of Greenbrier Creek is also used locally. For purposes of description we will use the Park Service maps as references, calling the lower portion the Little Pigeon and the portion above the junction the Middle Prong.

The Little Pigeon is stocked with trout by the state for several miles downstream from the national park lands, but these miles provide very limited public access. Above the park boundary the river is big water all the way up to the junction of the Middle Prong and Porters Creek.

Rainbow trout are the most common species in the Little Pigeon, but browns have moved up from stockings below the park as well. The average trout will be only 6 to 8 inches, but the water is big enough to accommodate much larger fish. There is plenty of room for casting on the river, with the only interference likely to come from the tubers, waders, sunbathers, and swimmers in the lower stretches. This can be a problem all the way up the main river.

Another aspect of fishing the Little Pigeon is the presence of a large number of huge boulders. This is a good stream for combining some trout fishing with rock climbing. Wading upstream will often put one in a position of detouring out of the water or climbing over rocks that range from the size of a pickup truck on up to the size of an 18-wheeler.

The water of the Little Pigeon is exceptionally clear for such a large stream, plus the sand and gravel bottom is quite barren of any aquatic vegetation. It appears that the stream probably suffers from something of a fertility problem, even by southern Appalachian standards, which explains why the average fish appears to be so small on the flow.

Access to the Little Pigeon River is via Greenbrier Road. It begins as a paved road running south from a point near the junction of US 321 and TN 416 on the northern edge of the national park. The last 2.8 miles of the road up to the head of the main river is gravel. The only camping available in this part of the park is of the primitive back-country type, located upstream of the end of the roads.

MIDDLE PRONG LITTLE PIGEON RIVER

USGS Mount Guyot • DeLorme 45

The Middle Prong is the main headwater of the Pigeon River, above the junction with Porters Creek at Greenbrier Cove. The lower section of the creek is paralleled by Greenbrier Road, then is followed for 1.5 miles by the Ramsey Cascade Trail.

Even above Greenbrier Cove, the Middle Prong is a large- to medium-size stream that is much like the Little Pigeon River itself. Huge boulders fill the stream bed, while wild rainbows hide in its pools. This far up the watershed brown trout are much less common than on the Little Pigeon. Water clarity and stream fertility also mirror that of the main portion of the river.

Casting room is plentiful for a couple of miles, up to the junction with Buck Fork. Above this point the Middle Prong and all of its feeders, including Buck Fork, are brook trout waters flowing off the slopes of Mount Chapman and closed to all fishing. The only other sizable tributary of the Middle Prong is the Ramsey Prong, which is a small stream that enters the creek where the Ramsey Cascade Trail leaves the Middle Prong.

PORTERS CREEK
USGS Mount LeConte • DeLorme 45

Porters Creek is a small-size stream that empties into the Little Pigeon River in Greenbrier Cove. The creek's bed, while rocky, is not as rugged as that of the river. Flowing through a portion of the park known as Porters Flat, the stream drains the slopes below the Appalachian Trail on the rock outcropping known as Charlies Bunion.

Open enough for comfortable fly-casting for a couple of miles upstream of its mouth, Porters provides a bit more fertile fishery than the Little Pigeon. Most of the trout are small, only running in the 6- to 9-inch range. With the exception of the extreme headwaters area where some native brookies remain, the trout are all rainbows.

Access to Porters Creek is excellent. At the junction of the creek with the Little Pigeon, Porters Creek Road (gravel) runs off Greenbrier Road to follow the stream for 1.5 miles to a large parking area. From this point, Porters Creek Trail then parallels the stream for another 3.7 miles up to Porters Flat backcountry campsite at 3400 feet of elevation.

WEST PRONG LITTLE PIGEON RIVER
USGS Mount LeConte, Gatlinburg • DeLorme 44

Besides being one of the most visible waterways in the Great Smoky Mountains NP, the West Prong of the Little Pigeon River has so many differing regulations applying to different sections that it is a veritable fishery all by itself. The visibility is the result of its location along Newfound Gap Road (US 441/TN 71), which is the main transmountain thoroughfare across the park. Additionally, the river runs through both Gatlinburg and Pigeon Forge, which constitute two of east Tennessee's most popular tourist meccas. Eventually the river empties into the Pigeon River at Sevierville.

The variety of fishing regulations and opportunities results from the river having multiple masters. The National Park Service is in charge from the headwaters down to the park boundary. The city of Gatlinburg then takes over as custodian of the water, with differing regulations. Finally, below Gatlinburg, the TWRA manages the fishery. While management by committee, easy access, and convenient location hardly sound like the ingredients of a recipe for a good trout fishery, the West Prong defies that perception. It is, indeed, a stream that offers angling scenarios to fit the tastes of virtually any trout fisherman.

Formed deep in the national park by the junction of Walker Camp Prong and Road Prong near Chimney Tops at an elevation of 4500 feet, from its inception the river is of medium size. It quickly grows into a large stream as it flows down a corridor between Mount LeConte on the east and Sugarland Mountain on the west. In the upper reaches of the stream, the West Prong tumbles through a small gorge that is well below the level of the highway paralleling it. Small cascades and swift currents are common on the river, which, along with the necessary climb down to the water from the road, discourages most anglers. Fishing pressure is light in this area. Further downstream, around the Chimney Tops Picnic Area, the river is more accessible and easier to fish. Still, fishing pressure only rates as moderate even at the busiest seasons of the year. You will, however, encounter a lot of picnickers on the rocks or wading in the river in the spring and summer.

Rainbow trout predominate in the West Prong, a legacy of the days when a hatchery was operated at Chimney Tops and thousands of that species were released into the river each year. Occasionally brook trout wander down from feeder streams into the upper part of the river, and brown trout have moved up from stockings below the park to become fairly common in the lower section of the West Prong in the Smokies. Rainbows run anywhere from 6 to 12 inches in length in the park, but 3- to 4-pound fish have been reported. As with browns anywhere they are found, the possibility of fish up to five or six pounds exists in the West Prong.

Once out of the park, the West Prong flows along the main street of Gatlinburg as a big stream of 80 to 100 feet wide. It is managed within the city limits under an innovative fisheries plan. Beginning back in 1982 the city converted an old sewage-treatment facility into a trout hatchery, from which the river is heavily stocked on a put-and-take basis. Nine- to 12-inch rainbows (1000 per week) constitute the bulk of the fish planted.

These are released on Thursday each week from April through November. Some big-fish action is also provided by 300 to 400 trophy-size rainbows and brookies stocked weekly. This trophy fishery is reinforced by the holdover browns from earlier stockings.

Not all of these fish go into the West Prong, since portions of the

Roaring Fork, plus Dudley and LeConte creeks which flow in the city, are also stocked. Of these, Dudley and LeConte are a bit small to be of prime interest to fly casters.

All of the West Prong inside Gatlinburg is open to fishing under the city's general trout regulations, with the exception of the pool under the Mynatt Park Bridge. That spot is reserved for children under 12 years old.

The city waters are open to fishing year-round, but are closed on Thursdays during the months when stocking is taking place. The creel limit is five fish per day, with no minimum size limit on general-regulation streams. On the portion of the West Prong set aside for the youngsters, the creel limit is two fish per day (the young anglers can then, of course, move to general waters to finish filling their five-fish-daily limit). In addition to applicable regular Tennessee trout licenses, a city permit (good for the year) is required of all persons 9 to 64 years old, plus a daily permit. These city fishing permits can be purchased at the Gatlinburg Visitors Welcome Center. While this array of licenses and permits may seem daunting, the chance to catch large numbers of fish and big trout has proven popular with visiting anglers. In spite of the fact that most of the fishing pressure is exerted by bait-fishermen, there is still plenty of room on this large stream for the fly caster.

Once the West Prong of the Little Pigeon exits Gatlinburg and heads north for Pigeon Forge, it falls under the supervision of the state of Tennessee. It is stocked several times each year with both rainbow and brown trout, but much of the shore is on private land and not open to the public.

Access to the West Prong is excellent in the national park and Gatlinburg. The river is always in sight of US 441 and ample parking is available. Even in the gorge area of the upper park waters, walking paths have been built down to the water at several locations.

WALKER CAMP PRONG
USGS Mount LeConte • DeLorme 44

Walker Camp Prong is the major fishable headwater of the West Prong of the Little Pigeon River, since Road Prong which joins it to form the flow is a brook trout stream and now closed to all angling. Medium to small in size, Walker Camp Prong has a very rocky course that keeps foliage far enough back from the water to allow fly-casting in many places. The creek is located within the Great Smoky Mountains NP.

Over the years the fishing reputation of this creek has been rather dismal. Highway construction years ago breached the natural-acid deposits of the slate, schist, and phyllite rocks of the half-billion-year-old Anakeesta Formation that borders the stream. The leaching of acid into the water ruined the angling for a number of years and, undoubtedly, continues to keep Walker Camp Prong's flow a bit acidified. This limits the insect life in the creek, as well as the growth rates of rainbow trout.

Today, however, there appears to be no shortage of rainbows in the creek, although they do run rather small. On the other hand, Walker Camp Prong is now one of the better bets for catching a native brook trout in the park from water that is large enough for easy fly-casting. This is due to the fact that the species can tolerate more acid content in the water than can rainbows. The water condition in this creek appears to have acted to level out the playing field when it comes to competition between the brookies and rainbows.

Walker Camp Prong begins approximately 8.5 miles south of the Sugarland entrance to the park on Newfound Gap Road (US 441). The stream parallels the road for most of its fishable length.

ROARING FORK
USGS Mount LeConte • DeLorme 44

Roaring Fork is a small creek that is a tributary of the West Prong of the Pigeon River. In spite of its size, there are a couple of reasons why it merits being covered as a fly-fishing destination. Located to the east of the river and the Cherokee Orchard portion of the national park, the upper regions of the creek descend a very steep valley. As a result, there are many ledges, potholes, and plunge pools on the creek. This situation and the rocky nature of the stream bed make it possible to find casting room as far upstream as the beginning of the Grotto Falls approach trail. Further down toward the park boundary the creek drops into a gorge area that makes it difficult to reach.

While the fish in Roaring Fork are not large, they are plentiful. These wild, colorful rainbows of 6 to 9 inches show no hesitation to attack a wide variety of dry flies.

Below the park boundary the creek flows through Gatlinburg and is open under the city's special sport-fishing regulations. City permits are required, the creel limit is two fish per day with a 10-inch minimum size, and only single-hook, artificial lures are allowed. These restrictions are enforced down to the TN 73 bridge, with the rest of the creek down to the West Prong of the Little Pigeon open under Gatlinburg's general trout-fishing rules. Needless to say, with these regulations in the city, plus the national park rules further upstream, Roaring Fork is only lightly fished.

Access is good to most of the stream. The paved Roaring Fork Motor Nature Trail (one-way traffic and closed during the winter months) parallels the creek downstream from the Grotto Falls trailhead. Parking, however, is not abundant along the roadway, traffic moves extremely slowly, and the creek leaves the road in the gorge area near the park boundary. In Gatlinburg, the road becomes a two-way-traffic thoroughfare providing good access to the stream, but, again, parking is at a premium.

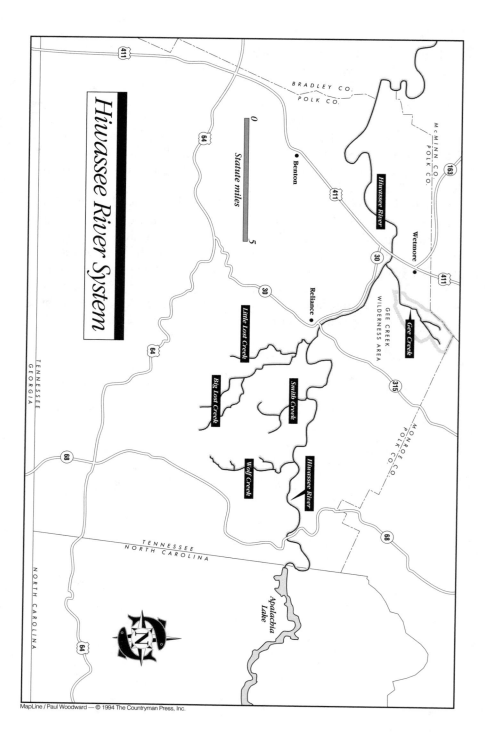

Hiwassee River System

Statute miles
0
5

BRADLEY CO.
POLK CO.

McMINN CO.
POLK CO.

Hiwassee River

Wetmore

• Benton

411

64

411

30

Reliance •

Little Lost Creek

Big Lost Creek

Smith Creek

Gee Creek

GEE CREEK
WILDERNESS
AREA

315

MONROE CO.
POLK CO.

163

30

411

64

68

Wolf Creek

Hiwassee River

68

TENNESSEE
GEORGIA

TENNESSEE
NORTH CAROLINA

NORTH CAROLINA

Apalachia
Lake

64

N

MapLine / Paul Woodward — © 1994 The Countryman Press, Inc.

32

Hiwassee River System

Located in southeast Tennessee, all of the trout waters in the Hiwassee River system are found within the boundaries of Polk County. All of these streams flow down the western slopes of the foothills of the Appalachians to empty into the Hiwassee River. Draining a large segment of the southern portion of the Cherokee National Forest, the Hiwassee system offers a wide variety of fisheries of differing quality and sizes. From big tailwaters with trophy regulations to small brooklets holding wild trout, the Hiwassee has something for everyone.

This description of the Hiwassee drainage will surprise many anglers, since the fame of the tailwaters on the river overshadow the other streams to the point that they are virtually unknown to many anglers. Indeed, all of the waters, other than those on the Hiwassee itself, receive only light to moderate angling pressure.

Besides the river itself, half a dozen other creeks feed into the main flow that are listed as trout waters by the TWRA. These are made up of several wild-trout streams as well as put-and-take stocked waters. A couple of them, Little Lost and Turtletown creeks, do not merit coverage as fly-casting destinations. In the case of Little Lost Creek, the stream is so small that it offers little casting room. As for Turtletown, much of the upper portion of the creek is on private land. The portion of the creek near the river is a sluggish lowland stream that is marginal at best. While it does receive hatchery stockings, it does not offer much of interest to the fly-fisher. This still leaves Big Lost, Gee, Smith, and Wolf creeks as tributary waters worth mentioning, along with three distinct sections of the Hiwassee River.

HIWASSEE RIVER
USGS Farner, McFarland, Oswald Bald • DeLorme 26

Mention the trout fishing on the Hiwassee River and the immediate response from any knowledgeable Tennessee angler will have something to do with the roughly eight miles of tailwater from the Apalachia Powerhouse down to US 411. The reaction is understandable since some fishermen consider the Hiwassee to be the successor to the Little Tennessee River as the South's best tailrace fishery. Many of the same folks who fished the Little Tennessee before it was inundated by the closing of the Tellico Dam back in the 1970s have now shifted their attention to the waters of Hiwassee.

While there is no question that the tailwater is a terrific trout fishery, the river actually has two other distinct and lesser-known angling areas. Add to this the different faces the tailwater presents to anglers depending on the water discharges at the powerhouse and one has an array of "Hiwassee" rivers from which to choose.

The actual trout waters on the Hiwassee start at the foot of Apalachia Dam right on the border between Polk County, Tennessee, and Cherokee County, North Carolina. Below the dam the river goes through an "S" curve that starts in Tennessee, crosses into North Carolina, and then back into Tennessee. From the last crossing the river flows for 10 miles to the west before it reaches the Apalachia Powerhouse.

This upper portion of the river is a medium-size flow spread out in a big channel and is better known for its smallmouth bass fishing than as a trout destination. This is due to the fact that very little water is released through the dam into the riverbed below. The bulk of the river water is diverted downstream through a pipe to the powerhouse, leaving the flow in the river as marginal trout habitat that is stocked several times during the year and managed under the state's general trout regulations. Most of the stream is open enough for fly-fishing. Its main characteristic that sets it apart from similar-size, put-and-take trout streams is the presence of a number of slow, extremely deep pools. These pools reach depths of 15 to 30 feet.

There are a couple of feeder streams that contain stocked or wild trout and empty into the river in this section, thus increasing the flow as it nears the powerhouse. Once below that point, the cold waters from the depths of Apalachia Lake are released into the river, bringing it back to the status of a large river of up to 100

Just upstream of the beginning of trophy-trout water at the Big Bend Recreation Area, the Hiwassee River is a big flow. It is also considered by many anglers to be the best tailwater fishery in the Southeast.

yards wide in places. It also becomes the premier trout water of southeast Tennessee.

As with all tailwaters, the flow fluctuates according to the need for generating electricity at the powerhouse. Fortunately, the Hiwassee is basically a broad, shallow river so that even at high water some portions can be waded (although extreme caution is advisable at these times). When the river is at low levels most of the tailwater is composed of smaller channels threading their way through the rocky riverbed. Though low water provides the best fishing conditions, veteran anglers of the river regularly take fish on higher levels as well, particularly when fishing from rafts, canoes, or float tubes.

The fish in the tailwaters of the Hiwassee consist of stocked rainbow and brown trout, but fish that hold over from season to season are common. More than 100,000 rainbows of nine inches in length are released into the river each year. The average Hiwassee trout will be from 10 to 14 inches long and often has taken on the shape of a football. The river is quite fertile, providing plenty of insect life to the fish, which accounts for their oval shape. In past years brook trout were also routinely stocked in the tailwater, resulting in the Hiwassee having produced the state-record brookie. Back in 1973 Jerry Wills hauled a 3-pound, 14-ounce brook trout from the river to set a mark that still stands.

From the powerhouse down to the Forest Service's Big Bend Recreation Site the river continues to be open to fishing under Tennessee's general trout regulations and creel limits. The next three miles down to the Louisville & Nashville railroad bridge just above the town of Reliance is managed under trophy-trout regulations. Artificial lures are mandated along this stretch, with a creel limit of two trout per day that must be a minimum of 14 inches long. These waters have been managed for trophy fishing since 1986 and the plan has worked well. Browns and rainbows of 16 to 20 inches are regularly hooked on this part of the Hiwassee and even bigger fish are taken occasionally.

Larger trout, whether in the trophy or open sections of the river, more often fall victim to fishermen during periods of high water. This is pretty typical of southern tailwaters where the larger fish do most of their feeding when they feel safer in the high waters.

From Reliance down to the US 411 crossing the fishing is again open under general regulations. The angling is very similar to that found above the trophy stretch, with plenty of 10- to 12-inch stockers present. There are some privately held lands along the river in the vicinity of Reliance, and just above US 411 the river flows out of the confines of the Cherokee NF.

Below US 411 the Hiwassee continues to be cool enough to support trout and is stocked, but access becomes a problem. Virtually all of the land is private, with little road access. The river is more suited for float-fishing and there is one unimproved boat ramp located near the junction of the Hiwassee and Ocoee rivers to the north of the town of Benton and downstream of the village of Patty. This portion of the river is not very accommodating to fly casters and gets little attention from them.

For the fly-fisherman targeting the Hiwassee, it is one of the rare streams of the southern highlands where hatches of aquatic insects provide some measure of predictability. Beginning in April, Blue-Winged Olives and caddis will be the mainstay of the daily activity, followed in May by sulphurs and Light Cahills. When no surface activity is visible, many anglers opt to float a size 12 to 14 Royal Wulff through the riffles.

Access to the upper portion of the Hiwassee above the powerhouse is fairly limited. The best access is along a short portion of TN 68 that parallels the river just downstream of Apalachia Dam. Also, FS 311 branches off TN 68 where the highway crosses the river. This Forest Service road hugs the northern bank of the river, going east to the state line. One other extremely rugged access point is located on the south shore off FS 23 further downstream.

From the powerhouse down to US 411 access to the Hiwassee is excellent. FS 108 runs along the north side of the river from the powerhouse down to Reliance. The only point at which it leaves the flow is the Big Bend section. There is, however, a foot trail along the three miles of water that are not at roadside. The John Muir National Recreation Trail follows the river through this stretch, which takes in most of the trophy-trout water. Parking areas are provided at Big Bend, Towee, and Hiwassee River recreation areas on this part of the river.

Below the bridge at Reliance, TN 30 parallels the south side of the Hiwassee. Due to the presence of some private land not all of the water is readily accessible. The water can be reached with ease in Reliance, or at Cherokee, Taylor Island, and Quinns Springs recreation sites by driving west along TN 30 from the town. A state-run campground is located on FS 108 at Gee Creek on the north side of the river, while the Forest Service maintains one at Quinns Springs.

The lower portion of the river below US 411 can only be fished by floating, since there is practically no shore access. The boat ramp at Boyd Bottoms can be reached by taking Clemmer Ferry Road west from the Benton town square. The road makes several sharp changes of direction along this route. At 1.7 miles turn left onto the road (it presently has no road sign) with a sign: Road Closed. At 0.75 mile the boat ramp is down the steep gravel spur on the right.

WOLF CREEK
USGS McFarland • DeLorme 26

Wolf Creek is the most easterly of the Hiwassee River tributaries that provide public fly-fishing possibilities. Flowing down a narrow valley between Ditney and Smith mountains, the creek enters the river from the south side, just to the northwest of the settlement of Turtletown.

Although a small stream, it has a fairly rocky course that leaves some portions open enough for limited fly-casting. Another attractive characteristic of this creek is that it is wild-trout water. Most of the fish encountered are small rainbows of 6 to 8 inches, but a larger fish, including an occasional brown, can turn up. While the average trout is not large, there are plenty of rainbows present, and they are not heavily fished. Wild-trout-water lure restrictions and reduced creel limits apply on the stream.

Wolf Creek is paralleled for 2.5 miles upstream of its mouth by FS 23. This gravel road is located up on the valley wall above the small gorge through which the creek flows. At 1.4 miles upstream the road crosses the creek, providing easy access around the bridge. By the time the road leaves the creek, the flow is too small to be of great interest to fly-fishermen.

SMITH CREEK
USGS McFarland • DeLorme 26

Traveling downstream, the next tributary of interest on the Hiwassee River is Smith Creek. One look at Smith and it is obvious why most anglers ignore it. At its mouth beside Apalachia Powerhouse it is very small. On the plus side, the creek has cut a deep, wide, rocky, and steep bed that is open enough for fly-casting.

The water in Smith Creek is usually crystal clear as it drops from pothole to pool over the mossy rocks. These tiny bits of holding water fairly teem with small wild rainbow trout. Though the creek is listed by TWRA as receiving stockings of adult hatchery trout, these fish are rarely in evidence. Rather, a lot of small 4- to 7-inch rainbows are present, with a fish of 8 to 10 inches occasionally seeming to appear from nowhere to take a fly drifted on the glassy water.

Smith Creek is not a primary fly-casting destination, but due to its location beside the powerhouse deserves to be mentioned. Access to Smith is via FS 23, which follows the creek for several hundred yards upstream from the stream's mouth. It is necessary to climb down a steep, rocky bank, however, to get to the water. Smith Creek is open under general state trout regulations.

BIG LOST CREEK
USGS McFarland • DeLorme 26

The largest of the Hiwassee feeder streams, Big Lost Creek provides varied opportunities to the fly caster. In its lower section below Big Lost Creek Campground at the FS 103 crossing, the creek is of medium size. Stocked regularly, the main creek, along with its tributary Little Lost Creek, yields rainbows and some browns in the 8- to 12-inch category. There are also some wild fish in both creeks. This section of Big Lost Creek and all of Little Lost Creek are open under general trout regulations. The main branch of the creek is canopied with foliage, but still has room for casting. Little Lost Creek does not offer much hope to the fly caster, since it is also canopied and quite small.

Above the Forest Service campground at FS 103, Big Lost Creek is managed as a wild-trout stream, under wild-trout regulations. A small stream, it rises several miles to the south on the slopes of Little Frog Mountain, but flows for some distance along a rather gently sloped valley. Most of the fish encountered here are rainbows of 6 to 9 inches. Very tight fly-casting conditions exist along most of the upper portion of Big Lost Creek.

To reach Big Lost Creek Campground, turn east from TN 30 onto FS 103. This intersection is several miles south of where the highway leaves the Hiwassee River at Reliance. There is a sign at the intersection for the campground. FS 103 will cross Little Lost Creek before reaching the main stream. These are the only road access points on the fishable portions of the creeks.

GEE CREEK
USGS Mecca, McFarland • DeLorme 26

Gee Creek has the potential to cause a great deal of trouble for an outdoor scribe who reports on it. It is a very small stream, but one that has a very high-quality wild-trout fishery—that is also relatively unknown. The folks who have already discovered the stream might take exception to anyone revealing the secret of Gee Creek's trout fishery.

The size of the creek is the main reason that Gee has not gained more renown. Most anglers see the stream at the Gee Creek Campground just off FS 108 on the north side of the Hiwassee River. Except during extremely wet weather, the creek is nothing more than a trickle of water. A couple of miles back up its valley in the Gee Creek Wilderness Area, however, the stream is quite different. Like many other southern Appalachian streams, once it hits the river bottom, much of the water soaks down into the fertile soil. Where it is tumbling down the rocky hillsides it actually has more water than it does further downstream.

By following the creek upstream to the edge of the wilderness area, fishable water can be found. While still small, the rocky stream bed is not as heavily canopied as most small brooks. Though quite tight, it can be fished with a fly rod. Flowing down through Forest Service lands off Hogback Ridge in the extreme northern tip of Polk County, Gee Creek usually surprises the first-time visitor. Within a series of potholes, riffles, and small cascades, wild rainbows of up to 10 inches are common. On one particularly fruitful trip to Gee Creek, my dry-fly offerings were snapped up by 25 wild trout in just two hours, with seven of those rainbows measuring 9 inches or larger.

Needless to say, Gee Creek is one stream where the practice of catch-and-release is almost an imperative. With its diminutive size it is susceptible to overfishing. Fortunately, Gee Creek is managed as a wild-trout stream, under single-hook, artificial-lure restrictions with minimum size and reduced creel limits.

Another reason the creek has remained a secret is the problem of finding access to it. There are a couple of miles of private land above the Gee Creek Campground, before the wilderness is encountered on Forest Service property. There are no intersecting roads between FS 108 on which the campground is located and the road that parallels the creek. This road presently has no signs identifying it, nor is the name listed on the maps.

To reach Gee Creek Wilderness Area, take US 411 north from the Hiwassee River. At the point at which TN 163 intersects from the west at the village of Wetmore, the road to the creek intersects from the east. Turn right onto this paved road and cross the L&N railroad tracks. The road then turns to follow the tracks back south toward the river. Eventually it will head east to Gee Creek, then follow that stream northward to the edge of the wilderness. The last couple of miles of the road are gravel. From the parking area at the end of the road, Gee Creek Trail follows the creek upstream into the wilderness area.

33

Little River System

The public trout waters of the Little River watershed are almost exclusively located in the Great Smoky Mountains NP. The drainage area of this system is the largest in the park, and is made up of the main stem of the Little River, plus its Middle and West prongs. Additionally, there are a number of tributaries within the park sporting such names as Jakes, Rough, and Spruce Flats creeks, or Fish Camp, Thunderhead, and Indian Flats prongs. These, however, tend to be small, tightly canopied flows or are brook trout streams closed to fishing.

The only water in this system not in the national park is the portion of the Little River from the park boundary down through the municipality of Townsend to the village of Walland. From there the river continues north as a warm-water stream to empty into Fort Loudoun Lake on the Tennessee River north of Maryville.

The Little River drainage is significant in both the natural and human history of the Smoky Mountains prior to and after the national park was established. The system was the site in 1986 to 1988 of the reintroduction of river otters to the park. They had last been confirmed in the area in 1936, just prior to the National Park Service taking charge. Some trout enthusiasts expressed concern over the stocking plan since the otters were commonly thought to feed heavily on trout. It was feared that the creatures would adversely affect the fishery in the Little River and its tributaries. Fortunately, as biologists argued at the time of the releases, otters much prefer crayfish, stone rollers, and suckers for food, only occasionally catching trout. There has been no adverse effect from the plantings, plus lucky anglers have had the opportunity to catch glimpses of these playful members of the weasel and skunk family frolicking along the river.

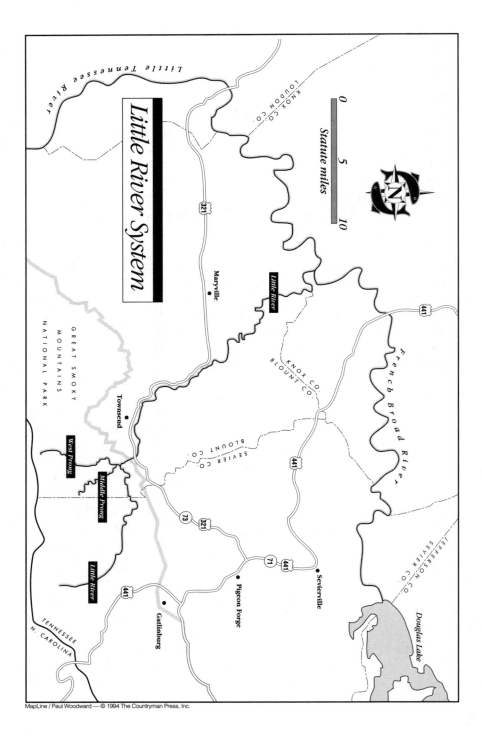

Little River System

Statute miles
0
5
10

Little Tennessee River

LOUDON CO.
KNOX CO.

321

Maryville

Little River

GREAT SMOKY
MOUNTAINS
NATIONAL PARK

Townsend

West Prong

Middle Prong

Little River

KNOX CO.
BLOUNT CO.

BLOUNT CO.
SEVIER CO.

French Broad River

441

441

73
321

71
441

Sevierville

Pigeon Forge

Gatlinburg

441

TENNESSEE
N. CAROLINA

SEVIER CO.
JEFFERSON CO.

Douglas Lake

MapLine / Paul Woodward — © 1994 The Countryman Press, Inc.

Man's intrusion into the Little River valley came in earnest in 1901 when the Little River Lumber Company purchased 85,000 acres along the river. For the next 40 years until the park was finally established, virtually the whole watershed was cleared of timber. A sawmill in the company town of Townsend (named for Col. W. B. Townsend, the president of the company) cut the trees into lumber on the river's bank. The Little River Lumber Company was the last logging operation to shut down in the Smoky Mountains; in 1939, just prior to the opening of the national park, their machinery finally fell silent. After removing the trees, the loggers left behind barren hillsides scarred by the skidders and the bed of the narrow-gauge railroads they built up the stream valleys. It is a tribute to the ability of nature to heal herself that the second-growth forests now have reclaimed those hillsides.

The Little River Basin has been visited by sportsmen seeking trout since very early in the twentieth century. In the course of time the early bait-anglers were joined by fly-fishermen attempting to emulate the success of early American fly casters like Theodore Gordon in New York's Catskill Mountains. A couple of innovations that have come down from these efforts are two fly patterns very closely associated with the Smoky Mountains and the Little River.

The first of these is a wet fly known as the Yellowhammer, or Yellarhammer. This fly is tied with a peacock herl body and was originally hackled with the wing feather of a yellow-shafted flicker. Since these birds are now a protected species, dyed feathers of other birds have to suffice for the angler.

The second fly is a dry pattern known as the Thunderhead, undoubtedly named for the mountain and stream of that name located in the Little River drainage. This one is an Adams pattern tied with a hair or Wulff-type wing.

The trout water of the Little River drainage will be described beginning with Little River and continuing in a westward direction to the Middle Prong and, finally, the West Prong of the Little River.

LITTLE RIVER
USGS Gatlinburg, Wear Cove • DeLorme 44

Draining off Clingmans Dome in the heart of the Great Smoky Mountains NP, the headwater streams that form the Little River begin their descent at over 5000 feet above sea level. With Sugarland Mountain to the east and Blanket Mountain framing its western side, the Little River begins at the confluence of Meigs Post Prong and Grouse Creek. Above this junction all the feeder streams harbor brook trout and are closed to angling.

The portion of the main stem of the Little River down to its junction with the Middle Prong is sometimes referred to as the East Prong. Regardless of what it is called, it is a tumbling mountain stream for its first five and a half miles down to the campground and ranger station at Elkmont. Besides occupying the site of one of the early logging camps on the Little River, Elkmont marks the general area where the river becomes big water. From this point downstream to the edge of the park the river is wide open with plenty of casting room. It also has long, deep holes that yield some of the largest trout taken in the Smoky Mountains each year.

If there is a true drawback to fishing the Little River, it is the easy access available to this lower section. During spring and summer the waders, tubers, and swimmers will be out in force along the section paralleled by Little River Road. Fortunately, the river is so long and big that even under these conditions the determined angler can still find an empty run or two on which to challenge the fish.

Wild rainbow trout of 7 to 10 inches are plentiful in the Little River, but the real attraction is the possibility of hooking one of the larger fish the stream holds. Rainbows of up to three or four pounds have come out of this river, along with browns of five to six pounds. Back in 1979 the Little River gave up a 16-pound brown that is the biggest trout ever reported in the park. The portion above Elkmont campground is rough, tumbling water more suited to the small rainbows. The entire length of the river is open to fishing under general park regulations.

A paved road follows the Little River to above the developed campground at Elkmont, leaving it at the junction with Jakes Creek. A gravel road continues on up the river for a short distance. Above the end of the road, the Little River Trail follows the river up to Three Forks backcountry campsite at 3400 feet of elevation. Fifteen primitive campsites are also located at Rough Creek, about halfway up to Three Forks.

On the river below Elkmont, access is good along the approach road to the campground. Further down, Little River Road (US 321) runs at streamside until the river leaves the park. Downstream of the park the river is predominantly on private lands.

A nice brown trout is led into the net on Tennessee's Little River.

PHOTO BY JIM CASADA

MIDDLE PRONG LITTLE RIVER

USGS Thunderhead Mountain,
Wear Cove • DeLorme 44

The Middle Prong of the Little River is the largest of the feeder streams entering the Little River. It is of medium size throughout, and borders on being large near its mouth. From its head at the junction of Lynn Camp and Thunderhead prongs the stream is open enough to accommodate fly-casting. The Middle Prong descends the valley between Meigs Mountain on the east and Defeat Ridge on the west. Its entire course lies within the Great Smoky Mountains NP.

The Middle Prong flows past the Tremont Educational Center and Ranger Station, but swimmers, waders, and fishermen use the stream less than the main stem of the Little River. Still, by Smoky Mountains standards, it receives moderate fishing pressure.

The bulk of the fish encountered on the Middle Prong are rainbow trout ranging in size from 6 to 9 inches. Occasionally an angler does get surprised by a mega–brown trout rising to a fly. Browns of more than 10 pounds have been reportedly wrestled from this stream in past years. The flow, however, does not have as many deep pools as the Little River, making these larger fish a rare commodity. Brook trout are sometimes found in the Middle Prong around the mouth of Spruce Flats Creek (closed to angling), about one and a half miles above Tremont. The Middle Prong is open under the park's general trout regulations.

Access to the Middle Prong is excellent. The water is paralleled by Laurel Creek Road for the first quarter mile upstream from the Little River. At that point the Middle Prong Road branches off to follow the stream for 2.0 miles up to Tremont as a paved track. Above the educational center the road changes to gravel as it follows the Middle Prong all the way to its beginning near Hornet Tree Top.

WEST PRONG LITTLE RIVER
USGS Thunderhead Mountain, Wear Cove • DeLorme 44

The final and smallest of the three prongs of the Little River, the West Prong is only a medium-size stream. Flowing in a northwesterly direction, it empties into the Middle Prong at the intersection of Laurel Creek and Middle Prong roads. Like the Middle Prong, all of the waters of the West Prong are located in the national park.

The West Prong is large enough to be fly-fished along the two miles of water that run at the roadside of Laurel Creek Road. At the point at which the road bears off to follow Laurel Creek toward Cades Cove, the West Prong climbs into the mountains. It flows to the west of Defeat Ridge while descending from the slopes of Thunderhead Mountain on the Tennessee–North Carolina border. Once away from the road the stream is a small creek, with tight fishing conditions.

Most of the trout in the West Prong are rainbows and the fishing is considered by some to be only fair in quality. Among the streams large enough for comfortable fly-casting, however, its upper section near the end of road access rates with Walker Camp Prong as the best bet in the park to encounter a brook trout. In this area the West Prong gets virtually no fishing pressure and below the road it is only lightly fished.

Access to the West Prong, other than along Laurel Creek Road, is via the West Prong Trail that begins at the Tremont center. A moderately strenuous 1.7-mile hike is required to reach the stream at the West Prong backcountry camping area. This is the only trail contact made with West Prong, and it is a small creek that is difficult to fly-fish at this point.

34

Little Tennessee River System

Mention the Little Tennessee River to any veteran trout fisherman in the southeastern U.S. and you are likely to be treated to a prolonged chorus of wailing and gnashing of teeth. The eulogies for the lost and greatly lamented brown trout fishery the river once supported have been continuous since the waters of Tellico Lake swallowed the stream back in the 1970s.

Why such an outpouring of grief, one might ask? For starters, it is not difficult to find biologists and fishermen alike who describe the Little T, as the regular anglers fondly called it, as having been the best water for big brown trout in the eastern U.S. The insect hatches that were produced on this extremely fertile flow were also legendary. With predictable, abundant hatches and brown trout that reached 20 to 25 pounds in size, is it any wonder that so many anglers grab for the sackcloth and ashes to mourn for the loss of the fishery?

In spite of the best efforts of fishermen and their unlikely ally, the snail darter, the gates finally closed on the Tellico project. When a $100 million project with heavy political support was at stake, frustrated anglers and an endangered finger-length fish could not stem the tide.

The really odd part of the history of trout water on the Little Tennessee River is that the stream originally was a warm-water lowland resource. Even in its headwaters near the town of Dillard in north Georgia, the Little Tennessee flows down a low-elevation valley as only marginal trout water. From there it courses to the northwest across the toe of North Carolina and skirts the Smoky Mountains finally to cross into Tennessee just downstream of Tapaco, North Carolina.

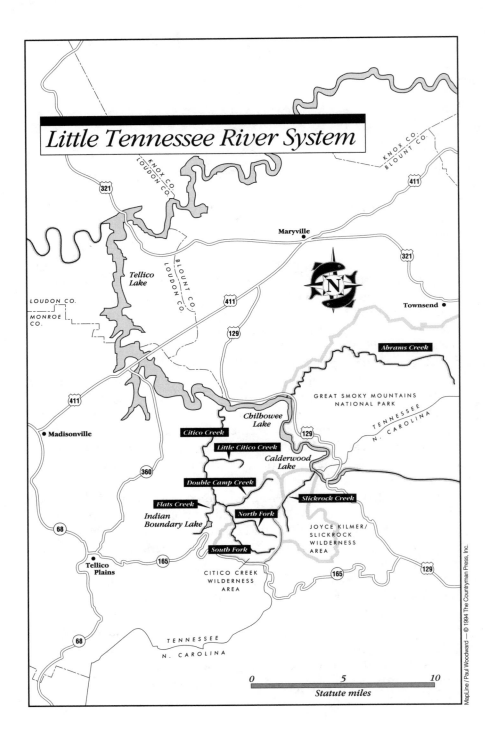

Little Tennessee River System

Beginning in 1919 with the construction of Cheoah Dam, the Aluminum Company Of America (ALCOA) and the Tennessee Valley Authority (TVA) began the process of harnessing the Little Tennessee for power generation. By the mid-1960s Calderwood (ALCOA), Chilhowee (TVA), and Fontana (TVA) lakes had been added along the Little T. In the process a fine tailwater trout fishery had been created from the Chilhowee Dam down to Fort Loudoun Lake at the mouth of the Little Tennessee. When the Tellico Dam project was completed this stretch of free-flowing trout water on the Little T disappeared.

What remains of the trout water in the Little Tennessee system is still substantial and varied. The streams range from the heavily stocked waters of the Citico Creek basin to the wild and pristine flows of Slickrock and Abrams creeks. Altogether there are seven trout-bearing tributaries of the Little Tennessee River in the Volunteer State. Of these, Jake Best Creek which flows into Citico Creek is the only one that is too small to interest fly casters.

The streams that constitute the trout fishery on the Little Tennessee system are Abrams, Double Camp, Flats, and Slickrock creeks, plus Citico Creek and its North and South forks. These will be covered starting at the North Carolina border and moving down the course of the Little Tennessee.

SLICKROCK CREEK
USGS Tapoco • DeLorme 27

For a description of Slickrock Creek see chapter 20 covering the Little Tennessee River system in North Carolina.

ABRAMS CREEK
USGS Cades Cove, Calderwood • DeLorme 43

Abrams Creek is a medium to small stream that drains the northwestern corner of the Great Smoky Mountains NP. Flowing from east to west, it finally turns to the southwest running along the park's western border and empties into Chilhowee Lake on the Little Tennessee River. The entire length of the creek is located inside the national park boundaries.

The deep pools at the foot of the waterfalls on Slickrock Creek are excellent places to find the stream's legendary brown trout.

    If there is one thing that characterizes Abrams Creek, it is the abundance of its ecosystem. Whether the subject is the trout, insects, or mammals, the valley of Abrams Creek has always been a wonderland of variety and plenty. The headwater of Abrams begins on the north slope of Mount Squire on the Appalachian Trail. Beginning as Anthony Creek, the flow is soon joined by other unnamed brooks to form Abrams, just upstream of Cades Cove.

    This plush valley did not go unnoticed by the early settlers of the Smoky Mountains. The area of Cades Cove was inhabited by as many as 700 people during pioneer times. Today the cove is one of the major tourist attractions of the park due to its being maintained as a living-history exhibit. Rather than the natural landscape so prevalent in the rest of the Smoky Mountains, Cades Cove is managed as a primitive highland farming community. For that reason white-tailed deer, black bear, wild hogs, and smaller animals are plentiful in the valley.

    Among the animals encountered here are beavers, which disappeared from east Tennessee as early as the 1890s. In 1966, however, the creatures reappeared in the park, probably after migrating westward from North Carolina. The lower elevations of Abrams Creek and Cades Cove have been identified as the most suitable habitat in the park for these animals.

The first reintroduction of river otters in the Smokies also took place on Abrams Creek in the late 1980s. Today these frisky critters are doing well along the stream.

The most recent restocking of a native animal that had become extinct in the national park was the release of several red wolves in the Cades Cove area in 1992. While the jury is still out on this species' survival here, a small population does exist along Abrams Creek.

There have even been occasional reports of sightings of cougars in the Cades Cove vicinity. The National Park Service, however, considers the big cats to have been eradicated from the Smoky Mountains in 1920.

Not all of the animal life that thrives in the Abrams Creek watershed is above the water line. The shovel-nose salamander, though now known to be quite widespread in the southern Appalachian streams, was first identified through specimens captured in Abrams Creek in 1937. Another aquatic creature of this stream that barely avoided oblivion is the Smoky madtom, a tiny member of the catfish family. In 1957 a project was begun to remove rough fish from Abrams Creek and the Little Tennessee River, to prepare for the closing of the dam on Chilhowee Lake. This would, supposedly, create pristine habitat for rainbow trout to be stocked in the new reservoir. The waters of both flows were treated with rotenone and a few specimens of the madtom were picked up from Abrams Creek. These were shipped to the Smithsonian Institution in Washington in the mid-1960s where they were identified as a new species. They were also declared extinct since these were the only known examples ever collected.

Fortunately, a small population of the Smoky madtoms were found living in Citico Creek in 1980. In 1986 some were transplanted to Abrams and are thought to be doing well, although they are such a secretive fish that it is difficult to make a judgment.

This discussion of the abundance of diverse life in the Abrams Creek drainage should serve as a reminder to anglers to tread gently when visiting. The impact of man has taken a toll on this area that is now beginning to be reversed. It would be a shame if we as fishermen delayed the progress.

What about the trout fishery? Again, unique features of this drainage make the trout fishing outstanding. Above Cades Cove the creek is small and has a rainbow trout population similar to other streams of its size in the Smokies. Once the flow reaches the cove, however, much of it goes underground where it mingles with the waters of half a dozen feeder streams that enter from different directions. When the creek exits the cove, the subterranean flow rejoins the stream on the surface, but after filtering through the limestone deposits, the natural acidity of the water has changed. The pH levels increase from around 6.0 to much milder levels of around 8.0.

This more alkaline flow is a boon to the stream's insect life. Both mayflies and caddis flies abound, but it is the abundant caddis hatches for which Abrams Creek has become known. Especially on the portion for a few miles downstream from Cades Cove to Abrams Falls, the number and size of trout in the creek have traditionally been extraordinary. The resultant reputation of the fishery, however, has led to heavy fishing pressure in recent years. Coupled with possible silting problems associated with the cattle pastured in the cove, this pressure has led to some regular anglers downgrading their rating of the stream.

The portion of Abrams Creek running through Cades Cove is small, level, bushy, and heavily fished near the roads. Both rainbow and brown trout are present, with the majority being rainbow trout, usually in the 7- to 9-inch range. Once the creek leaves Cades Cove, it begins to gain size quickly along the four and a third miles down to Abrams Falls.

This is the section that most fishermen are speaking of when they wax poetic about the great angling on the stream. Rainbows up to four pounds have been taken from this stretch and smaller fish are quite abundant. There are a couple of distinct bends in the creek that create loops away from the adjacent hiking trail. These more remote areas are of particular interest to the angler looking for solitude and less-harried trout. One is just above the falls and is appropriately dubbed the Falls loop, while the other is sometimes called the Horseshoe and is further upstream.

Once below the 25-foot drop of Abrams Falls, brown trout turn up more often. Although there is an excellent pool at the foot of the cascade, this is a favorite spot for hikers to swim or wade the creek during warm weather.

Below Abrams Falls the creek runs through an area known as Little Bottoms and then through the Abrams Creek Campground. By this point it is beginning to border on becoming a large stream. Below the campground, access is quite limited with neither road nor trail crossings. This remote location and the long, deep pools make lower Abrams a good possibility for large fish.

To get to Abrams Creek, the easiest approach to the upper reaches is the Cades Cove Loop Road. This is, however, a one-way, one-lane thoroughfare. Expect the going to be quite slow on it as the sightseeing public takes its collective time. The Abrams Falls Trail follows the creek downstream from the parking area on the loop trail to connect with the Little Bottoms Trail that skirts the lower part of the creek to the Abrams Creek Campground. There are also some backcountry campsites along the Little Bottoms Trail. Entry to the Abrams Creek Campground is via Happy Valley Road off US 129.

CITICO CREEK
USGS Whiteoak Flats • DeLorme 27

Citico Creek is a large stream that drains the Citico Creek Wilderness Area to flow northward, emptying into the Little Tennessee River at the head of Tellico Lake. This stream, however, is much more often associated with the Tellico River because of the fishing regulations that it shares with that flow.

In order to fish in Citico Creek and its tributaries from the mouth of Little Citico Creek up to the junction of the North and South Fork of Citico Creek, it is necessary to have a Tellico-Citico trout permit. The funds raised with this special daily fishing permit support very heavy, weekly stocking of the stream. Regular state creel limits of seven trout of any species apply, with the only minimum size limit being 6 inches on brook trout. Natural baits are also legal and since the streams are stocked on Thursdays, they are not open to fishing on that day or Friday (unless those days fall on state or federal holidays). The portion of Citico Creek below Little Citico Creek is not trout water.

Although the bulk of the fish in the creek are stocked rainbows of 9 to 12 inches, Citico also supports wild trout, especially in the upper reaches of the stream. Brown trout are also present along the flow. Expect to meet plenty of bait-fishermen on the nine miles of this stream open to fishing under the special-permit system. Fortunately, the creek is large and long enough to find room for some fly-casting on most days.

There are two Forest Service campgrounds on Citico Creek. One is located at the mouth of Double Camp Creek and named Double Camp. The other is at the mouth of Jake Best Creek and, appropriately, is the Jake Best Campground. A number of designated primitive campsites are also spread along the stream.

Access to Citico Creek is via Citico Creek Road, which is shown as FS 35-1 on some maps but marked as FS 35 on the road signs. It parallels the creek along its entire length from Tellico Lake up to within a quarter-mile of the point at which North and South Citico creeks join. This last quarter-mile has a short spur road (FS 29) along it up to the junction.

The closest location to Citico Creek where a Tellico-Citico trout permit can be purchased is at the Green Cove Trailer Park and Motel store on the Tellico River, but permits can also be purchased at most bait shops or sporting-goods outlets in east Tennessee that sell regular fishing licenses. Still, if you are going to fish Citico, plan ahead to pick up a permit since Green Cove is quite a distance from the creek.

SOUTH FORK CITICO CREEK
USGS Whiteoak Flats • DeLorme 27

The South Fork of Citico Creek flows northward through the 15,891-acre Citico Creek Wilderness Area, and is the main headwater of Citico. It is a large- to medium-size, rough-and-tumble stream with a very rocky stream bed.

This creek is open under wild-trout regulations and contains mostly rainbow trout. These fish are usually in the 7- to 9-inch range. Some browns also turn up, and there is plenty of room for casting, especially on the lower reaches near its mouth.

Access to the South Fork is via foot travel up the trail at the end of FS 29. About a quarter mile up Citico is the junction of the North and South forks. From there FT 105 crosses a wooden bridge over the North Fork to parallel the South Fork into the wilderness area.

NORTH FORK CITICO CREEK
USGS Whiteoak Flats • DeLorme 27

The North Fork of Citico Creek is a medium-size flow that runs from east to west, joining the South Fork to form Citico Creek. Only slightly smaller than its sister stream, it also has a rocky, tumbling course that originates deep in the Citico Creek Wilderness Area.

Wild rainbow trout abound in the North Fork, with fish of 7 to 9 inches being common, especially in the creek's lower reaches. An old concrete dam is located about fifty yards upstream of the confluence of the North Fork with the South Fork.

Although the two streams look very similar, they can be quite different in character on any given day of fishing. On one visit I had fished up the South Fork for perhaps a quarter of a mile, raising only two small trout that I failed to hook. In the process I managed to spook a number of fish in pools after drifting my fly through them. It was obvious the trout were there, but I could not interest them.

Being rather disappointed with the action, I walked back to the junction of the streams and turned up the North Fork. Using the same Royal Wulff that had been ignored on the South Fork, I proceeded to catch and release seven rainbows in 15 minutes before even reaching the old dam. It is hard to believe that the distance of only a few hundred yards could make that much difference in trout behavior. I guess that is why we call fly-casting an art. It certainly is not a science!

The North Fork of Citico Creek is open under wild-trout regulations and provides room to permit easy casting, particularly in its lower portion.

To reach the North Fork of Citico Creek, follow the trail at the end of FS 29 up to the junction of the North and South forks. From that point, FT 98 parallels the North Fork into the wilderness area.

DOUBLE CAMP CREEK
USGS *Whiteoak Flats* • *DeLorme 27*

This small- to medium-size feeder stream empties directly into Citico Creek at the Forest Service campground that is named for it. There are a total of three and a half miles of fishable water on Double Camp, up to the second bridge on FS 59 (Double Camp Road), which runs at streamside. Above this point the creek is no longer large enough to offer any fly-casting opportunities.

Open under the Tellico-Citico permit regulations, the stream is stocked with mature trout. It has some natural reproduction as well, so expect to find small rainbows also.

Although the access is easy via FS 59, the creek is rough, rocky, and, in places, steeply graded. Falls, rock slides, and plunge pools are very common on the last mile of Double Camp before it empties into Citico Creek.

Double Camp Creek can be reached by traveling south on Citico Road (FS 35) for 7.0 miles above the beginning of trout water at the mouth of Little Citico Creek. FS 59 enters from the east at the campground.

FLATS CREEK
USGS Whiteoak Flats • DeLorme 27

Flats Creek is a quite small stream of only passing interest to fly-fishermen. The creek's headwaters are impounded in Indian Boundary Lake at the Forest Service recreation site of that same name. Below the lake, Flats Creek is stocked and open to fishing under Tellico-Citico permit regulations.

The portion immediately upstream of its mouth on Citico Creek offers a few pools and runs that can be cast to with a fly, but the rest of the stream is heavily canopied.

There is no trail along this stream. Access is at the mouth of the creek where it flows to the east under FS 35 into Citico Creek. This junction is roughly 1.0 mile downstream from Double Camp Creek.

35

Nolichucky River System

The Nolichucky River system drains a large portion of northwest North Carolina and northeast Tennessee. From the point at which it is born at the junction of the Cane and North Toe rivers on the border of Yancey and Mitchell counties in North Carolina, the Nolichucky is a big river. It is not, however, considered trout water anywhere along its course through Tennessee. After entering the Volunteer State just south of Erwin in Unicoi County it eventually meanders into Hamblin County where it empties into the French Broad River in Douglas Lake.

On the Tennessee portion of the Nolichucky there are a dozen tributaries that the TWRA lists as trout waters. Of these, five are stocked streams that have very little public access. Devils Fork, North and South Indian creeks, plus Camp and Spivey creeks are all limited to access at some roadside right-of-ways and bridge crossings. None represent realistic fly-fishing destinations. Also, Dry and Higgins creeks are listed as wild-trout streams open under special regulations. Unfortunately, both flow through some private land and are very small where they offer public access. All of these streams listed above are located in Unicoi County, with the exception of Camp and Dry creeks, which are in Greene County.

The remaining streams in the Nolichucky system that merit mention are Clark, Horse, Rocky Fork, Sarvis Cove, and Squibb creeks. The descriptions of these creeks will begin with the ones nearest the North Carolina border and be followed by those downstream on the Nolichucky.

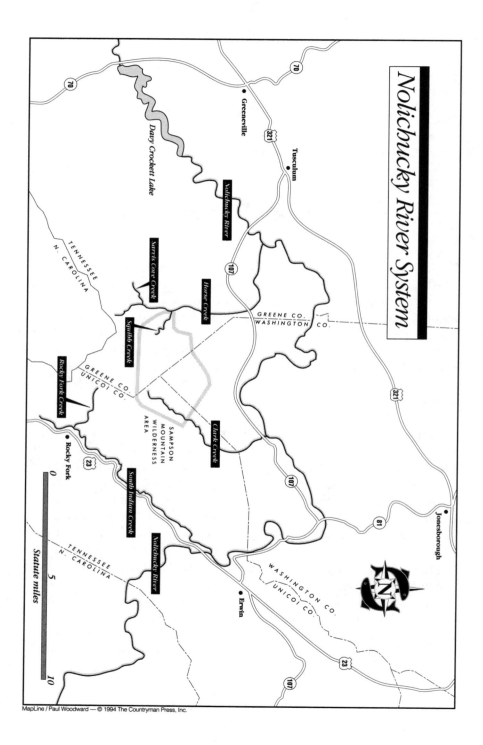

Nolichucky River System

Greeneville

Tusculum

Davy Crockett Lake

Nolichucky River

TENNESSEE
N. CAROLINA

Sarris Cove Creek

Horse Creek

GREENE CO.
WASHINGTON CO.

Squibb Creek

GREENE CO.
UNICOI CO.

Rocky Fork Creek

SAMPSON
MOUNTAIN
WILDERNESS
AREA

Clark Creek

Rocky Fork

South Indian Creek

Nolichucky River

TENNESSEE
N. CAROLINA

Erwin

Jonesborough

WASHINGTON CO.
UNICOI CO.

N

0

5

Statute miles

10

MapLine / Paul Woodward — © 1994 The Countryman Press, Inc.

ROCKY FORK CREEK
USGS Flag Pond • DeLorme 62

Located in the extreme southern end of Unicoi County, Rocky Fork Creek lies quite close to the North Carolina border. It is also by far the best trout stream to be found in the Nolichucky system. This small stream provides a couple of miles of public access and is loaded with wild rainbow trout.

Rocky Fork is one of the few streams in this part of Tennessee that is open to public fishing along its entire length. Rising near the point at which the boundary of Greene and Unicoi counties intersects with Madison County, North Carolina, Rocky Fork flows in an arc around the north side of Flint Mountain.

For the first mile upstream from the stream's mouth on South Indian Creek, Rocky Fork is paralleled by Rocky Fork Road. The creek runs along the road right-of-way through this area, descending a steeply inclined creekbed. Small drops, plunge pools, and potholes are plentiful with the boulder-strewn bed remaining open enough for limited casting room. Having the paved road at streamside, plus a couple of bridge crossings, provides such easy access that fishing pressure is moderate. Though plentiful, the rainbow trout in the lower part of the creek are usually small. Fish of 6 to 8 inches inhabit virtually every nook and cranny in the flow.

Where Rocky Fork Road bears away from the stream, a gravel road continues up the creek. This road, however, is blocked by a locked gate. The land along the creek is owned by the SF Rocky Fork Holding Company, but is open to public fishing. All access above this point is limited to foot travel. The stream bed levels out, but the holding water continues to be loaded with rainbows. In fact, some trout in the 9- to 10-inch range turn up along here, probably because the creek gets less pressure on the walk-in area.

Fly-fishing on the portion of the creek above Rocky Fork Road is difficult due to the creek's small size and the tight canopy of foliage along the flow. Rocky Fork Creek is open to fishing under special native-trout regulations.

Rocky Fork can be reached by traveling to the south on US 23 from Erwin. At the village of Rocky Fork, turn right onto Rocky Fork Road. The creek is located to the right side of this road.

CLARK CREEK
USGS Flag Pond, Telford • DeLorme 62, 63

This small stream rises in Unicoi County in the shadow of Rich Mountain. It then flows northward, skirting the southwest face of Embreeville Mountain as it crosses into Washington County. Finally, Clark Creek empties directly into the Nolichucky River.

The public fishing area on the creek is located upstream of the Clarksville Iron Furnace historic site. All of the creek above this point is on Forest Service land in the Cherokee NF.

Above the national forest boundary Clark Creek runs through a gently graded valley. Always in sight of the gravel Forest Service road, there are a large number of primitive campsites along the shore. This part of the creek receives regular stockings of catchable-size rainbow trout. The worn condition of the banks indicates that fishing pressure is heavy during the spring and summer.

Although the creek is not particularly crowded with foliage, it is still a very small stream for the two and a half miles to the point at which the road is blocked. Fly-fishermen particularly have a problem fishing this stream when the campers, who are mostly bait-fishermen, are out in force. Water temperatures indicate that this water is only marginal trout habitat, as well as being a marginal fly-casting destination.

Above the barrier across the road, foot travel is possible upstream. The creek is very small, but open enough to permit fly-casting. There are a number of old in-stream structures in the creek, but in such poor repair they are of little aid to the trout today. Surprisingly, a few small wild rainbows turn up on this part of the creek. Along its entire length, Clark Creek is open under Tennessee's general trout regulation.

Clark Creek is accessible via Clarks Creek Road which runs south off TN 107 where the highway parallels the south side of the Nolichucky in Washington County. Clarks Creek Road changes to gravel and becomes FS 25 when it enters the Cherokee NF.

HORSE CREEK
USGS Greystone, Chuckey • DeLorme 62

Horse Creek is a medium to small stream that empties into the Nolichucky River a few miles upstream of Davy Crockett Lake. Its entire watershed is located in Greene County. The only portion open to public fishing is located on Cherokee NF lands in the extreme headwaters of the creek. This part of the creek is quite small.

Due to its size, under ordinary circumstances, Horse Creek would not merit much attention, especially from fly casters. However, its unique regulations require mentioning it. From the point at which the creek exits Forest Service land, up to the mouth of Squibb Creek, Horse Creek is reserved for fishing by children under 13, persons over 65, or disabled individuals.

This regulated portion of the creek runs through the Horse Creek Recreation Area. The site provides picnic and camping grounds, plus two locations where the stream has been dammed to provide swimming pools. All of these are handicap-accessible. A trail and fishing piers have been installed to open the creek to wheelchairs for fishing. To add to the appeal, a large number of in-stream structures have been installed to provide better holding water for trout.

This project is a cooperative effort of the Cherokee Chapter of Trout Unlimited, the Fish America Foundation, Greene County government, Robert Merrel Construction Company, the Boy Scouts of America, the TWRA, and the U.S. Forest Service. In all, there are three-quarters of a mile of stream in this special-regulation area.

This lower portion of public water is stocked with catchable-size rainbow trout. Both natural and artificial baits are legal. From May 1 through September 30 each year the creel limit is two fish per angler per day. During the rest of the year the general trout regulation creel limit of seven fish per day applies.

Although it receives very little angling attention, the portion of Horse Creek above Squibb Creek is open for fishing to all anglers. The stream is fairly high-quality trout water with some natural reproduction. It is a very small stream, but has a lot of potholes containing mostly wild rainbows of 6 to 8 inches. Of course, some stocked fish will move up into this area as well. Much of the creek is canopied, but short stretches will emerge into small clearings offering a couple of pools that are castable. It is possible to find these openings for three-quarters of a mile above the restricted area, up to the mouth of Sarvis Cove Creek. This upper part of Horse Creek is open under general trout regulations.

Although Horse Creek does not qualify as a primary fly-fishing destination, for the fly-fisherman vacationing with a family that includes children, senior citizens, or a handicapped individual it does provide sections that have something for everyone.

To reach Horse Creek Recreation Area, follow the signs south on Horse Creek Road from TN 107 east of Tusculum. The road is designated as FS 94 beginning at the edge of the national forest and runs through the recreation area. At the upper end of the site, the road continues and is listed on maps as being for four-wheel-drive vehicles. It is, however, in such bad repair it is little more than a hiking trail. It continues to follow the creek all the way to its source. From the fly-fisherman's standpoint, however, at the fork of the road after the fourth ford on Horse Creek, the upper limit of fishable water has been reached.

SQUIBB CREEK
USGS Greystone • DeLorme 62

This is a very small feeder stream that enters Horse Creek about 100 yards above the end of the Horse Creek Recreation Area. It is a high-quality trout stream, containing wild rainbow trout that rarely top 7 inches in length. It is also so tightly canopied that it is of little interest to most fly-fishermen.

Rising to the east of Horse Creek in the 8300-acre Sampson Mountain Wilderness Area, Squibb Creek exits the preserve only a few yards short of its mouth. The major attraction of this creek is its fishing regulation. It is open under special wild-stream tackle rules, but using the general trout creel limit of seven fish per day. Of these seven fish, however, only three may be brook trout. The obvious indication is that some native brookies may exist upstream in the dapping water.

To get to Squibb Creek, follow FS 94 upstream of the Horse Creek Recreation Area. A footbridge crosses the creek where FT 23 enters the road. This trail follows Squibb Creek up into the wilderness area.

SARVIS COVE CREEK
USGS Greystone • DeLorme 62

Sarvis Cove Creek is another small tributary of Horse Creek that offers some marginal benefit to fly-fishermen visiting the area. The stream enters Horse Creek from the west roughly three-quarters of a mile south of the recreation area.

Not as steeply graded as Squibb Creek, Sarvis Cove Creek provides more small pools and pockets for trout. Unfortunately, it is even more heavily canopied than that former stream. Most of the trout are small rainbows of under 8 inches.

Again, the main reason for mentioning this flow is that it is open under the modified special wild-stream regulations. The general creel limit applies, but only artificial lures with single hooks may be used. Only three brook trout may appear in the day's catch, which would again indicate that the adventurous angler may find some of these natives far upstream.

To reach Sarvis Cove Creek continue up FS 94, crossing four fords on Horse Creek to where the road forks. The mouth of Sarvis Cove is not visible from the road. At the fork, go right for 0.25 mile to a parking area and primitive camping site at streamside. This spur road parallels Sarvis Cove Creek, but is blocked at the camping area. Upstream the creek has foot access via FT 22 and then FT 14 when the two trails intersect.

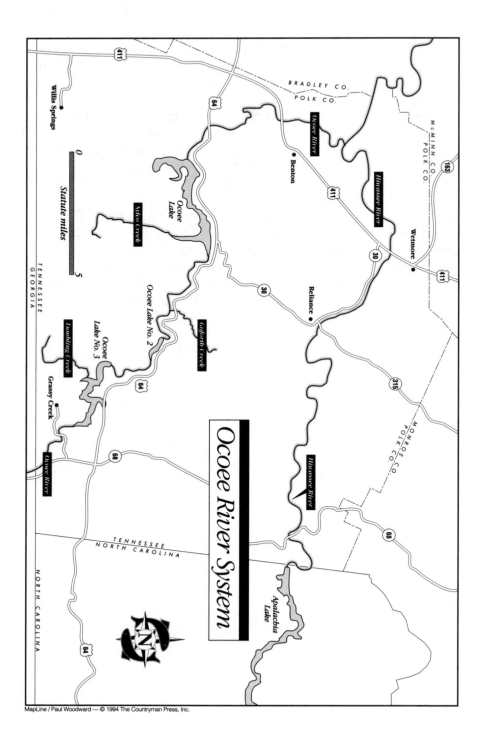

Ocoee River System

MapLine / Paul Woodward — © 1994 The Countryman Press, Inc.

36

Ocoee River System

The Ocoee River is a rarity among the rivers of the southeast in that it undergoes a name change when it crosses a state boundary. The headwaters portion located in north Georgia is known as the Toccoa River (see the Toccoa's description in section one), but once it crosses into Tennessee at Copper Hill the stream is then known as the Ocoee.

From the Copper Basin area of southeast Tennessee the river flows to the northwest to join the Hiwassee River in the vicinity of Boyd Bottoms. Along its course the Ocoee is not trout water, and, in fact, is almost not a river. A series of three impoundments interrupt the stream's flow. These reservoirs are designed for electric power generation, but they utilize pipelines and flumes in the process that leave long stretches of the riverbed virtually dry. Downstream from the dam at Ocoee Lake No. 2 the river is a torrent when the turbines are not turning, but will also be virtually dry when water is diverted to the flume for power generation.

As a result of this extensive management of the river's flow, there is no fishery, but there is a world-class white-water kayaking and rafting run below the dam at Ocoee Lake No. 2 when water is allowed to flow down the riverbed. This stretch of water is so challenging that it is the site of the white-water canoe and kayak events for the 1996 Olympic Games that are being hosted a hundred miles south in Atlanta.

As far as trout water is concerned, there are a number of feeder streams that enter the river and are stocked with trout by the TWRA. Due to the relatively low elevation of all the streams in the area, only one, Tumbling Creek, has a very high-quality fishery. Three others, Rough and Big creeks on the south side plus Rock Creek on the north, are small, canopied, and, in the case of Big Creek, extremely inaccessible. For these reasons they do not qualify as fly-casting destinations.

This leaves, in addition to Tumbling Creek, only Goforth and Sylco creeks that merit description.

The streams will be covered starting at the Georgia border and working downstream along the Ocoee.

TUMBLING CREEK
USGS Ducktown • DeLorme 26

Tumbling Creek is a small stream that rises across the state boundary in northwest Georgia. From there it runs almost directly north to empty into Ocoee Lake No. 3. Licklog Ridge borders the stream valley to the west, separating Tumbling Creek from both the Cohutta and Big Frog wilderness areas. The entire Tennessee portion of the creek is located in Polk County and the Cherokee NF.

The lower portion of the creek near the lake is in a relatively level valley that provides a number of slow, crystalline pools. This mile-and-a-half section is paralleled by FS 221 with the Forest Service's Tumbling Creek Campground at streamside. The wading in this portion of the creek is quite easy and the stream gets heavy fishing pressure in spring and summer. Although the creek is stocked with mature rainbow trout by the TWRA, it contains high-quality trout habitat and wild fish are also present. The stockers run in the 9- to 10-inch range, while the wild rainbows are 6 to 8 inches in length.

Upstream of the campground, there is a stretch of private land, but still further up another two miles are on public land. This final stretch up to the Georgia border contains more of the wild fish. Along here FS 65 is the gravel road that skirts the creek's shore.

Access to Tumbling Creek is via FS 221 from the village of Grassy Creek to the west of TN 68. The other end of FS 221 is at the crossroads of Willis Springs to the east of US 411 at the village of Conasauga. This area to the south of the Ocoee River is rugged and has little access. Expect slow going over gravel roads throughout the area, especially when approaching Tumbling Creek from the west.

GOFORTH CREEK
USGS Caney Creek • DeLorme 26

Entering the river below Ocoee Dam No. 2 in the portion of the river known for its white water, Goforth Creek is a small, steeply dropping creek. This boulder-strewn flow has some good-looking pools and holding water near its mouth. Also, due to the rocky nature of the stream bed, room to fly-cast is adequate.

The TWRA stocks Goforth Creek with catchable-size rainbow trout several times during the spring and summer. The water, however, reaches temperatures in the summer that make it marginal trout habitat. This is probably due to the low elevation of Goforth Creek's valley as it skirts to the west of Brock Mountain. This stream is only marginal as a fly-casting destination.

Access to the lower end of Goforth is off US 64 which follows the north shore of the Ocoee River. Although there is some access to the upper reaches of the creek via a jeep trail marked as FS 185 (this road does not connect to US 64), the creek is too small to offer much of an opportunity to the fly caster.

SYLCO CREEK
USGS Parksville • DeLorme 26

This small stream has a very wide rocky bed that leaves plenty of room for casting. The valley through which it flows is quite gently sloped, and the stream is easily waded. There is not a great deal of holding water on the flow, however.

Sylco Creek's flow seems marginal from the standpoint of trout habitat, but it does have some small wild rainbows present. The TWRA adds catchable-size rainbows to the fishery in the creek as well. The only time that Sylco Creek is attractive as a destination is just after it has been stocked. The rest of the time the trout population appears sparse.

There is a Forest Service campground located on FS 55 at the upstream limit of the fishable area of the creek. Sylco Campground is just north of the point at which FS 55 intersects FS 221, and provides a good headquarters for exploring this region. Just south of the campground FS 55 veers away to the west, leaving the stream. From this point maps show FS 302 as a road following the creek all the way down to Lake Ocoee. It, however, more closely resembles a pig path that should only be challenged with rugged four-wheel-drive vehicles or on foot.

To reach Sylco Creek travel east from Willis Springs on FS 221 to the point at which FS 55 joins from the north. Follow FS 55 north to the campground and the creek.

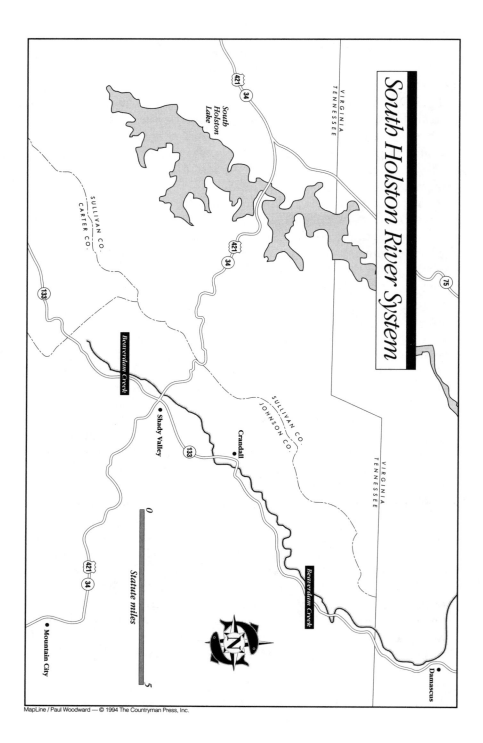

South Holston River System

South Holston Lake

VIRGINIA
TENNESSEE

SULLIVAN CO.
CARTER CO.

SULLIVAN CO.
JOHNSON CO.

Beaverdam Creek

Shady Valley

Crandall

Beaverdam Creek

VIRGINIA
TENNESSEE

Mountain City

Damascus

Statute miles

0

5

N

MapLine / Paul Woodward — © 1994 The Countryman Press, Inc.

37

South Holston River System

The South Holston River rises in southern Virginia and flows down through the Widner Valley to empty into South Holston Lake as it crosses into Tennessee. Mention of trout fishing in the South Holston River system immediately brings to mind the tailrace of the river below South Holston Lake in Sullivan County. That reaction is understandable since this stretch of tailwater down to Bluff City, just above Boone Lake, provides one of the better trout fisheries in Tennessee.

This stream, however, flows down a valley that is west of the Appalachian range, and, while it is close to the uplands, it does not flow through any of the mountains. The character of the river is that of a lowland stream, and not freestone trout water. For that reason the river itself does not qualify for coverage.

There are three tributaries of the South Holston that are recognized as trout water by the TWRA. All are located to the east of the river, nestled in the northeast corner of the Volunteer State. Laurel Creek is the most easterly of these, flowing between the Iron Mountains and Fodderstack Mountain before running into Virginia to bisect the town of Damascus on its way to the South Holston. Laurel Creek and its feeder stream Gentry Creek are both stocked with trout by the TWRA, but both are located primarily on private land with only road-crossing public access. This leaves only Beaverdam Creek as legitimate public trout water in the South Holston River system.

BEAVERDAM CREEK
USGS Laurel Bloomery • DeLorme 70

Beaverdam Creek begins when several forks of the creek join at the south end of the Iron Mountains. From there it flows down a level course through Shady Valley as it heads north to join Laurel Creek in Damascus, Virginia.

The portion from its headwaters down to the village of Crandall flows almost exclusively through private holdings, much of which is farmland. Beaverdam then enters a section of the Cherokee NF that continues along its shore all the way to the state border. For the fly caster, only the six miles of water on Forest Service land is of interest.

Along its entire length, Beaverdam Creek is managed under wild-trout regulations and receives no stockings of trout. In the area where the creek is on public land, it is of medium size, offering plenty of room to cast. Besides being a gentle flow, the waters do not seem particularly cold in the spring and summer. The presence of large numbers of snails on the streambed rocks, and some extremely slick algae indicates that this is not prime trout water. The algae also makes this a very slippery and treacherous stream to wade.

At the point at which Beaverdam Creek enters public land it tumbles through some shoals before running under TN 133. This stretch upstream of the bridge is the only portion not at roadside on the public lands. It appears to get less fishing pressure, and tends to hold more of the wild rainbow trout present in this stream. There are undoubtedly also brown trout in the creek, but all of the trout share the water with large populations of dace, darters, and other minnows. This is usually an indication that conditions are approaching marginal levels for the cold-water species.

Just before the creek enters Virginia, it cuts through the Forest Service's Backbone Rock Recreation Area. The road that parallels the creek runs through the "Backbone Bridge," which is actually a tunnel piercing a ridge of rock that the creek skirts around. Just north of the tunnel there is a campground and picnic areas. In this vicinity the creek apparently gets heavy fishing pressure.

Access to Beaverdam Creek is easy via TN 133 which runs at streamside for the entire length of the creek on national forest land between Crandall, Tennessee, and Damascus, Virginia.

38

Tellico River System

The trout waters of the Tellico River basin are some of the most celebrated in the southeastern United States. Second only to streams of the Smoky Mountains in renown, they have plenty of history and lore associated with them. Much like the Smoky Mountains streams, these rivers, creeks, and brooks have been attracting sport fishermen since early in the twentieth century. Beginning just after 1900 local anglers were being hired by visiting fishermen to guide expeditions into this wild, rugged, and bear-infested area.

Like the rest of southern Appalachia, the Tellico's virgin forests also beckoned timber companies during these same decades. As a result the hillsides suffered from extensive logging operations. Today the watershed is protected within the Cherokee NF in Monroe County, with some portions of the basin also in the federally managed Bald River Gorge Wilderness Area. Special regulations that apply on all of the streams in the Tellico system continue to attract anglers while generating cash for the local economy.

Along with the remnants of logging dams and old narrow-gauge railroad beds, another vestige of the early days of the Tellico can be found resting in virtually every southern fly caster's collection of nymphs. The Tellico Nymph has been used for decades to entice both the stocked and wild trout from streams throughout the region.

This heavily weighted nymph is tied with a yellow rayon under-belly that is ribbed with peacock herl. Brown cock forms the hackle at the eye of the hook, while natural guinea fowl hackle is used for the tail. In sizes 8 to 16, it is one of the most consistently productive subsurface flies I have discovered for southern Appalachian trout.

Besides the Tellico River itself, the TWRA lists eight tributary

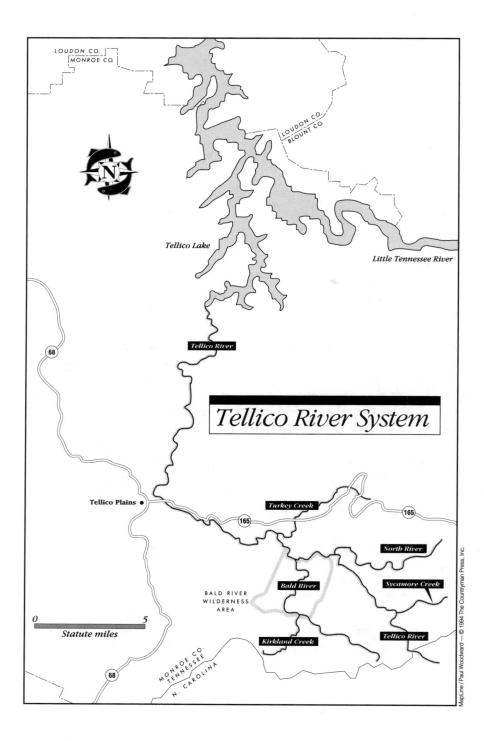

LOUDON CO.
MONROE CO.

LOUDON CO.
BLOUNT CO.

Tellico Lake

Little Tennessee River

Tellico River

68

Tellico River System

Tellico Plains •

Turkey Creek

165   165

North River

BALD RIVER
WILDERNESS
AREA

Bald River

Sycamore Creek

Tellico River

0   5
Statute miles

Kirkland Creek

MONROE CO.
TENNESSEE
N. CAROLINA

68

MapLine / Paul Woodward — © 1994 The Countryman Press, Inc.

streams as trout water. All of these streams are managed under some form of special regulations, but since these vary from creek to creek they will be discussed in the sections on those specific waters. Three of the creeks, however, are so small and cramped with foliage that they do not merit consideration as fly-fishing destinations.

Brooks Creek is a tributary of the Bald River, which in turn empties into the Tellico. This tiny flow enters the Bald up in the river's headwaters and is managed under the TWRA's wild-stream regulations. Only single-hook, artificial lures are allowed, the creel limit is three trout per day, and rainbow and brown trout must be 9 inches long. Brook trout must be 6 inches in length.

Rough Ridge Creek is the most southerly of the feeder streams entering the Tellico River, as this tributary runs from east to west along the Tennessee–North Carolina border. It meets the Tellico in the Forest Service's State Line Recreation Area campground. Too small for comfortable fly-casting, Rough Ridge is open to fishing with single-hook, artificial lures only, the creel limit is seven (only three may be brook trout), and there is no size limit on browns or rainbows. The statewide brook trout size limit of six inches applies.

Finally, Henderson Branch is open under the special Tellico-Citico permit regulations (see the Tellico River description below for permit and closed-season details). Natural baits may be used, the creel limit is seven fish, with the brook trout minimum size limit at six inches.

The remaining streams in this system are the Tellico, North, and Bald rivers, plus Kirkland, Sycamore, and Turkey creeks. These will be described starting with the Tellico and then moving downstream through its tributaries.

TELLICO RIVER
USGS Big Junction, Bald River Falls • DeLorme 27

The Tellico River is one of the largest natural trout streams in the Volunteer State. Although the river rises on the slopes of McDaniel Bald in North Carolina, it becomes a medium-size stream when it is joined by Rough Ridge Creek at the state line. From that crossing, there are 13.7 miles of recognized trout water down to the mouth of Turkey Creek in Tennessee. Trout are also found further down the river, but not in large numbers and the waters are marginal.

The Tellico is one of the most popular and heavily fished trout streams in the southern Appalachian region. The main reason for this popularity is the heavy stocking of adult trout in the river, plus the special regulations that the waters are managed under.

The Tellico River and several of its tributaries, as well as Citico Creek (which was discussed earlier in the Little Tennessee River system), are open year-round under the Tellico-Citico trout regulations. The streams are stocked Thursday of each week, and, as a result, angling is not allowed on Thursdays and Fridays. All natural baits that are legal under Tennessee trout rules may be used, the creel limit is seven fish per day, and the only minimum size limit is 6 inches on brook trout. In addition to the applicable state fishing license, a Tellico-Citico daily fishing permit is required.

The real key to why the river attracts so much angling pressure is the 150,000 mature trout stocked in the drainage each year. To facilitate plantings of this magnitude, the Tellico Fish Hatchery is located on the river at Pheasant Field near the mouth of Sycamore Creek. Another drawing card for fishing the Tellico is the fact that many of the stocked fish are in the 12- to 14-inch range. The bulk of these trout are rainbows, but there is a healthy holdover population of big brown trout.

The brown trout taken over the years on the Tellico have become legendary in eastern Tennessee. A number of fish in the 20-pound range have been reported, while browns of 8 to 10 pounds are caught each year on the Tellico. The deep pools in the middle to lower portion of the river are the best areas to encounter these magnum-size trout.

At a mile and three-quarters upstream of Turkey Creek is Bald River Falls at the mouth of that stream on the Tellico. This spectacular cascade is mainly of interest to the angler on the Tellico because of the traffic jams of sightseers that occur on the bridge over the Bald River below the falls.

A further quarter of a mile upstream is a large waterfall on the Tellico itself. There is a sign at streamside warning that seven people have drowned at that point on the river. Needless to say, care is called for around the falls.

The Tellico Fish Hatchery is located 10.6 miles upstream of Turkey Creek and the Forest Service State Line Campground is located at the North Carolina border 13.7 miles from Turkey Creek. The state boundary also marks the upstream limit of practical fly-fishing water. Below the fish hatchery the Tellico is big water, while from the hatchery up to the state line the flow is of medium width. The whole stretch from Turkey Creek up to State Line Campground offers room for easy casting.

All of the managed waters on the Tellico River are paralleled by FS 210, which is paved all the way from TN 165 up to State Line Campground. Other Forest Service campgrounds are located on the Tellico at Spivey Cove, Davis Branch, and Big Oak. Sites for primitive camping are also designated all along the river.

The Tellico-Citico daily permits can be purchased at the Green Cove Trailer Park and Motel. The store is 9.0 miles upstream from Turkey Creek, and is also a good place to look at the photos hanging on the wall of the many big trout the Tellico has given up over the years. Tellico-Citico permits can also be purchased at many outlets throughout eastern Tennessee that sell regular fishing licenses.

SYCAMORE CREEK
USGS *Big Junction* • *DeLorme 27*

In traveling down the course of the Tellico River, the first tributary that is encountered which provides enough room for fly-fishing is Sycamore Creek. This medium to small stream enters the river from the eastern side, after flowing down from the Big Junction area at the border of Monroe County, Tennessee, and Graham County, North Carolina.

The creek is open to fishing under modified wild-trout regulations and does not require the purchase of a Tellico-Citico permit. Only artificial lures with single hooks are legal, but the creel limit is still seven fish. Only three may be brook trout, which must be 6 inches or more in length. There is no size limit for brown or rainbow trout.

The lower portion of Sycamore Creek, which is the only part large and open enough to interest most fly-fishermen, is in a relatively level valley, and does not possess as much holding water as is common on more steeply inclined flows. Expect to find mostly small wild rainbows in the 6- to 8-inch range.

Access to Sycamore Creek can be gained by crossing the Tellico River from FS 210 at the entrance to the Tellico Fish Hatchery. Just across the bridge, a road runs upstream along the river, but is gated. A walk of about 200 yards up this road leads to the mouth of Sycamore Creek. The road then continues up the creek, providing foot access. Several maps of the area show this trail as Sycamore Road or FS 61, but, as noted, it is closed to vehicular traffic.

NORTH RIVER
USGS *Big Junction, Bald River Falls* • *DeLorme 27*

The next fishable tributary of the Tellico encountered as one moves downstream is the North River. It, along with the Bald River, is one of the two main feeder streams of the upper Tellico basin.

The area around the North River has a long tradition among eastern Tennessee bear hunters. The campsites along the river were the scenes of gatherings of hardy mountain men and their bear hounds that produced hunting stories still repeated around campfires today. The surrounding ridges and mountains are just as wild and rugged as were those old-time bear hunters.

Most of those campsites, which are plentiful and well marked, are now filled during the spring and summer by anglers seeking to challenge the wild rainbow and brown trout in the North River. Open to fishing under standard wild-trout regulations, the river has a reputation for producing plenty of small, wild, and spunky rainbow trout. It does not, however, produce large fish with any regularity.

For the first three and three-quarter miles upstream of the river's mouth on the Tellico, the stream is of medium size, steeply graded, and tumbling. This portion of the North River is the best fly-casting area for the fisherman interested in catching lots of fish. The rainbows are thick and usually willing to rise to a variety of attractor flies.

Beginning at the Forest Service's North River Campground the river valley levels out considerably. Above this point the stream has a completely different character. While still medium in size, it has a number of 40- to 60-foot-long pools. There has also been extensive stream renovation work done here. In-stream structures are common. This is the best area to stumble onto a brown trout or two on the North River. Additionally, there is one stretch of water where the road paralleling the river goes up on the mountainside, making access less available. No doubt this is a good spot to find a few less-harried trout.

At six and a half miles upstream from the Tellico, the road leaves the North River to wind over several ridges. At this point the river is beginning to get small with a heavy canopy of foliage. The fishing is difficult, but the trout are still present. When the river and road rejoin a mile further up at Big Indian Branch, the North River is no longer large enough to be fly-cast.

While scouting this upper end of the river, however, I received a vivid reminder of just how wild the area remains. Having parked my car near the bridge of Big Indian Branch, I intended to walk down this small feeder to the North River. The gravel forest road was raised about a yard above the level of the surrounding ground, so I had to jump down to begin the trek. Immediately upon landing, a tan-colored blur darted from the bush at my feet, headed for the river. Too big for a rabbit or squirrel and too small for a bear, at first I thought it was a small wild hog. As it bounded across the North River it presented a broadside view that identified it as a bobcat.

The road I had just dropped down from receives a respectable amount of traffic in the spring. In fact, I had passed several vehicles coming from the opposite direction just before I parked. It was hard to believe that a shy creature like a mountain bobcat had been crouching virtually on the road's shoulder, oblivious to the commotion of the passing traffic. That is, unless it was just waiting for me to hop on it. A few feet to my right and the expression "hop on it" would have been much too true. Undoubtedly I would have been hopping even higher trying to get back off the critter!

Access to all of the fishable portion of the North River is available from North River Road (FS 217). This road joins FS 210 at the river's mouth, 5.5 miles upstream of Turkey Creek.

BALD RIVER
USGS Bald River Falls • DeLorme 27

The Bald River is a primary tributary of the Tellico River that drains the valley to the west of the Tellico, between Waucheesi Mountain on the west and Chinquapin Ridge on the east. The major characteristic for which this flow is best known is 120-foot-high Bald River Falls. This cascade is located at the mouth of the river, directly beside FS 210. Few visitors to this area explore any more of the Bald River besides this attraction.

Above the falls the river traverses the Bald River Gorge Wilderness Area. The river valley certainly lives up to its name, sporting steep rocky walls and unspoiled scenery. The river is big water through the gorge, offering plenty of room for casting. To get up to this part of the stream from FS 210 requires a very steep 0.25-mile hike to the picnic area at the lower end of the gorge. From there, FT 88 offers foot access as it follows the river for roughly five miles to FS 126 at the other end of the gorge.

Fishing pressure for the wild rainbows in the gorge appears to be almost nonexistent. There are just too many other streams in the area that are easier to reach, so most anglers do not expend the effort needed to get into the Bald River Gorge. The trout in the gorge run a bit larger than the wild trout on the North River, but don't match the stockers on the Tellico in size.

Upstream of the gorge, the Bald River is paralleled for 1.5 miles by FS 126 (Smith Field Road). Holly Flats, a Forest Service campground, is located at the point at which the river enters the gorge. Along here the stream is of medium size, flowing through a level valley.

Since this part of the Bald River has easy access and is near the campground, the fishing pressure is greater. The trout encountered tend to be smaller as well. Most of the rainbows are only 6 to 8 inches. Above the point at which the flow leaves FS 126, the Bald River is too small and tightly foliated to be of interest to fly-fishermen.

To reach the upper portion of the Bald River and Holly Flats Campground, turn west from FS 210 onto FS 126. This intersection is 9.7 miles south of the mouth of Turkey Creek on the Tellico River.

KIRKLAND CREEK
USGS Bald River Falls • DeLorme 27

Kirkland Creek is the only feeder stream of the Bald River that provides any appreciable fly-casting opportunities. It is, however, only a marginal opportunity itself. The stream drains the northwest face of Wolf Ridge, flowing on a northward course to intersect the Bald River just upstream of Holly Flats. There is a small parking area beside the river on FS 126, but Kirkland enters from the opposite side, requiring one to ford the Bald to get to it.

Kirkland Creek is quite small even at its mouth and would not merit mention except for a few unusual circumstances. The valley it is located in is quite level, giving the creek a meandering, almost pastoral quality. A number of in-stream structures, such as wing dams and anchored logs, have been installed to provide some holding water for trout. These have apparently worked since the creek has plenty of small wild rainbows.

Unfortunately, the canopy of vegetation is so thick that only occasional openings offer the chance to toss a cast. Also, since much of its flow is slick or calm water, stalking the trout is quite difficult. Expect to spook far more than you will catch. This is a creek to try when fishing on the upper Bald River, but not one to make a special trip to visit.

Like the Bald River, the creek is open to fishing under standard state wild-trout regulations. Access to Kirkland is along FT 85, which parallels the creek upstream from the parking area on FS 126 at the Bald River.

TURKEY CREEK
USGS Bald River Falls • *DeLorme 27*

This small stream is the last feeder of the Tellico encountered before the end of recognized trout water when traveling downstream. Entering the river from the northwest, the lower portion of the stream from TN 165 down to FS 210 at the Tellico provides some very tight fly-casting conditions.

Turkey Creek is open to fishing under the Tellico-Citico permit regulations and is stocked with mature trout. It is another creek that merits exploring only as a sidelight to a fishing trip to the Tellico. It is not a primary destination.

Access to Turkey Creek is via FS 210 at the creek's mouth, 4.5 miles east of the junction of FS 210 and TN 165 in Monroe County. The creek can also be reached by traveling north from that road junction along TN 165. This highway crosses the creek, which is very small at that point. Upstream of TN 165 Turkey Creek is on private property, but downstream it is in the Cherokee NF.

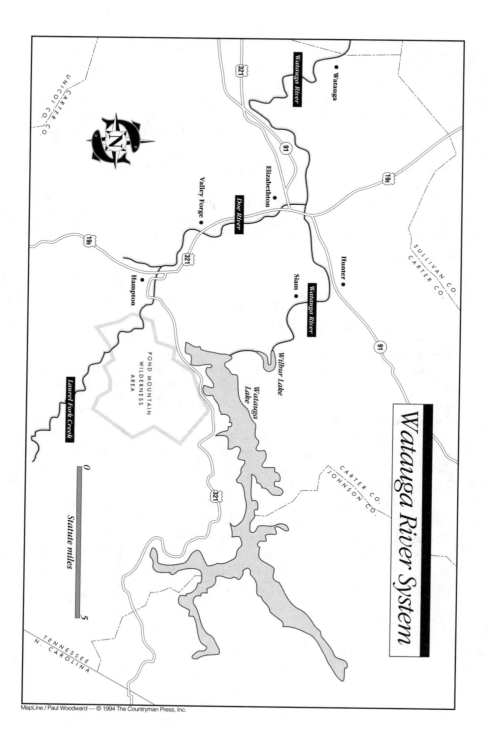

Watauga River System

Watauga River

• Watauga

321

91

19E

Elizabethton

Valley Forge •

Doe River

Hunter •

Siam •

Watauga River

Hampton •

19E

321

91

UNICOI CO.
CARTER CO.

SULLIVAN CO.
CARTER CO.

CARTER CO.
JOHNSON CO.

Wilbur Lake

Watauga Lake

POND MOUNTAIN
WILDERNESS
AREA

Laurel Fork Creek

321

0

Statute miles

5

TENNESSEE
N. CAROLINA

MapLine / Paul Woodward — © 1994 The Countryman Press, Inc.

39

Watauga River System

The trout waters of the Watauga River system are located in the upper northeast corner of the Volunteer State in Carter and Johnson counties. Although the fishing waters of the Watauga system appear substantial on first glance at a map, that judgment does not hold up to closer scrutiny.

The Watauga River rises in North Carolina, crossing into Tennessee just north of US 321 in Johnson County. Almost immediately the river disappears into the depths of Lake Watauga, which in turn spreads its waters across the border into Carter County. Below Watauga Dam the river goes through Wilbur Lake, a small electric-power-generating impoundment. The tailwaters below this reservoir are the only trout water on the Watauga itself.

The Doe River, Roan, Hampton, and Stony creeks are all feeders of the Watauga River that are listed by the TWRA as trout water and are stocked with catchable-size fish. None of these, however, provide much in the way of a public trout fishery. All four run through private lands, with only the occasional bridge crossing or highway right-of-way presenting the opportunity for public access to the fishing water. None of these merit coverage as fly-fishing destinations. This leaves only Laurel Fork to complete the scant list of public fishing locations in the Watauga River system.

WATAUGA RIVER
USGS Elizabethton, Johnson City • DeLorme 63

The Watauga River below Wilbur Dam is a large stream, character-ized by long, deep pools. In all there are 10 to 12 miles of trout water on the river, stretching all the way down to the village of Watauga at the Carter and Washington county border. All of the river's trout water is located in Carter County.

Along the course of the Watauga's tailwaters, the stream passes through the area known as Siam, then runs through the towns of Hunter and Elizabethton. Just downstream of Elizabethton, the Watauga passes the historic site at Sycamore Shoals, where the fron-tier settlers mustered before crossing the Appalachian Mountains to help defeat the British in the Battle of Kings Mountain during the Revolutionary War.

Much of the country traversed by the Watauga is flat, providing little shoal water. In fact, the only real connection to Appalachia is that the tailwater originates at a gap in the Iron Mountains, then skirts between Holston Mountain to the north and Lynn Mountain to the south. The rest of the flow is in relatively level lands. Most of the river is best suited to float-fishing due to its size and depth.

One spot along the flow that does offer some wading possibilities is around the Siam Bridge. This old metal span is the first bridge below the dam and offers some public bank access on the north shore. Even on high water levels, it is possible to wade some of the river here, although parts of the flow will still be out of casting range. The shore is clear of trees, so it is possible to let out some line for long casts.

Wilbur Dam Road follows the river upstream from the Siam Bridge, but due to private lands along the shore, the only good ac-cess to the water on this road is at the foot of the dam on the south bank. Additional south bank access is located under the bridge in the town of Hunter. On the rest of the river anglers are limited to road crossings for access.

The Watauga is stocked with both rainbows and brown trout. The river is noted for producing good catches of the stockers and yielding some trophy-size browns. The bulk of the anglers encountered on this stream are bait casters, but the river is large enough that there is still room for fly-casting at virtually any time.

A fly caster tries his luck below the Siam Bridge on tailwaters of the Watauga River.

One of the more popular flies on the Watauga is the Elk-Hair Caddis, fished in sizes as small as 18. When the water is falling in the river, this fly can be very effective in the spring and early summer. Although falling water provides the best angling, the river remains clear enough for fishing even when water is being released from Wilbur Dam. Once the late-summer heat sets in the trout become quite picky about flies and often rise only to well-presented midges in size 20 or smaller.

On the Watauga, Tennessee's general trout regulations apply, including the seven-fish creel limit, with the only minimum size restriction being 6 inches on brook trout. There is, however, a quality trout fishing area designated on the river from the Smalling Bridge below Sycamore Shoals down to the bridge in Watauga. The creel limit along here is two fish per day, with a 14-inch minimum size limit on all trout species. Only artificial lures are permitted on this two-mile stretch of river.

To reach Wilbur Dam Road along the Watauga, travel north from the town of Hampton on US 321 to Siam Road at the village of Valley Forge. Turn to the northeast on Siam Road and drive to the bridge over the river. From this point Wilbur Dam Road runs east along the south shore of the Watauga up to the dam.

LAUREL FORK CREEK

USGS White Rocks Mountain, Watauga Dam,
Elizabethton • DeLorme 46, 63

Laurel Fork Creek is the premier wild-trout stream of the northeast corner of the Volunteer State, but it also offers a section of water that is stocked with mature trout. Located in Carter County, the creek rises in the shadow of Big Pine Mountain near the North Carolina border, then flows to the northwest skirting just north of White Rocks Mountain.

One thing that sets Laurel Fork apart from other streams in this portion of the state is the fact that rainbow, brown, and brook trout can be taken from the stream—and all could be wild fish! In the headwaters of the creek, native brookies still exist, while further downstream in the designated wild-trout area brown trout make up about 90 percent of the population. There are some rainbows in here as well, but below Dennis Cove Campground where the creek goes through the Pond Mountain Wilderness Area, wild rainbows become more common.

In the headwaters where the brookies roam, Laurel Fork is very small, but it becomes a medium-size stream long before it reaches Dennis Cove. This middle section offers plenty of casting room due to the large boulders located around many of the pools. This casting room is also present on the lower reaches of the creek.

In the last decade, for unknown reasons, brown trout have become prevalent in the wild-trout portion of the creek that begins at a cable crossing a half mile upstream of the Dennis Cove Campground. These browns usually run from 7 to 11 inches, but as is the story anywhere brown trout are present, larger fish are a definite possibility. In the part of the stream from the cable crossing down to Dennis Cove and continuing for a mile and a half further downstream, rainbow trout are stocked on a put-and-take basis. Once the creek enters the 6600-acre Pond Mountain Wilderness Area, no fish are stocked, but populations of both browns and rainbows exist. These fish also attain large sizes due to low fishing pressure that results from the difficult access to this part of the creek.

A couple of things to take note of on Laurel Fork are the presence of Laurel Falls on the lower part of the stream in the federally managed wilderness area, and the unusually slick rocks on this creek. It is wise to use caution when near the falls or anytime wading the stream.

From its mouth up to the designated wild-trout waters above Dennis Cove, Laurel Fork is open to fishing under general trout regulations (this includes the portion in the Pond Mountain Wilderness Area). As mentioned earlier, above the cable crossing upstream of Dennis Cove, wild-trout regulations apply.

Access to Laurel Fork Creek is via Dennis Cove Road, which runs south off US 321 at Hampton. The road joins the creek at the point the Appalachian Trail crosses both the road and creek. The trail provides the only access to the lower portion of the creek as they run parallel into the wilderness area.

Dennis Cove Road continues to run alongside the creek up to the Forest Service campground at Dennis Cove. From that point, FT 39 provides a footpath up into the wild-trout and headwaters areas.

Appendix

Map Sources

Some of the publications listed below are produced free of charge by public agencies, but others require a fee to purchase. Contact the individual companies and agencies for details.

Atlantic Mapping Company
392 Fairgrounds Street
Marietta, Georgia 30060
(404) 426-5768

Atlantic Mapping produces a Guide to North Georgia Wildlife Management Areas map, which covers most of the locations containing public trout waters in Georgia.

Blue Ridge Parkway
National Park Service
700 NW Bank Building
Asheville, North Carolina 28801
(704) 298-0398

A brochure is available containing a map of the parkway through both North Carolina and Virginia. Also ask for a copy of the parkway fishing regulations.

Cherokee Fish Management Enterprise
P.O. Box 302
Cherokee, North Carolina 27819
(704) 497-5201

The Eastern Band of the Cherokee Indians provides a brochure containing the fishing regulations and a map of the open streams on the Qualla Reservation at Cherokee, North Carolina.

County Maps
Thomas Publications Ltd.
Puetz Place
Lyndon Station, Wisconsin 53944
(608) 666-3331

This private company produces books containing individual county maps. They presently offer maps of Kentucky, North Carolina, South Carolina, and Tennessee. These are particularly helpful in that they show county and state route numbers on secondary roads.

DeLorme Mapping Company
P.O. Box 298
Freeport, Maine 04032
(207) 865-4171

Another private company, DeLorme produces an *Atlas & Gazetteer* for a number of states. These are the most comprehensive maps available from private sources. They show names for secondary roads, numbers for Forest Service roads and trails, plus stream locations. The *Atlas & Gazetteer* is presently only available for North Carolina and Tennessee.

Georgia Department of Natural Resources
Wildlife Resources Division
2070 US Highway 278 SE
Social Circle, Georgia 30279
(404) 918-6400

The WRD distributes photocopied maps of individual Wildlife Management Areas (WMA) in the north Georgia mountains. These are not packaged, so WMAs must be requested individually.

Great Smoky Mountains National Park
National Park Service
Gatlinburg, Tennessee 37738
(615) 436-5615

The NPS distributes two maps that are of use to trout anglers. Request the Great Smoky Mountains Trail Map, as well as the Great Smoky Mountains National Park Fishing Regulations. The former shows the trails that approach the wilderness streams in the park, while the latter brochure has a map of the trout streams, including those presently closed to angling.

North Carolina State Parks
P.O. Box 27687
Raleigh, North Carolina 27611
(919) 733-4181

This agency can provide maps of South Mountain State Park and Stone Mountain State Park, both of which contain trout streams.

North Carolina Wildlife Resources Division
512 N. Salisbury St., Room 458
Raleigh, North Carolina 27611
(919)733-3391

The NCWRC produces a booklet entitled "Hunting and Fishing Maps for North Carolina Game Lands." It contains maps of all the game lands in the state and is quite helpful in finding which streams are located on publicly controlled property.

South Carolina Wildlife and Marine Resources Department
P.O. Box 167
Columbia, South Carolina 29202
(803) 734-3888

The SCWMRD publishes the *South Carolina Wildlife Facilities Atlas.* This book contains individual maps of all the counties in the state, and is helpful in locating South Carolina Heritage Trust Preserve lands. The agency can also provide the booklet, "Brook, Rainbow and Brown Trout in South Carolina," which contains maps showing the location of all of the state's trout waters.

Tennessee Wildlife Resources Agency
Central Office
P.O. Box 40747
Nashville, Tennessee 37204
(615) 781-6500

This agency distributes a brochure entitled "Trout Fishing in Tennessee." Contained in the publication are maps showing the locations of all of the state's cold-water fisheries.

United States Forest Service
Region 8
1720 Peachtree Street NW
Atlanta, Georgia 30309
(404) 347-2384

The Region 8 office oversees all of the national forests (NF) in the states covered in this book. They have maps available for Georgia's Chattahoochee NF, Kentucky's Daniel Boone NF (both north and south portions), North Carolina's Nantahala and Pisgah (Grandfather, Toecane, and French Broad ranger districts on one and the Pisgah Ranger District on another) NFs, South Carolina's Sumter NF, and Tennessee's Cherokee NF. They also have maps available for most federal wilderness areas, or wild-and-scenic river corridors located in these states.

United States Geological Survey
Map Distribution
Federal Center Building 41
Denver, Colorado 80225
1-800-USA-MAPS or (303) 236-7477

The USGS distributes free indexes to topo maps and order blanks for those quadrangle maps for all of the states covered in this book. Request the index for the states for which you need maps.

Index

Also from the Countryman Press and Backcountry Publications

The Countryman Press and Backcountry Publications, long known for their fine books on the outdoors, offer a range of practical and readable manuals on fish and fishing.

We publish many guides to canoeing, hiking, walking, bicycling, and ski touring in New England, the Mid-Atlantic states, and the Midwest.

Our books are available at bookstores, or they may be ordered directly from the publisher. For ordering information or for a complete catalog, please contact:

The Countryman Press
c/o W.W. Norton & Company, Inc.
800 Keystone Industrial Park
Scranton, PA 18512
http://web.wwnorton.com